Eblaitica:
Essays on the Ebla Archives
and Eblaite Language

Volume I

Publications of the
Center for Ebla Research at New York University

Eblaitica: Essays on the Ebla Archives and Eblaite Language

Volume I

Edited
by

Cyrus H. Gordon
Gary A. Rendsburg
Nathan H. Winter

EISENBRAUNS
WINONA LAKE, INDIANA
1987

Printed in the United States of America

Library of Congress Cataloging in Publication Data

Eblaitica : essays on the Ebla archives and Eblaite language.

(Publications of the Center for Ebla Research at New York University)
Includes bibliographical references.
1. Ebla (Ancient City) 2. Ebla tablets. 3. Eblaite language.
I. Gordon, Cyrus Herzl, 1908- . II. Rendsburg, Gary.
III. Winter, Nathan H. IV. Series.
DS99.E25E35 1987 939′.4 86-29139
ISBN 0-931464-34-X

In Memoriam

Mr. David Rose
24 December 1891 – 16 July 1986

through whose vision and generosity
the Center for Ebla Research was established

זכר צדיק לברכה

Contents

Abbreviations

AB	Anchor Bible
AHw	W. von Soden, *Akkadisches Handwörterbuch* (Wiesbaden, 1965–81)
AfO	*Archiv für Orientforschung*
AJA	*American Journal of Archaeology*
AnOr	*Analecta Orientalia*
ARET	*Archivi reali di Ebla – Testi*
AS	Assyriological Studies
BA	*Biblical Archaeologist*
BHS	*Biblia Hebraica Stuttgartensia*
CAD	*The Assyrian Dictionary of the Oriental Institute of the University of Chicago*
CAH	*Cambridge Ancient History*
CRAI	*Comptes rendus de l'Académie des inscriptions et belles-lettres*
CRRA	*Compte rendu de la . . . Rencontre Assyriologique Internationale*
FAOS	*Freiburger Altorientalische Studien*
Fara	A. Deimel, *Die Inschriften von Fara*, 3 vols. (Leipzig, 1922–24)
GAG	W. von Soden, *Grundriss der akkadischen Grammatik* (*AnOr* 33; Rome, 1952)
IAS	R. D. Biggs, *Inscriptions from Tell Abū Ṣalābīkh* (Chicago, 1974)
IB	*Interpreter's Bible*
ICC	International Critical Commentary
IRSA	E. Sollberger and J.-R. Kupper, *Inscriptions royales sumériennes et akkadiennes* (Paris, 1971)
JAOS	*Journal of the American Oriental Society*
JBL	*Journal of Biblical Literature*
JCS	*Journal of Cuneiform Studies*
JEA	*Journal of Egyptian Archaeology*
JEOL	*Jaarbericht van het Voorazaiatische-Egyptisch Geselschap "Ex Oriente Lux"*
JNES	*Journal of Near Eastern Studies*
JPSV	*Jewish Publication Society Version* (1917)
JQR	*Jewish Quarterly Review*
JSS	*Journal of Semitic Studies*
KJV	*King James Version*
LAK	A. Deimel, *Liste der archäischen Keilschriftzeichen* (Leipzig, 1922) (=*Fara* I)

MAD	I. J. Gelb, *Materials for the Assyrian Dictionary*, 5 vols. (Chicago, 1952–70)
MARI	*Mari: annales de recherches interdisciplinaires*
MDP	*Mémoires de la Délégation en Perse*
MEE	*Materiali epigrafici di Ebla*
MSL	B. Landsberger, *et al.*, *Materialien zum sumerischen Lexikon* (Rome, 1937–)
MUSJ	*Mélanges de l'université Saint-Joseph*
NAB	*New American Bible*
NJPSV	*New Jewish Publication Society Version* (1962–82)
OA	*Oriens Antiquus*
OAIC	I. J. Gelb, *Old Akkadian Inscriptions in Chicago Natural History Museum* (Chicago, 1955)
OECT	*Oxford Editions of Cuneiform Texts*
Or	*Orientalia*
PBS	*Publications of the Babylonian Section of the University of Pennsylvania Museum*
PRU	*Le palais royal d'Ugarit*
RA	*Revue d'assyriologie et d'archéologie orientale*
RBI	*Rivista Biblica Italiana*
RGTC	*Répertoire Géographique des Textes Cunéiformes* (Wiesbaden, 1977–)
RLA	*Reallexikon der Assyriologie*
RSP	Y. Rosengarten, *Répertoire commenté des signes présargoniques sumériens de Lagaš* (Paris, 1967)
SEb	*Studi Eblaiti*
SKL	T. Jacobsen, *The Sumerian King List* (Chicago, 1939)
SMEA	*Studi micenei ed egeo-anatolici*
TIT	T. Jacobsen, *Toward the Image of Tammuz*, ed. W. L. Moran (Cambridge, MA, 1970)
UET	*Ur Excavations, Texts*
UF	*Ugarit-Forschungen*
UT	C. H. Gordon, *Ugaritic Textbook* (Rome, 1967)
VS	*Vorderasiatische Schriftdenkmäler*
WZKM	*Wiener Zeitschrift für die Kunde des Morgenlandes*

Introduction

CYRUS H. GORDON

The Center for Ebla Research was evoked by the discovery in 1974 and 1975 of the Ebla Archives by the Italian expedition led by Professor Paolo Matthiae of the University of Rome.[1] The unearthing of a great Early Bronze Age library electrified scholars engaged in the study of the Ancient Near East. I was attracted particularly to the problem of reconstructing the Eblaite language. The chairman of my department, Professor Nathan Winter, was most encouraging. Financial and moral support came soon thereafter from an enlightened philanthropist, the late Mr. David Rose, of Rose Associates in New York City.

Shortly after the discoveries, attempts were made to classify Eblaite, and there were advocates both of East Semitic and of West Semitic affinities. Eblaite is indeed a border language, with isoglosses in both directions. Its precise classification, however, is less important than its reconstruction.

The contributions that individual scholars are able to make depend largely on their background. Training in Mesopotamian cuneiform is basic. Other kinds of expertise in the Ancient Near East are also valuable in varying degree. In an age of less specialization—well before our knowledge explosion—all Assyriologists were conversant with Hebrew. Now there are cuneiformists who are unacquainted with Hebrew, as well as Hebraists ignorant of Akkadian. Such specialists can make contributions of a detailed and specific nature. Scholars with broader training must beware of inadequate control of the component materials that they compare. Yet, comparison is necessary for understanding the Ancient Near East because movement, trade, and interpenetration were so common. As a result, "The World of the Old Testament" is virtually coextensive with "The Cuneiform World."

No element remains the same in both the culture from which, and the culture into which, it is borrowed. (However different Eastern Orthodoxy and New England Protestantism appear, they both stem from the same Christianity. Would a "wild man from Borneo" perceive the common origin shared by Hagia Sophia and a wooden Congregational church in New Hampshire?)

[1] The general introductions to Ebla are: Paolo Matthiae, *Ebla: An Empire Rediscovered*, trans. Christopher Holme (Garden City, NY: Doubleday, 1981); and Giovanni Pettinato, *The Archives of Ebla*, with an Afterword by Mitchell Dahood (Garden City, NY: Doubleday, 1981).

The materials discovered at Ebla require specialized and comparative studies. Each scholar does the best he can with what he has.

As a Semitic language, Eblaite can be illuminated by any other Semitic language from Akkadian to Egyptian. Arabic, for example, will play a major role in our understanding of Eblaite, even though written Arabic does not begin until almost three millennia after the passing of Eblaite. To draw on Hebrew does not imply that Eblaite is Hebrew or even Canaanite. The earliest Hebrew records are about a thousand years later than the last texts in Eblaite. Pretending to know everything significant that happened in the interim may be an art, but it is not a science.

The reconstruction of Eblaite draws on various types of evidence from the Ebla tablets. The bilingual texts provide the Eblaite translation of many Sumerograms whose meanings are known. This is of obvious value for establishing some of the Eblaite vocabulary. But the meanings of other words, as well as the morphology and syntax, often come from translatable phrases imbedded in texts consisting largely of Sumerograms. Thus, in an Eblaite incantation, *an-na gú-wa-ti-ma i-za-ba-dè-ga*[2] means 'I have seized thee' (='I have thee in my power'). The pronoun *anna* 'I' shows that the verb is in the first person even though its prefix is *i-* (instead of *a-*). The accusative independent 2 m.s. pronoun *kuwati* is resumed by *-ka* suffixed to the verb. But the fact that the meaning and etymology are clear does not mean that we understand the forms. The pronoun 'I' is usually written *an-na* in Eblaite, less often, *a-na*. In the hitherto known Semitic languages, the *n* of this pronoun is not doubled. However, the orthographic norm in Mesopotamian cuneiform is: while a singly written consonant can be phonetically single or doubled, a doubly written consonant is phonetically geminated. Support for Eblaite *anna* may be forthcoming from the rare Hebrew accusative *-annī* 'me'[3] instead of the common *-anī*. The *i-* of *i-za-ba-dè-ga* 'I have seized thee' has been explained by Edzard in accordance wth Barth's law of vocalic sequence because the thematic vowel is *-a-*. Contrast *a-za-me-du* (ARET V, 17, text 1:I:1) = *ᵓaṣmidu* 'I have tied' (where the thematic vowel is not *-a-*, but *-i-*). The *-a-* of the second syllable is orthographic but not phonetic; the system of writing calls for signs of the consonant + vowel type, which conceals the presence of closed syllables. The connecting vowel (*-e-*) of *i-za-ba-dè-ga* (*ᵓiṣbaṭeka*) recalls the Hebrew pausal form אשמְרֶךָ. Thus, even when we can translate Eblaite accurately, the explanation of the grammatical details may require some recondite (and at times debatable) comparative data.

Even when the spelled-out words in Eblaite are minimal, it is possible to arrive at sound conclusions for describing Eblaite. This applies particularly to the syntax, because the Sumerograms in an Eblaite text appear in Eblaite word

[2] Dietz Otto Edzard, *Archivi Reali di Ebla—Testi* (ARET) V: *Hymnen, Beschwörungen und Verwandten* (Rome: Missione Archeologica Italiana in Siria, 1984), Text 4:II:2–4.

[3] Cf. forms like דָּנַנִּי "he has judged me" (Gen 30:6). Ps 118:18 is interesting in that it includes both forms (*-annī* and *-anī*): יַסֹּר יִסְּרַנִּי יָּהּ וְלַמָּוֶת לֹא נְתָנָנִי "Yah has verily chastised me but not delivered me to Death." For *-annī*, see further Gesenius-Kautzsch-Cowley § 26g.

order. The sentence *wa* DU$_{11}$-GA EN means 'the king said.' The only Eblaite word in this sentence spelled phonetically is *wa* = Semitic *wa* 'and.' The verb (DU$_{11}$-GA) and subject (EN) are Sumerograms. The construction is the one that appears in Hebrew as ויאמר המלך 'the king said,' in which the word order is fixed: (*wa* + verb)—(subject). Similarly *wa* ÍL IGI-IGI *wa* NAM-KU 'he lifted his eyes and swore,' is like Hebrew וישא עיניו וירא 'he lifted his eyes and saw.'[4] This establishes the so-called waw-conversive construction for Eblaite, the first time it appears in any known Semitic language. Note that the only phonetically written word in these sentences is *wa*. For further details, see pp. 21–22 below.

Ugaritic texts were first discovered in 1929. By 1940, a detailed *Ugaritic Grammar* was published. This was possible because so many of the Ugaritic tablets are in parallelistic poetry closely related to Old Testament poetry. Other types of Ugaritic texts, such as the numerous administrative lists and even bilingual texts, did not contribute as much to the reconstruction of the grammar as the literary texts with their parallelism. So far, in the extensive archives of Ebla, there is little evidence of literary compositions to provide the basis for any prompt and comprehensive reconstruction of Eblaite. The task will take a long time and require hard work on the part of many who labor in the fields of Assyriology and Semitics.

Eblaite, as recorded in the tablets from Ebla, is not a homogeneous local vernacular. It has close affinities to the local Semitic dialects attested during the early Bronze Age at Mari, Abu Salabiḫ, Kish, and other Mesopotamian sites. Indeed, Eblaite words are sometimes identical with Old Akkadian. Accordingly, Eblaite (especially in the bilingual texts) looks like the Semitic lingua franca used in the cuneiform world during the middle of the Early Bronze Age. There would be some chronological justification for calling Eblaite "Old Semitic," but this might convey the misimpression that Eblaite is "Primitive Semitic" (the hypothetical parent of the Semitic family), which it is not. So we will adhere to the label "Eblaite" to designate the mixture of Semitic dialects written by the scribes of Ebla in the twenty-third century.

The influence of cuneiform centers like Ebla was largely intellectual. The presence of Sumerian loanwords (like the architectural term *haykal* 'temple, palace' and *nomina agentis* forms like *naggâr* 'carpenter') in Arabic, Hebrew, Syro-Aramaic, and Ugaritic goes back to the Early Bronze Age when scribal activity was already intense in Syrian cities like Ebla and affected the urban civilizations of Syria-Palestine. We must reckon with the intellectual impact of the cities that fostered cuneiform scribes in the Early Bronze Age. The scribal schools reflect a far-flung educational system, often using the same textbooks (for example, the sign-list found both at Abu Salabiḫ and Ebla). Faculty and student exchange throughout the interregional system is also attested.[5] While in general all the then-known arts and sciences of the Ancient Near East were

[4] For the documentation, see Cyrus H. Gordon, "The 'Waw Conversive' from Eblaite to Hebrew," *Proceedings, The American Academy for Jewish Research* 50 (1983) 87–90.

[5] For the professor of mathematics who describes himself as a "scribe of Kish," and for the young scribes who came from Mari, see Pettinato, *The Archives of Ebla*, 239–40.

fostered at the cuneiform academies, it is philology that was central, demonstrated by the presence of sign-lists, syllabaries, bilingual vocabularies, and so forth. The bilinguals of Ebla and the quadrilinguals of Ugarit reflect the linguistic sophistication of the cuneiform cities of the West. The magnitude of the scribal impact is indicated by the fact that by the Amarna Age Mesopotamian cuneiform had become the written lingua franca of the entire Near East, from Egypt to Mesopotamia, including the East Mediterranean and Anatolia as well as Syria-Palestine.

The Center for Ebla Research is pleased to publish here a number of articles by Professor Alfonso Archi, the epigrapher of the Italian expedition at Ebla. The other articles are by members of the Ebla Seminar at New York University, with an additional contribution from a London colleague.

In February, 1983, Professors Matthiae and Archi visited New York University with members of their Ebla team. Dr. Matthiae delivered an illustrated lecture on the archeology of Ebla, while Dr. Archi addressed the Seminar and gave a public lecture on Eblaite.

In December, 1982, and January, 1983, I visited Syria to see the excavations at Ebla, accompanied by Joan K. Gordon, who served as photographer. Dr. Adnan Bounni, the Director of Syrian Excavations and Archeological Studies, was exceedingly kind in facilitating arrangements. The Director General of Syrian Antiquities and Museums, Dr. Afif Bahnassi, graciously saw to it that I visited the sites and museums, as well as met the Syrian archeologists and curators. The excavations of Ebla, Ugarit, and Ras ibn Hani were of special concern to me. At the Aleppo Museum, I was admitted to the underground treasure room where I could examine and handle tablets of the Ebla archives.

I owe a debt of gratitude to New York University, which provides the academic institutional base for the Center, thus supplying the indispensable general library, office space, utilities, classrooms, and so forth. Beyond that, the Center requires the aegis of a School within the University. The School of Education, under the leadership of Dean Robert A. Burnham, provided this haven. Moreover, the Center had to be sponsored departmentally. My Professorship at New York University, in the Department of Hebrew Culture and Education, calls for graduate teaching in the languages and cultural history of the Bible World. This means training Ph.D. candidates in Hebrew, Ugaritic, Aramaic, Arabic, Assyriology, and Egyptology. The distinctiveness of the program consists in the study of varying combinations of such subjects, not in isolation, but as interrelated facets of the Ancient Near East. The Chairman, Professor Nathan H. Winter, was supportive from the start, when I joined his Department in 1973, and gladly embraced the Center for Ebla Research subsequently, for the contribution that Ebla can make to our understanding of the Bible World. Thus, I had on hand a group of graduate students, some of whom I had already trained in cuneiform studies and who were prepared to add Eblaite to their repertoire. Without them, the Center could not function as a training ground.

Ebla Studies must reckon with the Ebla tablets as the point of departure. Individually, we bring to bear on the Ebla archives whatever collateral information we control. But simultaneously, the Ebla tablets are already shedding light on the whole gamut of Semitic studies. For example:

1. In Ugaritic and Minoan, the word for 'wine' is pronounced not *yayn*/*yên* but *yan* (written *ya-ne* in Minoan).[6] The development *ay* > *a* is now attested in Eblaite; e.g., the tree called *bîn* (< **bayn*; like *bît* < *bayt*) is written *ba-ne* in Eblaite. The same development occurs sporadically in Hebrew; thus, instead of the normal מאין 'whence?' we find מאן anomalously in 2 Kgs 5:25, where the *ktiv* is מֵאָן and the *qre* is מֵאַיִן. So we can now trace the shift of *ay* > *a* from Iron Age Hebrew, through Late Bronze Ugaritic and Middle Bronze Minoan, back to Early Bronze Eblaite.

2. In Ugaritic and Minoan, merchandise can be said 'to go out' (as distinct from the more logical 'to be brought out/issued' by someone). This idiom is attested in Eblaite,[7] showing that the Late Bronze Age idiom in Ugaritic goes back, not only in Sumerian but also in Semitic, to Early Bronze Age Ebla (with Minoan again in between).

Eblaite, as a new branch of Semitics, will have a growing impact on our understanding of Arabic, Ethiopic, Northwest Semitic, etc., including the Semitic stratum of Egyptian.

The Center and its publications do not intend to engage in any kind of special pleading. We are interested in truth, based on primary sources, wherever it may lead. This declaration should be unnecessary in the twentieth century, but a new and far-reaching discovery can give rise to misunderstandings and suspicions which must be laid to rest from the start.

Among those who have contributed to this volume are some whose names do not appear on the title page or in the table of contents. Especially worthy of mention are two participants in the Ebla Seminar at New York University, namely, Sharon Keller, a graduate fellow in the Ebla center, and Dr. Meir Lubetski, whose keen observations on the Eblaite language and onomasticon will be published in the near future. But we cannot state too emphatically that the existence as well as the accomplishments of the Center for Ebla Research we owe to Mr. David Rose, whose wide-ranging intellectual interests spontaneously embraced Ebla without any persuasion from anyone.[8]

[6] Cyrus H. Gordon, *Evidence for the Minoan Language* (Ventnor, NJ: Ventnor, 1966) 28–29 (§ 123).

[7] For Ebla examples of È 'to go out' (with merchandise as the subject), see tablet TM.75.G.1394: v. IV:20–V:8 (transliterated and translated by Pelio Fronzaroli, *SEb* 4 [1981] 168–69). For the same idiom in Minoan and Ugaritic, see Cyrus H. Gordon, "Further Notes on the Hagia Triada Tablet No. 31," *Kadmos* 15:1 (1976) 28–30.

[8] Since this volume first went to press, Joan K. Gordon died, after a long illness, on 25 September 1985. Tributes to her will appear in the near future.

In September, 1986, my professorship at N.Y.U. was transferred to the School of Arts and Science, and with it the Center for Ebla Research.

Ebla and Eblaite

ALFONSO ARCHI

In a well-known article of about twenty years ago, I. J. Gelb, after an accurate examination of the relevant epigraphic material, came to the following conclusions: "Our sources pertaining to the West Semites in Syria and Palestine flow almost uninterruptedly from the Old Babylonian period on. Two important conclusions can be drawn on the basis of the study of geographical names and of other, less important considerations: 1) The Semites entered Syria in mass in the Old Babylonian period, encountering a population of unknown, but certainly not Hurrian, ethnic affiliation. 2) The Semites must have been established in Palestine long before the Old Babylonian period, and nothing prevents us from assuming that they may have been native to the area from time immemorial."[1]

Now, with the discovery of Ebla, we have recovered ample written documentation which is older by several centuries than the Old Babylonian sources concerning Syria. The texts are to be dated approximately to the first half of the 24th century, more or less before the time of the reign of Sargon of Akkad (and we may confidently enough estimate that they cover an uninterrupted period of about 50 years). Since the picture that emerges from these texts is that of a relatively stable political situation—one of whose strengths was widespread urbanization—we can maintain that this culture developed, in its most fundamental aspects, at least some decades earlier, probably about halfway through the third millennium. This state of affairs was the creation of a Semitic language speaking people.

The history of Semitic populations was for many years described as a succession of waves of nomadic migrations which took place throughout the millennia: from Arabs to Arameans and, still earlier, Amorites. The Amorites would therefore have been the very first Semites to reach Syria. But during the last ten years a reinterpretation of the information which the documents from Mari provide has (a) shown that one must not mistake pastoralism for nomadism, and (b) illustrated how pastoralists in fact coexisted with sectors of settled population. With Ebla, however, it now appears that the social pattern

* Text of a paper read at New York University and several other universities in the Spring of 1983.

[1] I. J. Gelb, "The Early History of the West Semitic People," *JCS* 15 (1961) 45.

built around village and pastoral life represented by the regions around Mari during the second millennium was not shared by all the Semitic language speaking peoples on the margins of the great Sumerian and Akkadian centers. Numerous urban centers populated by Semites—who cannot, however, be identified with the Amorites—flourished in the pre-Sargonic age in the whole of Northern Syria west of the Euphrates. Furthermore, the Semites were not the original inhabitants of Syria. Many place names and various divine names which cannot be analyzed as Semitic illustrate that originally there must have been a non-Semitic population in Syria.

A name both classifies and defines. For this reason it is necessary to avoid giving names which already have precise meanings to things which can be defined only partially. If one considers that scholars (even though at times for different reasons) have not reached agreement in considering as Canaanite the language of Ugarit, it makes no sense to use the term "Early Canaanite" for the language of Ebla. Those who have done so have used incomplete (at times also inconsistent) linguistic evidence derived from cultural data (which almost always in fact are presumed data, particularly as far as religion is concerned). In this sense, the tendency to find linguistically direct genealogies has also played a part in the debate; on the contrary, it is now clear that the Semitic languages, in areas which knew neither unification nor political continuity, are only segments of an extensive reality which developed differently in different regions and periods. It is clear that to call the language the evidence for which comes from the archives of Ebla, "Eblaite," is only stating a fact at an elementary level. Yet this name may convey the misconception that the language was limited to Ebla. I believe indeed that the language of Ebla was spoken in the whole of Northern Syria. On the other hand, it is also true that even if one cannot speak of an Eblaite empire, Ebla certainly exercised a large influence over the whole area, but we do not know for how long. Only if the epigraphic documentation should increase substantially (and it is not unlikely that archives of the Eblaite age will someday be discovered in the Jezireh or that the third millennium texts from Mari will increase in number) and the picture of history should in that way change will it be appropriate to reopen this question.

What then is the linguistic material at our disposal? First of all, there are about 1,200 words in the bilingual lexical texts, the so-called "dictionaries." The Eblaite scribes constructed a series (arranged according to the initial signs) of more than 1,500 Sumerian words, which are only partially glossed with the corresponding Eblaite words. The corpus is formed by four texts which are duplicates, two of which are represented by one large table each (about twenty columns on the obverse and the same on the reverse), one by two tablets, and the last by five tablets of medium size. Sixteen other tablets are abstracts from this series. The information here cited concerns the texts which have been reconstructed and restored. Larger numbers of texts which have been cited even recently refer in fact to the fragments (about 140), to be considered separately. The name "dictionary" sounds in itself reassuring, being by definition the means which enables us to overcome lexical difficulties. But here we must avoid deluding ourselves. Sumerian words which are familiar to us have similarly clear Eblaite equivalents (for example, Sum. sa-šu = Ebl. *ma-da-nu*, cf. Akk. *matnum* 'sinew'; in Sum. 'sinew of the hand'). But we do not know the meaning of a large number of the Sumerian words (indeed, some compound words occur in fact only at Ebla), so that at times the Ebla gloss, by providing the opportunity to make comparisons with other Semitic languages, sheds light on the Sumerian.

These lists constitute an unprecedented work of lexicography. The Eblaite scribes had (in one way or another) to solve a large number of problems. Not all the lexical equivalents can have been so immediately obvious as in the case of Sum. šeš-mu = Ebl. *a-ḫu-um* 'brother.' And if in this case we have a real overlapping, at times the semantic fields of the two terms coincide only in part: Sum. šà-gal 'great stomach, belly,' but also 'fodder,' = Ebl. *kar-su-um*, cf. Akk. *karšum* 'stomach.' Or the Eblaite term may have a more restricted connotation than its Sumerian counterpart; e.g., Sum. šà = Ebl. *ʾà-da-ru*$_{12}$*-um*. The Sumerian means 'heart' and corresponds to Akk. *libbum* 'heart' or *qerbum* 'inside(s),' while the Eblaite corresponds to the Ugaritic and Hebrew *ḥeder* 'room,' Arabic *ḫidr* 'inside of a building,' Ethiopic *ḫadara* 'to live.' Sometimes the Eblaite scribes, like the Akkadian, use two words for Sumerian compound words: Sum. igi-íl 'to lift the eyes' = Ebl. *na-zi-i a-na-a*, corresponding to Akk. *našûm ša īni*.

The lexicon of the glosses is almost always independent of the Akkadian tradition. For example, the corresponding word to the Sum. balag 'lyre,' is *kinnārum*, a word common to all Semitic languages (excluding Ethiopic), while Akkadian has a loanword from Sumerian: *balaggum*. Of course, there are loanwords from Sumerian for some technical terms in Eblaite as well, like *ma-la-ḫu-um* 'boatman, sailor' (Akk. *malāḫum*, WSem. *mallāḥ*) from the Sum. ma-laḫ$_4$. Nevertheless, overall, the glosses of the lists are indeed representative of the Eblaite lexicon, their choice not having been influenced by elaborations of the Mesopotamian school.

Because this lexical series is reproduced in several tablets, the same word is often found with graphic variations. This is of great help in determining the exact spelling of the word. The sign LUM, which often appears in a final position, can be read, for example, *gúm* and *núm* as well as *lum*. A variant for the third consonant of a word means in many cases that the interpretations theoretically possible must be multiplied by three. Fortunately, at times there is a variant without mimation, *lu*, *gu*, *nu*, which clarifies the problem. But there are cases which are still more complicated. The sign NI can be read in five different ways: *ni*, *ì*, *li*, *ʾa*$_y$, *bu*$_x$; the last two are new to us, being attesed only at Ebla. In general, the Eblaite syllabary (that is to say, the phonetic values of each sign) has many points of contact with the Akkadian; the Eblaite, however, belongs to another tradition (that of Kish or another one developed in Syria, at Mari or Ebla?) which includes a number of Sumerian phonetic values

(EN = ru_{12}; NAP = *nap*, etc.). To determine correctly the syllabic values of the signs is the point of departure in interpreting the language. It is primarily for this purpose that the lexical lists are of inestimable value.

Up to now it has been difficult to estimate the extent of Eblaite vocabulary in the economic texts. We have many thousands of tablets and fragments, drawn up, however, in rather repetitive patterns. And in this case the impact of Sumerian technical expressions is so great that the Sumerian terms are more numerous than the Eblaite. There is more variety in the lexicon of the letters and the royal decrees (ca. 100 in number) and the mythological texts (ca. 20). Here, however, the difficulties of interpretation are even greater.

Personal names provide the only source at our disposal for Amorite, and the most important for Old Akkadian as well. Even though the Eblaite documentation is rather rich in different kinds of texts, even here personal names provide pronominal and verbal forms which do not in general appear in economic texts or even in letters. More than 2,000 Eblaite personal names have so far been published, and it is reasonable to expect this number to double within a few years. For a point of comparison we might bear in mind that the large volume dedicated to the Amorite names by I. J. Gelb and his collaborators assembles 6,500 names, coming from numerous archives, as many Mesopotamian as Syrian, which cover a period of about eight centuries.[2]

About 800 place names have been published and it is possible that this number too will be doubled. Many of these names refer to small places in the environs of Ebla, as we may conclude from the type of document involved (agricultural products come in large part from the villages in the region of Ebla, while the exchange of clothes and metals covers a vast area, even as far as the Tigris). This part of the documentation is difficult to evaluate, since many names (most of which are impossible to locate geographically) may be from regions outside the linguistic area of Ebla. Furthermore, as has already been noted, many of these names do not seem to be Semitic and probably come from a pre-Eblaite phase.

The divine names (about 100), which are so important in determining the nature of Ebla's culture, are much less important for the study of the language. Semitic divine names, when they are involved, are difficult to analyze. But we must bear in mind that the first of the most important divinities of the *city* of Ebla—the one who presides over oaths, namely, Kura—does not seem to be Semitic (the other two are the Weather-god Adad, and the Sun-god, always written in Sumerian, ^{d}U t u, so that we do not know the Eblaite reading). Many of the others are found in the Semitic religion of Mesopotamia (Dagan, Eštar, Išḫara), while others, Rašap and Kamiš, as is well known, are attested later in western areas. Perhaps not Semitic and therefore no longer attested after the third millennium is another extremely important divinity: NI-*da-kul*, whose cult centers are found in the Orontes valley. Two other gods, Adamma and Ašdabi, are included in the pantheon of the Hurrians of Syria and Anatolia in the second millennium. The god Yaw (whose name is considered an archaic form of

[2] I. J. Gelb, *Computer-aided Analysis of Amorite* (AS 21; Chicago, 1980).

Yahwe) is not attested in the Eblaite offering lists. The element *-ià* (NI), which appears in personal names and was interpreted as a shortened form of Yaw, is in fact to be read *-ì* or *lí*, because it often alternates with *-Il* in the same tablet in the name of the same person, such as in *Ḫa-ra-Il*/*Ḫa-ra-ì*/*lí* 'El/God has chosen.'[3]

In his two studies on Ebla, Gelb introduced and developed the concept of "Kish tradition," later replaced by "Kish Civilization."[4] It is certainly true that Ebla participated in the culture which flourished at Kish, the famous Mesopotamian city. First of all, the texts found at Ebla reflect some of the characteristics of the writing system created at Kish, adapting the Sumerian system to a Semitic language (e.g., the use of certain syllabograms: $iš_{11}$ = LAM×KUR; of certain logograms: dùl 'statue,' AB×ÁŠ 'elder'). It is also true that Ebla and Mari, in the north, and Kish and Abu Ṣalabiḫ in the south, are linked by scribal contacts, either directly or indirectly. Some Sumerian unilingual lexical lists from Ebla (and at least one literary text) are faithful copies (and perhaps among them there are also some originals) of texts which come (via Mari) from the Kish area. The signs are of the same shape and size, and at times the number of cases for each column is also the same. It is now well known that one text reproduces a mathematical progression compiled by a certain Išma-I(l) 'scribe of Kish.'[5] In fact, the economic texts show how frequent the contacts between Ebla and Kish were (from a cursory reading it has been possible to find about 100 references to Kish).

Gifts were exchanged between the two kings (Ibbi-Zikir, for example, on the occasion of the marriage of one of his daughters, Ḫirdut, sent clothes and two lapis lazuli and gold bracelets to the king of Kish). Unfortunately, no names of the kings of Kish are attested (they would have permitted an important synchronism between Kish, Mari, and Ebla). All we know is that two brothers of the sovereign who was contemporary with Ibbi-Zikir were called, respectively, *I-rí-sum* and *Bù-šu-um* (incidentally, all the personal names of people from Kish attested at Ebla show that in the former city only the Akkadian language was in use). But all of another group of documents, in particular the bilingual lexical texts which undoubtedly are one of the major linguistic achievements of the entire third millennium, are without doubt of the Ebla school. Another aspect to be considered is that, while it is true that the decimal system was in use both at Ebla and Abu Ṣalabiḫ, it is very likely that it was originally common to all the Semites. As far as the system of measures is concerned, we do not in fact know if at Kish the mina was valued at about 470 grams, as at Ebla, or (as is more probable) at 504 grams, like the Sumerian. But it is in its religion that the originality of the Eblaite culture is revealed. The statement that "the divine element ᵓIl (later Semitic ᵓEl), who is found in numerous names of the Mesopotamian Semites in Early Dynastic times is also

[3] A. Archi, *Biblica* 60 (1979) 556–60; and A. Archi, *BA* 44 (1981) 145–46.

[4] I. J. Gelb, "Thoughts about Ibla: A Preliminary Evaluation, March 1977," *Syro-Mesopotamian Studies* 1:1 (1977); I. J. Gelb, "Ebla and the Kish Civilization," in *La lingua di Ebla*, ed. L. Cagni (Naples, 1981) 9–73.

[5] A. Archi, *SEb* 3 (1980) 64–65.

at home at Abu Ṣalabiḫ and Ebla,"[6] does not more than define a common level in Semitic religious experience; it is certainly not sufficient for positing the existence of religious communities in the areas where the names are found.

However, to participate in certain aspects of a culture does not mean to share the same language. As Gelb writes: "The identification of 'Kishite' and Eblaic does not appear likely. Alone, the long distance between Kish and Ebla militates against such a possibility and the assumption of a unifying chancery language is negated by the fact that Kish and Ebla represent distinct political entities."[7]

It is generally accepted that the homeland of the Amorites was in the desert of Northern Syria, west of the Middle Euphrates (the Akkadian king Šar-kali-šarri achieved a victory "over the Amorites in the mountain of *Ba-sa-ar*," and *Ba-sa-ar* is identified with Jebel Bišri). What information, then, do the archives of Ebla provide about the Amorites? Is it possible to make a synchronic examination of Eblaite and Amorite? With regard to the material culture, a type of dagger (gír), by far the most common, is called mar-tu, without the determinative KI, which is used for place names. One cannot be certain that this really refers to daggers of an Amorite type, particularly as the qualification *Mar-tu/tum*^{ki} is in general very rare. It has not hitherto been possible to find more than about 30 attestations of this geographical name. From these we may deduce that (1) the region of Martu was not far from Emar (and therefore near Jebel Bišri), and (2) it was ruled by a king (the title is expressed both by the term used at Ebla, Sum. en, and therefore to be read *malikum*, and by that in use in Mesopotamia, Sum. lugal). This latter fact is certainly surprising, because this title presupposes a social system based on urban structures. On the other hand, everything hitherto known indicates that the Amorites had a tribal system. The Eblaites, then, ignored the specific title of the Amorite heads of tribes but made the chiefs' functions equivalent to those of a king. But it is certainly not chance that the references to Amurru are so rare (Emar and Mari, on the other hand, are attested several hundred times). It is evident that the Amorites, because they lived in a semi-nomadic or pastoral state, were on the periphery—as much from the geographical as the political point of view—of the connections the Eblaites had with the other peoples. The personal names qualified by the appellative "Amorite" which are known to me are no more than twelve and are not, furthermore, very significant. Certainly the name of a king of Martum, lugal *Mar-tum*^{ki} in an Ebla tablet, that is, *A-mu-ti*, is found later in a text of Ur III in the form *Ià-a-mu-tum*; and later on in Old Babylonian times there are more names of the type *Ia-mu-tu* + DN (this illustrates, by the way, how initial *a-* in Eblaite can be read as *ia-*). But other names could be Eblaite or even Akkadian: *Puzur*$_4$*-ru*$_{12}$, and *A-bu-mu-du*. And some others, like *I-ku-tu-a-bu* and EN-*zu-ru*$_{12}$, are not easy to interpret. In short, we have very little information about Amorite from the Ebla texts.

[6] Gelb, "Ebla and the Kish Civilization," 63.
[7] Ibid., 70.

Let us consider some points in the morphology of the Eblaite language.[8] For the independent personal pronoun we have the 1 c.s. *an-na* and 2 m.s. *an-da*, as in Arabic and Ethiopic. By contrast, in Akkadian (and in certain forms of the Ug. and Heb. pronoun) we have in the 1 c.s. the additional element *-k*: *anāku*, and in the 2 m.s. we have the assimilation of *n*: *attā*. Other Eblaite forms are 2 m.pl. *an-da-nu*; 3 m.s. *su-wa*; 3 f.s. *si-a*; 3 m.pl. *su-nu*. Spellings SA/SI/SU are used for the Proto-Semitic /*š*/. In the forms with sibilants, therefore, there is agreement between Eblaite and Akkadian, Amorite, South Arabian (with the exception of Sabean), and Egyptian. As in Akkadian, the pronoun was declined, as shown by the 3 s. forms *su-wa-ti* (gen.-acc.); *su-wa-si* (dat.).

Personal pronoun suffixes include 1 c.s. *-i*/*-a* (*áš-da-a*) (as in Akkadian and Arabic); 2 m.s. *-ga*; 3 m.s. *-su*, 3 f.s. *-sa* (Akkadian: *-šu*, *-ša*; Arabic and Hebrew: *-hū*, *-hā*); 1 c.pl. *-na*/*-nu* (*áš-du-na*, *áš-du-nu*) (Akk.: *-ni*/*-na*; Arabic, Ethiopic: *-na*); 3 m.pl. *-su-nu*, 3 f.pl. *-si-na* (as in Akkadian). Like Akkadian, Eblaite has different forms for the dative and the accusative. For the dative, the following forms are attested: 2 m.s. *-kum* (maškim-*kum*; ì-na-sum-*kum*); 3 m.s. *-su-um*, both of which correspond to the Akkadian forms. The following are accusative forms: 1 c.s. *-ni*; 2 m.s. *-ga*, 2 f.s. *-gi*; 3 m.s. *-su*; 2 m.pl. *-gú-nu*; 3 m.pl. *-su-nu*; and perhaps 3 f.pl. *-si-na-at*.

The forms of the determinative-relative pronoun also correspond to the Akkadian and Amorite: m.s. *šu* (nom.), *ši* (gen.), *ša* (acc.); f.s. *ša-du* (nom.), *ša-ti* (gen.); m.pl. *šu-ti* (gen.-acc.); f.pl. *ša-du* (nom.) *ša-ti* (gen.-acc.). For the interrogative, the forms of the animate pronoun 'who?' must be *ma-nu* (nom.), *ma-na* (acc.), but these are uncertain attestations. The inanimate 'what?' in the nom. is *mi*(*n*) (*mi-ga-Il* /*min-ka-ᵓIl*/ 'What is yours, O El?'; *mi-kum-*ᵈ*Ku-ra* /*min-kum-Kura*/ 'What is with you, O Kura?'), presumably with the variants *mi*/*me-nu*. The acc. is *mi-na*, and the dat. (with adverbial function) *mi-ne-iš*. This constitutes a further tie with Akkadian, while Amorite, Arabic, and Hebrew have *ma*. Eblaite and Akkadian, because they are archaic languages, decline this pronoun.

We have the following data for the indefinite pronoun. Definitely attested is the animate nom. *ma-nu-ma* (*áš-ti* dam-guruš *ma-nu-ma* ná 'Whoever lies with the wife of a worker . . . .'). The acc. *ma-nu-ma* is not certain. The inanimate nom. is *mi-nu-ma* (*mi-nu-ma* ì-na-sum ì-na-sum dumu-nita-dumu-nita PN 'Whatever will be given to the sons of PN').

Forms of the independent possessive pronoun have not yet been identified at Ebla, though they are attested in Old Akkadian. Altogether, the system of pronouns seems to be strictly parallel to that of Old Akkadian.

With regard to noun morphology, we note several matters briefly. The dual in the economic texts is expressed by spellings of the type *ab-si*-2; *sa-ḫa*-2 (cf. *sa-ḫa-wa*). In the lexical lists on the other hand, the dual genitive is frequently

[8] For Eblaite grammar, see P. Fronzaroli, *SEb* 5 (in press); and Gelb, "Ebla and the Kish Civilization."

expressed phonetically: *ma-wu i-da-a* (Sum. a-šu-luḫ) /*māw-ū yid-ayn*/ 'water for the hands'; *ḫu-ma-zu a-na-a* (Sum. igi-du_8-du_8) /*ḫumaṣ-u* ᶜ*ayn-ayn*/ 'deprived of the eyes.'

Since mimation is not expressed regularly, only from context can it be decided whether nouns whose last sign is CV(*u*) have the ending /*ū*/ of the plural.

Besides the nominative case ending, the genitive is also well attested (e.g., *ti-a-ma-tim* 'of the sea'). However, no clear attestation of the accusative is known.

The dative-terminative suffix /*iš*/ occurs (as in Akkadian) with infinitives (ì-na-sum *a-ga-mi-iš* engar-engar). This takes an adverbial meaning with adjectives (*ar-ḫi-iš ar-ḫi-iš* 'very rapidly').

The construct state is not always expressed in writing. Besides forms like *ḫa-za-nu* GN 'mayor of GN,' we have *ma-lik-tum*/*ba-da-lum* GN 'queen, merchant of GN,' and also *ma-lik* GN. It is clear that, like certain Sumerian terms that were used by the Eblaite scribes as nouns and, without verbal prefixes, also as verbs (ná 'bed, to sleep'), Eblaite terms could also function as logograms in scribal usage. The problem is made more complex by the unsystematic use of mimation. However, phrases like *ba-da-gu da-ne-um* 'to decide a judicial case' contain examples of the construct, because the ending lacks mimation.

The predicate state has the same termination as the construct, e.g., *A-bu*-DN. But as in Old Akkadian, there is a second form in *-a*, e.g., *A-ba*-DN, *A-ḫa*-DN 'DN is a father, a brother.'

For examples of the absolute state, we have nominal stems without endings for divine names, e.g., ᵈ*Ga-mi-iš*, ᵈ*Ra-sa-ap*; for geographical names, e.g., *A-da-bí-ik*ᵏⁱ, *A-da-ti-ik*ᵏⁱ; and also for month names, e.g., iti *za-*ᵓ*à-na-at*. The latter also take forms with the ending vowel and mimation as well: *A-da-bí-gú*ᵏⁱ, *A-da-ti-gú*ᵏⁱ, *za-*ᵓ*à-tum*.

In the case of the verb, we must limit ourselves to the most relevant facts. It is held that the original prefix of the 3 m.s. was *ya-*, which in Akkadian changed to *yi-*. The form attested at Ebla is *yi-*: *Ib-ri-um* /*yibrium*/ 'he has seen,' from **br*ᵓ; *I-bí-Da-mu* /*yibbi*ᵓ DN/ 'DN has called'; *I-i-da-du* /*yiḫyi*-DN/ 'may he live, O DN!'. On the other hand, we have seen that Amorite *A-mu-ti* is an example of how *ya-* could be expressed by *a-*. Furthermore, the sign NI+*a-* (*Ì-a-du*, *Ì-a-sa-du*, etc.) could be used. It is therefore certain that we must not read /*yabrium*/. Once more there is morphological agreement between Eblaite and Akkadian.

In the West Semitic and Arabic perfect the *qatal* forms generally indicate completed action. Eblaite has such forms which do not seem to have the functions of a stative; thus, terms like *Ḫa-ra-Il* /*ḫāra*-DN/ 'DN chose,' exist alongside forms like *Iḫ-ra-Ma-lik*. This example provides a correspondence between Eblaite and West Semitic.

A few words can be added on the verbal stems. Besides the B (or G) stem, Bt is also well attested: *Iš-da-ma* /*yištama*ᶜ/ 'he heard.' For the D stem, one could consider the infinitive and the present-future of *$q\d{t}r$*: 'to burn' *ga-du-ru*$_{12}$ *u*$_9$*-ga-da-ra* /*qaṭṭuru*(*m*) *yuqaṭṭārā*/. The Š stem is attested in the infinitive: *sa-ḫu-sum*, from *ʾḫḏ 'to keep.' For Št, see the verbal noun *du-uš-da-gi-lu-um*, from *ʾkl 'to eat.'

Finally, we may list the prepositions: *in*, locative and temporal (as in Old Akkadian); *al*, locative (as in other Semitic languages); *si-in*, directive; ʾ*a*$_y$(NI)*-na* 'to' (as in Akkadian); *iš*, *iš*$_{11}$*-ki* 'in favor of'; *áš-ti*, *áš-da* 'by' (Akkadian *ište* and *itti*); *áš-du*, ablative (Old Akkadian *ištum*); *mi-in* 'from' (as in Arabic and Hebrew).

So, a series of morphological elements is common to both Eblaite and Old Akkadian. On the other hand, from the lexical point of view (even though Eblaite lexicographic studies are only at the beginning), one can already say that a whole series of isoglosses ties Eblaite to Northwest and Southwest Semitic. We can well omit Kulturwörter like *kinnārum* 'lyre' (Akk. *balaggum*); and *ar-za-túm*, Sum. GIŠ-nun-mí, a conifer which is widespread in the Syro-Palestine area, see Heb. ʾ*erez*, Syr. ʾ*arza*, Ar., Eth. ʾ*arz*. But let us consider instead terms like the verb *ḥāyā* 'to live,' a form of which has been previously examined; or *ur-pù-um*, Sum. ab-lá, 'window,' see Ug. *urbt*, Heb. ʾ*ărubbā* (Akk., differently, *aptum*); or *ba-da-lum* 'merchant,' see Ar. *badal* 'to barter,' while the root **bdl* 'to substitute, separate' is widespread in the whole western area. If Eblaite must be classified on the basis of morphology as a language which is parallel to Old Akkadian, the lexicon nevertheless indicates that it was a language of a population whose cultural development was different from that of the Akkadians.

What was the area over which the language of Ebla was spread? The material at our disposal for such an enquiry consists only of personal names, and there are grave disadvantages in depending on them alone. Although it is true that the place of origin of many people is given, it is also true that for the vast majority of place names it is not possible to establish the location. And if we want to proceed in a methodologically correct way, it will be necessary to exclude from the corpus of genuinely Eblaite names all those for which the provenance is not given.

The vast majority of the names are Semitic. There is not a single Hurrian name, although some people are said to come from places which must certainly be located between the Habur and the Tigris. But the publication of the third millennium texts from Gazur (later Nuzi) caused E. Speiser to retract his theory that the original population of Northern Mesopotamia consisted of Hurrians. Among the personal names attested at Gazur no more than two or three can even hypothetically be considered Hurrian. The Ebla documentation confirms that the Hurrians did not reach the Habur area before the end of the Akkadian dynasty.

It is not easy to identify a single city on the Mediterranean coast with city-names in the Ebla texts with sufficient certainly to have a basis of comparison for personal names in that area. It has been suggested that we read *Du-lu*^{ki} 'Gubla,' that is, Byblos; and one expects Byblos to be attested at Ebla.

But this reading is ruled out by the fact that at Ebla the name never ends in *-a*; and, furthermore, it has still not been demonstrated that the first sign, DU, can be read *gub*. Nevertheless, at Dulu, beside the cult of the god Adad, there is evidence of the cult of a god ^{d}NE-*ti-a-du* (called 'God of Dulu,' dingir *Du-lu*^{ki}, not otherwise known). In the personal names, gods like El (*En-na-il*), Ma-lik (*A-zi-Ma-lik*; *Ìr-an-Ma-lik*; *Zi-dam-Ma-lik*), and Kamiš (*I-ti-*^{d}*Ga-miš*) occur. Among the other personal names we may note *A-mu*, *Ar-ra-du-lum*/*Ar-ra-ti-lum*, *Gú-ru-du*, *Ḫa-ba-ti-a-dar* (cf. Eblaite *Ḫa-ba-ti*, Ur III *Ḫa-ba-ti-a*, OB Mari *Ḫa-ba-du-*DINGIR), *Lu-sa-ra-du*/*Lu-wa-sa-ra-du*/*Mu-sa-ra-du*. The second element of the latter names is to be identified with *šarratum* 'queen' (see Sargonic *Ma-ma-sa-ra-at*). As 'queen' at Ebla is *maliktum*, these names appear to follow an East Semitic tradition. With *Mu-zi*, compare OB Mari *Mu-zi-ya*. Overall, the names of persons associated with *Du-lu*^{ki} are analogous to those of Ebla and are to be interpreted as Semitic. For the northern region, we may cite names from Karkemiš, such as *ʾÀ-daš*, *I-zu-kum-ì*, *Ìr-an-da-ar*, *Zé-da-ar*, *Zi-i-sar*; and names from Harran, such as *En-na-ni-Il*, *Ar-si-a-ḫu*, *Su-a-ḫu*, and *Zu-ga-*LUM, *maliktum* 'queen' of Harran. Apart from this last name, all the others are also attested at Ebla.

For the Tigris and Habur area, let us look at Kakmium (a city which is well known from the Mari texts as Kakmum). Many theophoric names have, as the second element, the god Malik: *Ar-ra-Ma-lik*, *Du-bù-ḫu-Ma-lik*, and *I-ti-Ma-lik*. But we also note Damu: *Ib-gi-Da-mu* and *Iš*$_{11}$*-gur-Da-mu*; and Zikir: *Du-bí-Zi-kir* and *Il-ba-Zi-kir*. All of these names are also well attested at Ebla. At Emar (Meskene) on the Euphrates, theophorous names with Damu are very frequent for the royal family: *Iš*$_{11}$*-gi-Da-mu*, *Ru*$_{12}$*-zi-Da-mu*, and *Sur*$_{y}$*-sa-Da-mu*. Furthermore, there are names with Malik, e.g., *A-bù-Ma-lik* and *Ib-du-Ma-lik*.

Taken as a whole, it seems that throughout Northern Syria, from Ebla to the Euphrates and the Tigris, the same names or name-types were used. Therefore, the evidence is that the same language and the same tradition prevailed. At Mari, names like those of Ebla, such as *Ìr-an-Ma-lik*, are still found. But, in general, the Ebla tradition is different, with, for example, compound names with the god Dagan: *En-na-Da-gan* and *Bù-da-*^{d}*Da-gan*; and above all with the Sun-god: ^{d}Utu*-a-ḫu* and *Puzur*$_{4}$*-ra-*^{d}Utu. Finally, several names have as the first element the preterite of *šaṭāpum* 'to preserve': *Iš-dub-bù* and *Iš-dub-*NI. In this there is a point of contact with the names of Kish attested from the Eblaite documentation, like *Iš-dub-*^{d}Utu. There are many names at Kish which follow a tradition different from the Eblaite, like the theophoric names with Suʾen, the Moon-god: *Ìr-an-Zu-i-nu* and *Du-bí-Zu-i-nu*. There is also *I-rí-su*, not attested at Ebla, but found only in Sargonic texts. However, there are some names which are analogous to those of Ebla: *I-da-*NI (well attested in Presargonic and Sargonic texts, and also at Ebla: *I-da-Ma-lik*) and *Iš-má-*NI (Old Akkadian from Kish: *Iš-má-*DINGIR; at Ebla: *Iš-má-Da-mu*/*Ma-lik*).

We must therefore conclude that on the sole basis of personal names it would be very difficult to distinguish the language of Ebla from the Old Akkadian of Kish. The North Syrian tradition of personal names is not, however, the same as that of Mari and Kish. Ebla and Kish represent, then, two different cultures.

Eblaitica

CYRUS H. GORDON

The use of É to represent a laryngeal followed by a vowel or diphthong was widespread in the cuneiform tradition.[1] Otherwise, Sumerian É-GAL could not have come into West Semitic as *haykal* 'temple, palace,' cf. idigna = *ḥiddeqel* 'Tigris.' For an example of É = *ha* in Eblaite, note the bilingual equation al-DU = *É-a-gu-um*,[2] to be normalized *hâkum*. The Eblaite root 'to go' is the same as Aramaic *hâk* 'to go'; note Biblical Aramaic יהך 'he will go' and the infinitive (with the preposition) למהך 'to go' (Ezra 5:15; 7:13). Since Hebrew הלך 'to go' has לך in the imperative (and, accordingly, ילך in the imperfect), it is possible to explain הלך as a conflation of two roots, הך and לך, both meaning 'to go'; the conflation might well have been facilitated by their identical ending in *-k*.[3] For É = *ḥa*(*y*) in Eblaite, note also ŠÀ = É-*da-ru*$_{X}$*-um*, corresponding to Hebrew חדר 'room.'[4] But the most interesting example of É = *ḥa*(*y*) is present in the bilingual equation EN-KI = *É-um*.[5]

The name of the god EN-KI means 'Lord of the Earth' in Sumerian. The Semitic Akkadians called him *É-a*, which has been taken to mean 'House of Water.' However, É 'house' and A 'water' are Sumerian, not Akkadian. A case can be made for 'House of Water' because sea is down like earth, rather than up like sky. Moreover, Enki's shrine is surrounded by water.[6] But Ebla has added a new dimension to the discussion of Enki = Ea; for EN-KI = Eblaite *É-um* in the bilinguals. The *-um* is the Semitic nominative ending with mimation, so that *É* stands for the divine name stripped of the case ending.

If EN-KI were simply translated into Akkadian, it would be *Bêl-irṣitim* 'Lord of the Earth.' But the case of *É-a* is quite different. We shall turn to West Semitic for the solution.

[1] Sooner or later this will have to be reflected in Assyriological transliteration and normalization.

[2] *MEE* 4, p. 308, #984.

[3] OT *hâk* is limited to Ezra (5:15; 7:13). Daniel has הלך throughout, with no examples of *hâk*.

[4] *MEE* 4, texts 4–6, p. 14, v. III: 8–9.

[5] *MEE* 4, p. 290, #803. Elena Arcari, *Or* 53 (1984) 443 (as David Owen calls to my attention) notes that *É-um* may "possibly" stand for *ḥayyum*.

[6] Often represented on cylinder seals; for a literary reference, note Gilgamesh Epic XI:42. The *a* of *É-a* indicates the ending phonetically (i.e., *É-a* = *ḥa*(*y*)*ya*); the iconography of the watery shrine is thus secondary, prompted by the scribal "popular etymology" of É-A as 'House of Water,' for in Sumerian, É = 'house' and A = 'water.'

At Ugarit, the most active god of fertility is Baal 'the Lord,' who is specifically *Bᶜl-arṣ* 'Lord of the Earth,' the precise equivalent of EN-KI. Enki[7] and Bᶜl-arṣ both have among their functions the fertility of plants and animals.

The myths about Baal stress the theme of the dying or disappearing god[8] whose resurrection or reappearance is necessary for the return of fertility. The saddest moment in the religion is the disappearance or death of Baal, signifying the onslaught of famine: *kmt aliyn bᶜl kḫlq zbl bᶜl arṣ* (*UT* 49:I:13–14) 'for dead is Almighty Baal, perished is the Prince, Lord of the Earth.' The most joyous moment is the discovery that Baal has returned to life to inaugurate a new cycle of fertility: *kḥy aliyn bᶜl kiṯ zbl bᶜl arṣ* (*UT* 49:III:8–9, 20–21) 'for Almighty Baal is alive; the Prince Lord of Earth, exists.'

Accordingly, the *É* in *É-um*/*É-a* reflects West Semitic *ḥy* 'he lives' or 'is alive.' The name *É-a* can only be West Semitic; for the root *ḥyy*/*ḥwy* 'to live' is replaced by an entirely different root (*blṭ*) in Akkadian.

The early presence of West Semitic gods or divine epithets in the Akkadian pantheon is not surprising. The West Semitic Dagan has long been known as the tutelary god of the Akkad Dynasty. Now it turns out that *É-a*, who alone among the gods saved humanity from annihilation in the days of Utnapishtim, has the West Semitic name *Ḥay*(*y*)*a* = *É-um* (nom. *Ḥay*(*y*)*um*) 'The Living One.'

It is possible that Philippi's Law is operative sporadically in Eblaite; an example is SIG$_4$-TUŠ-GAR = *li-ba-tum* 'brick.'[9] *Li-ba-tum* (< *libittum*[10] < **libin-tum*[11]) reflects Philippi's Law, whereby in an accented, originally closed syllable, short *i* shifts to *a* in Northwest Semitic. Thus *bint-* (so in Arabic) appears as *bat* in Hebrew.[12] Similarly, *libittu*, affected by Philippi's Law, would become *libattu*.

The fact that both *li-ba-tum* and *li-bi-tum* occur (*MEE* 4, p. 213, #146) suggests that both Northwest Semitic (*libattum*) and East Semitic (*libittum*) variants occur in Eblaite.[13]

[7] For Enki's concern with plant and animal fertility, see S. N. Kramer, *Mythologies of the Ancient World* (Garden City, NY: Doubleday, 1969) 100.

[8] For the theme of "The God who Disappears" in Hittite mythology, see H. G. Güterbock in *Mythologies of the Ancient World*, 143–48.

[9] *MEE* 4, p. 213, #146.

[10] As in Akkadian.

[11] Cf. Hebrew לְבֵנָה (< **labinat-*).

[12] The norm in cuneiform spelling is that long sounds can be written singly or doubly. (Orthographic doubling normally implies phonetic doubling.) There is a way of checking this in Akkadian, because short, unaccented vowels are dropped between single consonants (except in the ultima). Thus, the present future tense is *iparras*, regardless of whether it is written *i-pa-ar-ra-as* or *i-pa-ra-as* because the second *a* is not dropped in the plural *iparrasū*, even though it can be written *i-pa-ra-su*. Contrast *paris*, which has the plural *parsū*.

[13] The normal treatment of *pataḥ* in Hebrew calls for lengthening to *qameṣ* in pause. However, a "Philippi's Law *pataḥ*" remains unchanged by pause. Thus בַּת remains בַּת in pause (2 Sam 12:3); whereas עַם 'people' becomes עָם in pause (Isa 3:7). Similarly, זָקַנְתִּי (< **ḏaqintī*, note זָקֵן) retains the *pataḥ* in pause (Gen 18:13) vs. pausal שָׁמָרְתִּי (Ps 119:67; as against non-pausal שָׁמַרְתִּי [< **šamartī*, note שָׁמַר]).

The position of Eblaite between East and West Semitic may be illustrated by the problem posed by the adverb *en-ma* 'so says . . . .': Akkadian *um-ma X-ma* 'so says X' is used like Hebrew נאם 'so says (X),' but a genetic connection between them looks phonetically so remote that no one associated them. However, Eblaite *en-ma X* 'so says X' bridges some of the gap, at least with regard to the first consonant.

In Hebrew נאם refers almost exclusively to divine utterances: e.g., נאם יהוה 'so says Yahweh.' At Ebla, *en-ma* is used in ordinary prose, referring to human speakers.[14] In the OT, the few applications of נאם to human speakers are limited to poetic contexts (Num 24:3, 4, 15; Prov 30:1; 2 Sam 23:1). Numbers 24 deals with Balaam, who hailed from Euphrates country not too far from Ebla; and Prov 30:1 has to do with משא, a northern city-state—the name, if not the actual place, occurs in the Ebla archives.[15] But since 2 Sam 23:1 refers to David, we should not push northern origins too far.

It is the syllabification[16] of *nĕ᾽ûm* that makes squaring it with *en-ma* so difficult. Transposing the א and נ in *en-ma/nĕ᾽ûm* is rather jarring. Accordingly, we are posing a problem rather than claiming to solve it.

Wa is an ancient morpheme, though its use as a conjunction is an innovation. Its function as a tense indicator prefixed to verbs can now be traced back to Eblaite.

In Sumerian the verb comes at the end of the sentence. In Eblaite (which is written largely in Sumerograms) a construction like *wa* DU$_{11}$-GA EN[17] 'the ruler said' is to be compared with ויאמר המלך (1 Kgs 1:16) 'the king said.' With Eblaite *wa* ÍL IGI-IGI EN *wa* NAM-KU, 'the ruler raised (his) eyes and swore' we compare וישא עיניו וירא (Gen 18:2) 'he raised his eyes and saw.'[18]

[14] E.g., *en-ma Ib-ri-um sí-in* en 'so says Ibrium to the ruler' (D. O. Edzard, "Der Texte TM.75.G.1444 aus Ebla," *SEb* 4 [1981] 35–59; note column I'10–13 on p. 37). Constance Wallace independently suggested a connection between *en-ma* and נאם in my Ebla seminar at New York University in 1983.

[15] Thus *maš-a*^{ki} (Pettinato, *MEE* 1, p. 278).

[16] Another example of discrepancy in the syllabification is Sumer = "Babylonia." Thus, in Gen 11:1–4 שנער is the land of the Tower of Babel, where the inhabitants built great constructions of baked bricks. שנער definitely designates Babylonia (Gen 11:9) and can hardly stand for anything except "Sumer." The most troublesome discrepancy between שנער and "Sumer" is the syllabification. The laryngeal ע is less surprising in the light of the laryngeals in words borrowed from (or through) Sumerian into West Semitic, as pointed out above.

[17] Edzard, "Der Text TM.75.G.1444 aus Ebla," 35–59. The above example, and the following one, are on p. 38. The construction occurs repeatedly in TM.75.G.1444.

[18] See further, Gordon, "The 'Waw Conversive' from Eblaite to Hebrew," *Proceedings of the American Academy for Jewish Research* 50 (1983) 87–90. There are several essential pieces of information regarding *wa*. For example, the initial *w-* has not shifted to *y-* in Northwest Semitic *wa*, because, when the shift was operative, the *w* was not initial. *Wa* is cognate to the existential particle *ỉw* in Egyptian. For existential *wa* in Semitic note Arabic *wallâh* "by (the existence of) God!' like *ḥayât allâh* 'by the life of God.' A Hebrew example is צר וסביב הארץ (Amos 3:11) 'a foe is round about the land.' *W-* in the so-called conversive tenses is the tense indicator and not a conjunction. Biblical books begin with וַיִּקְרָא (Lev 1:1) 'he called' or וַיְהִי (Ruth 1:1) 'it happened,'

The prefixing of *wa* to a verb at the head of the phrase or sentence in Eblaite, is the earliest known occurrence of the so-called "waw conversive" in the Semitic languages. Hitherto, this phenomenon was limited to Hebrew and a number of other Northwest Semitic dialects, such as Moabite, Phoenician, Ugaritic, and most recently, the Balaam inscriptions from the Jordanian site of Deir ᶜAlla in ancient Gilead. It has not been pointed out so far in Akkadian, Arabic, or Ethiopic.

Briefly stated, the two forms of the "waw conversive" are illustrated by וָמֵת (Deut 19:21) 'so that he will die' and וַיָּמָת 'he died.' It is the *wa-* that makes וָמֵת futurative (for מֵת can be past, whereas וָמֵת is not); and it is the *wa+n-* that makes וַיָּמָת past (for יָמֹת 'let him die' or יָמוּת 'he will die' are futurative, whereas וַיָּמָת cannot be). So both varieties of "waw conversive" are in reality compound verbs in which the first element is the time indicator. Syntactically, these compound verbs must head the sentence or phrase. Thus, Hebrew tolerates קרא משה or משה קרא but once we employ וַיִּקְרָא, וַיִּקְרָא מֹשֶׁה 'Moses called' is obligatory; מֹשֶׁה וַיִּקְרָא* is ruled out.

Among the bilinguals published by Pettinato in *MEE* 4 is the equation BURU4-MUŠEN = *a-a-tum.*[19] The BURU4 bird is here defined as *a-a-tum* in Eblaite = Hebrew אַיָּה. The precise ornithological identifications of bird names must ultimately be left to specialists in bird terminology. Non-specialists use such terms more loosely than ornithologists. The אַיָּה is a bird of prey (sometimes identified with the black kite) whose flesh may not be eaten according to Pentateuchal law (Lev 11:14; Deut 14:35; etc.). We should not expect scientific exactness from scribes whose business it was to produce bilingual lists. By the same token, translators of ancient texts have to provide a translation (right or wrong) for the words in the original.

A number of trees listed in bilingual texts published in *MEE* 4 are of interest for a variety of reasons.

One such tree is GIŠ-AD 'the father tree' = *adu.*[20] As is often the case with Eblaite words, this one is borrowed from Sumerian. In Ugaritic, *ad* = ᵓ*adu* 'father' is a synonym of *ab* = ᵓ*abu* 'father.' In Hebrew, the short noun ᵓ*ad-* is augmented with the suffix *-ôn* (< *-*ân*); thus ᵓ*ādôn-* 'lord.'

For the notion that a tree could sire a human being, note Jeremiah's reference (2:27) to superstitious people who say to the tree "Thou art my father" (אמרים לעץ אבי אתה).

---

where 'and . . .' would be meaningless. See also *UT* §§ 12:1; 19.779. E. J. Revell shows no awareness of this Egypto-Semitic and inner-Hebrew evidence in his "Stress and the WAW 'Consecutive' in Biblical Hebrew," *JAOS* 104 (1984) 437–44.

[19] *MEE* 4, p. 352, #049.

[20] Text 32 on p. 59 (v. 1:2) GIŠ-AD (:3) *a-du*; texts 4–6 on p. 11 (VII:12) GIŠ-AD (:13) *a-du* (also text 9–ll:v. III′3′–4′ on p. 24).

Another noun referring to a tree is also borrowed from Sumerian into Eblaite: GIŠ-NUN 'the lordly tree' = *nu-nu* (text 4: r, II:12–13).[21] In analyzing the name of Joshua's father, נון we must at least consider the possibility that it designates a large tree, perhaps the cedar (ארז) in the light of the following entry.

The feminine of GIŠ-NUN, namely GIŠ-NUN-SAL, is defined bilingually as Eblaite *ar-za-tum* (4: r. II:10–11; see also *MEE* 4, p. 252, #471). As E. Zurro[22] has pointed out, ארזה occurs in Zeph 2:14. In any case, Eblaite has ʾ*arzatu*(*m*), the feminine of ארז.

GIŠ-MA = *ti-ni-tum*[23] merits our attention. Semitic *ti-ni-tum* in the tree category can only mean "the fig." Note Hebrew תְּאֵנָה and Arabic *tīnat-*, *tīn-* 'fig, fig tree.' *Ti-ni-tu*(*m*) may have a bearing on the name of the West Semitic fertility goddess who first appears in Linear A Minoan as *ti-ni-ta*[24] and later becomes ubiquitous as תנת in Punic. The spelling of *ti-ni-tum*/*ti-ni-ta* allows (but does not require) the doubling of the *n*, so that the name could be Tinnit as well as Tinit.[25] Punic texts in Greek letters from El-Hofra, near Constantine in Algeria, render תנת as θινιθ.[26]

Various suggestions made concerning the derivation of Ti(n)nit are discussed by Robert Steiglitz in his "Neith Athena and Tinnit: Cultural Diffusion and the Maghreb in Antiquity" (*extrait Des Cahiers de Tunisie*, vol. 29 (1981) ##117–18, pp. 465–76). Scholars have attempted to derive Ti(n)nit from Late Egyptian *T*ꜣ*-Nt* 'The Neith' or *T*ꜣ*-Nṯrt* 'The Goddess.' An objection to a Late Egyptian origin is Minoan *Ti-ni-ta*, which occurs prior to the appearance of the Late Egyptian article *t*ꜣ 'the.' That Ti(n)nit might have acquired such Egyptian associations is possible, but a more fundamental association of the fertility goddess Ti(n)nit with 'fig' is likely.

The fact that the fig is full of seeds may be the natural basis for the fig symbolizing female sexuality. We may note in passing that fig leaves in Gen 3:7 cover the nakedness of Adam and Eve after they become sexually aware. Still more to the point, the Mishna (*Nidda* 5:7) compares the three stages of girlhood with the three stages of the maturing of figs; the first is פגה,[27] when the girl is but a child; the second stage is called בוחל, corresponding to the girl's puberty; the final stage of the fig is called צמל, corresponding to the maturity of the young

[21] Note the variant GIŠ-NUN = *nu-nu-mu* (alongside GIŠ-NUN = *nu-nu*, under #472a, p. 252; see also p. 13; text 4–6: IX′:33–34). Whether *-mu* stands for *-m*(*u*) = simply the mimation (*-m*) is problematic.

[22] E. Zurro, "Notes de lexicografía eblaita: nombres de árboles y plantas," *Aula Orientalis* 1 (1983) 263–69; see p. 263.

[23] *MEE* 4, p. 240, #368a.

[24] C. H. Gordon, *Evidence for the Minoan Language* (Ventnor, NJ: Ventnor Publishers, 1966) 39.

[25] There is no basis for the *a* in the commonly used form "Tanit."

[26] Reproduced on p. 289 in C. H. Gordon, "Northwest Semitic Texts in Latin and Greek Letters," *JAOS* 88 (1968) 285–89.

[27] פג first appears in Song of Songs (2:13): התאנה חנטה פגיה 'the fig tree sprouts its young figs.'

woman. The comparison of the fig with the sexual ripening of the girl is appropriate for the fertility goddess Ti(n)nit. We might add that פג may well be related to Latin *fic-us*, English *fig*. Sexual undertones are suggested in English "I don't give a fig" and German "einem die Feige weisen" designating an obscene gesture.[28]

GIŠ-ŠINIG = *i-ṣu ba-ne* (*MEE* 4, p. 11, VII:21–22) is of interest for phonetic reasons. Eblaite *ba-ne* reflects the shift from *-ay-* to *-a-*, paralleling Minoan *ya-ne* < *yayn-* 'wine.' In normal Akkadian the tree is pronounced *bînu* 'tamarisk(?).' Compare **baytu* 'house' > Akkadian *bîtu*. Eblaite has variant forms. Thus (text 32: v. II:1) GIŠ-ŠINIG = (:2) *ba-nu* and (text 35: r. I:2) GIŠ-ŠINIG = (:3) *ì-ṣú ba-nu-um*.

There are a number of cultic terms that merit discussion. For instance, ENSI = *sa-il-tum*.[29] The ensi priestess had among her functions the asking of a god or departed spirit a question on behalf of devotees. Hopefully, the question would be heard and answered favorably. Places frequented for such oracular responsa might appropriately be called אֶשְׁתָּאוֹל[30] (from שאל 'to ask') or אֶשְׁתְּמוֹעַ[31] (from שמע 'to hear').

When Odysseus went to Erebos to ask and learn about the future, the purpose of his journey was πυθέσθαι 'to inquire.' Specifically, he inquired of the spirit of the dead prophet Teiresias. The OT counterpart is the visit of Saul to the Witch of Endor so that he might inquire of the dead prophet Samuel.[32] His inquiry is expressed by the verb שאל 'to ask.' This explains the meaning of שְׁאוֹל 'Sheol' (The Underworld), which gets its name from the use put to it by the living, who inquire of the dead for knowledge and guidance. The asking must be through a professional intermediary. Women commonly filled this role,[33] and in Eblaite this sort of woman is accordingly called *sa-il-tum* 'asker (fem.).'

Another cultic term equated in the bilinguals is EZEN = *ì-sí-ba-tum*.[34] Since ezen is Sumerian for 'festival,' *ì-sí-ba-tum* should have the same or a similar meaning in Eblaite. In the OT, pagan festivals were to be shunned, and so they took on a pejorative flavor along with the idols associated with them. Accordingly, עֲצַבִּים 'idols, pagan deities' (e.g., Hos 4:7; 8:4; 13:2) may be the Hebrew reflex of the same root that appears in the Eblaite word for 'festival.'

[28] It has been suggested that German *fücken* and its vulgar English equivalent are cognate. Methodologically, it is well to reckon that such far-flung and varied elements, if related, may reflect the association of similar sounding words, and not necessarily words derived from the same source in accordance with phonetic law.

[29] *MEE* 4, p. 301, #907.

[30] E.g., Josh 15:33; Judg 13:28.

[31] E.g., Josh 21:14; 1 Sam 20:28.

[32] For documentation, see C. H. Gordon, *The Common Background of Greek and Hebrew Civilizations* (New York: Norton, 1965) 86, 260.

[33] The femininity of dream interpreters also characterizes ancient Mesopotamia. It is goddesses who interpret the dreams of Gilgamesh and of Gudea.

[34] *MEE* 4, p. 342, #1448; and p. 354, #007.

The deified ^{d}EDEN = *wa-pi*$_5$*-um*[35] may be considered cosmographic, designating personified Eden or Paradise. Thus, ^{d}Eden (the divine, personified Paradise) comes into Eblaite as 'The Beautiful One.' The root is *wpy* (the *w-* is preserved in Arabic and Ethiopic), which is familiar in Hebrew as יפה 'beautiful' (with the Northwest Semitic shift of *w-* to *y-*). Biblical 'Eden' (as in Gen 2:15 גן עדן 'the garden of Eden') is borrowed from Sumerian. That ^{d}EDEN is personified at Ebla makes it possible that for the author of Genesis גן עדן did not necessarily mean only 'the garden of the place Eden' but also the 'garden of the god Eden.'

The star ^{d}MUL = *kab-kab*[36] and constellation ^{d}MUL-MUL = *ka-ma-tu*[37] are members of the pantheon. The god ^{d}MUL refers to a specific star, like Kôkab among the Phoenicians, even as ^{d}MUL-MUL is the specific constellation *ka-ma-tu* (cf. כימה in Amos 5:8, Job 9:9, 38:31, generally translated as 'The Pleiades').

We may note that there was a system whereby a god was identified with a specific heavenly body and a specific number. Thus Anu = heaven itself = I; Sibittu = The Pleiades = VII; Inanna/Ishtar = the star Venus = XV; Utu/Shamash = the Sun = XX; Nanna(r) Sin = the Moon = XXX; etc. In Egypt, Ra^c is called "the one One." By the same token, when God is called אחד, the levels of meaning include not only the monotheistic oneness of God but also that as the first and foremost in the old pantheon he was number I like Anu and Ra^c.

The OT preserved other deified numbers. Beer-sheba cannot mean (as the OT popular etymologies would have it) either 'seven wells' or 'the well of the oath,' the first for grammatical, the second for lexical, reasons. It is a place name like Beth-El and means 'The well of the divine Seven.' Just as אליהו 'Elijah' means 'Yahu is divine,' אלישבע 'Elizabeth' means 'Seven is divine.' Nor can קרית ארבע mean 'four cities' grammatically; it means 'The city of the divine Four,' whom we know from the name of the Assyrian city Arba-Ilu 'Erbil' meaning 'Four is God.'

Isa 40:26 proclaims שאו־מרום עיניכם וראו מי־ברא אלה המוציא במספר צבאם לכלם בשם יקרא 'Lift on high your eyes and see who created these (heavenly bodies): He who brings out their host by number; all of them He calls by name.' This shows that in the conservative poetic tradition the Prophet reechoes the old concept that the personified stars had names and numbers. God Himself is One and His name is 'One,' as plainly stated in Zech 14:9 (ביום ההוא יהיה יהוה אחד ושמו אחד 'on that day Yahweh shall be one, and His name One').

Referring to a special and important god as "the Name" is common. השם 'The Name' refers to God in Lev 24:11–16. It is there decreed that anyone in Israel who reviles השם 'The Name' (24:11) shall be stoned to death because he curses אלהיו 'His God' (24:15). Similarly *rn* 'name' can refer to a god in Egyptian. This is common in Mesopotamia; e.g., the royal names in the First

[35] *MEE* 4, p. 290, #807. The fact that the root is not East but West Semitic shows that mimation in Eblaite does not necessarily imply borrowing from Akkadian.

[36] *MEE* 4, p. 288, #781.

[37] *MEE* 4, p. 288, #782.

Dynasty of Babylon: Sumu-la-ilu 'The Name is verily God,' and indeed, the name of the founder of the dynasty, Sumu-Abu, means 'The Name is Father' (cf. Hebrew names like אליאב 'Father is Divine,' David's older brother in 1 Sam 16:6).

At Ebla the Name is Tammuz; dumu-zi = *šu-um* (*MEE* 4, p. 317, #1084). This suggests a new aspect of Ezek 8:14, where the prophet is transported to Jerusalem by God: ויבא אתי אל פתח שער בית־יהוה אשר אל־הצפונה והנה־שם הנשים ישבות מבכות את־התמוז 'and He brought me to the entrance of the gate of the House of Yahweh which was to the north, and behold the women were sitting there weeping for "the Tammuz." Note that the article is used in התמוז, showing that תמוז is here a common noun used generically for 'god,' like בעל in הבעלים 'the Baals' = pagan male deities, or like אשרה in האשרות 'the Asherahs' = pagan goddesses. Now, since 'The Name' to a Hebrew designated 'Yahweh,' we can ask whether "Name = Tammuz" facilitated the paganizing custom of weeping for "the Tammuz."

There are two Eblaite values for ^{d}AK in the bilinguals: (1) *ša-du-um* and (2) *ri-ba-nu.*[38] *Šà-du-um* calls to mind שדי as in the combination אל שדי, often translated 'God Almighty.' *Ri-ba-nu* recalls a rabbinic designation of God, which appears in the Aramaic form רִבָּן and in Hebrew as רִבּוֹן (with the Canaanite shift of *â* to *ô*). The latter is built into divine epithets such as רבונו של עולם 'Master of the Universe.' Even as rabbinic terms, absent from the Bible, are attested at Ugarit,[39] we can expect rabbinic terms to be anticipated at Ebla.

The grammatical plural of 'god' (in Hebrew אלהים) can be treated as a singular referring to God. Contrast יהוה הוא האלהים 'Yahweh is the God' (1 Kgs 18:39) with the paganizing statement attributed to the Philistines: אלה הם האלהים המכים את־מצרים 'these are the gods who smote (pl.) Egypt (= the Egyptians).' In origin, אלהים 'God' is not a plural of majesty but reflects the treatment of the pantheon as a unit. The grammatical plural *ilâni* is treated as the singular God in an Akkadian text of Late Bronze Canaan,[40] a usage that may well be anticipated in the Ebla archives. D. O. Edzard transliterates and translates TM.75.G.144: XV:1–11 as follows (in *SEb* 4 [1981] 44):

(1)	giš ba-tuku	Es höre
(2)	^{d}Ku-ra	Kura,
(3)	*wa*	und
(4)	giš ba-tuku	es höre
(5)	^{d}Utu	die Sonne,
(6)	*wa*	und
(7)	giš ba-tuku	es höre

[38] *MEE* 4, p. 291, #810.

[39] B. A. Levine, *Survivals of Ancient Canaanite in the Mishna* (Ph.D. dissertation, Brandeis University, 1962).

[40] C. H. Gordon, "Observations on the Akkadian Tablets from Ugarit," *RA* 50 (1956) 127–33 (see p. 131). The passage is cited in n. 43 below.

(8) ^{d}ʾÀ-*da* Hadad,[41]
(9) *wa* und
(10) giš ba-tuku es hören[42]
(11) dingir-dingir die Götter.

Since individual gods (Kura, the Sun, and Hadad) are invoked to hear, DINGIR-DINGIR should also refer to a particular god. Sumerian usage does not favor reading DINGIR-DINGIR as ^{d}An, because An = Anu is written with the single sign DINGIR. Yet here the context favors taking DINGIR-DINGIR as the name of a god. This text is Eblaite, written as usual with a plethora of Sumerograms. DINGIR-DINGIR is a normal way of pluralizing DINGIR, so that DINGIR-DINGIR in Sumerian designates 'gods.' But, if we are dealing with the name of a specific deity in Eblaite, we cannot help recalling the morphologically plural Elohim (אלהים) that serves as the name of God in the OT. The morphologically plural *ilânu* occurs in an Akkadian tablet from Ugarit of the Late Bronze Age, referring to a particulary deity, as is demonstrated by the fact that it takes a singular verb, and it is therefore to be compared with Elohim.[43] DINGIR-DINGIR at Ebla may well reflect the same name in the Early Bronze Age. We need not delve into the problem of whether DINGIR-DINGIR // *Ilânu* //Elohim originally designated the personified pantheon. When Elohim and *ilânu* are treated as singulars, they refer to a particular deity. Accordingly, Elohim as the Hebrew name of God in the Iron Age can be traced back through *ilânu* at Ugarit in the Late Bronze Age to DINGIR-DINGIR at Ebla of the Early Bronze Age.

It should also be noted that, on the Stela of Naram-Sin, at the top of the mountain peak there are two stars which might stand for the god DINGIR-DINGIR = *Ilânu* = Elohim as well as for 'the gods = the pantheon.'

^{d}EN-LIL was pronounced *i-li-lu* in Eblaite.[44] The history of religions often illustrates the debasing of the great gods in an older religion to devils or demons in a younger religion. Thus, בעל זבוב אלהי עקרון (2 Kgs 1:2, 3, 6, 16) 'Baal-zebub, the god of Ekron' is debased to the king of the demons in the NT (Matt 12:24).[45]

The classical Aramaic for 'gods' (אלהין) often stands for 'pagan gods, demons' in Mandaic.

The Hebrew word for a pagan deity, or pejoratively, "a non-god" is אליל, pl. אלילים. Some have derived it from אֵל 'god'; others from אַל 'not.' But *I-li-lu* prompts another explanation: the great Mesopotamian deity ^{d}EN-LIL/*I-li-lu* was demoted to 'false god' in Yahwistic circles. In Ugaritic, *ill* (*UT* § 19.84) is a

[41] The spelling (^{d}ʾ*à-da*) reflects the pronunciation 'Hadda' rather than 'Hadad.' All the following variants are attested in Northwest Semitic: ʾ*Adad-*, *Hadad-*, ʾ*Ad*(*d*)-, and *Had*(*d*)-.

[42] Should be singular "es höre."

[43] C. H. Gordon, "Observations on the Akkadian Tablets from Ugarit," 131. The passage is *ša-a ṭup-pu an-na-am ú-na-ki-ir ilânu*${}^{meš\ nu}$ *šum-šu li-ḫal-li-iq* 'whoever alters this tablet, may God destroy his name.' Note that *Ilânu* is the subject of the singular verb *liḫalliq*.

[44] *MEE* 4, texts 4–6, v. X:10′–11′ and texts 9–11, v. II: 21–22 (pp. 17, 29).

[45] On the variants "Beelzebub/Beelzebul," see W. F. Albright and C. S. Mann, *Matthew* (AB; Garden City, NY: Doubleday, 1971) 152–62.

minor deity, midway, so to speak, between the exalted ^{d}EN-LIL and the degraded אליל.

The bilingual equation A-KUL = *ma-ba-lum*[46] translates Sumerian A 'water' + KUL 'heavy' into Eblaite as *ma-ba-lum*, which calls to mind Hebrew מַבּוּל (Gen 9:11; 10:1; etc.) 'deluge.'

Since TAR designates 'cutting,' the bilingual equation TAR-TAR = *ga-da-dum*[47] invites comparison with Hebrew התגודד (from גדד) 'to cut oneself.' Note Deut 14:1; 1 Kgs 18:29, etc., for the pagan rite of self-laceration.

Note the equation LÁ-LÁ = *ti-iš-tá-qì-lum*.[48] Since LÁ means 'to see, perceive,' the Eblaite may be cognate with Hebrew שֹׂכל 'insight, prudence, good sense.' Note especially Late Hebrew השׂתכל (normally written הסתכל) 'to look into, have a good look at.'

[46] *MEE* 4, p. 272, #640b.
[47] *MEE* 4, p. 375, #0419.
[48] *MEE* 4, p. 326, #1184.

WM- "and" in Eblaite and Hebrew

CYRUS H. GORDON

The comparative method does not justify reading one of the compared sources into the other; but the comparison of related sources may explain a crux in one source because the same feature occurs unequivocally in another.

That enclitic *-m* can be added to *w-* 'and' in Hebrew does not require Eblaite or any other outside source to prove it. But, the combination *wm-* is so rare in Hebrew that it has been misconstrued by commentators and translators for the more than two millennia of OT study. The first scholar to posit *wm-* in Hebrew was F. I. Andersen, fifteen years ago (see G. A. Rendsburg's article herein). What has at last demonstrated that *wm-* does occur in Semitic is its clear and well-documented appearance in Eblaite.

In retrospect, Hebraists need not have gone beyond the biblical text itself for understanding and interpreting *wm-* 'and, but, also' correctly. The fact is that until Eblaite familiarized us with the conjunction plus the enclitic, all of the biblical examples remained *cruces interpretum*.

Our review of the biblical examples of *wm-* begins with Ruth 4:5, where Boaz tells the next of kin to redeem the land if he insists, but (*wm-*) Ruth in any event has already been acquired in marriage by Boaz. The Hebrew is *wm-ᵓt rwt . . . qnyty* 'but I have acquired Ruth.' The *ktiv* (*qnyty* 'I have acquired') is correct; the *qre* (*ûmêᵓēt rût . . . qnyt* 'from Ruth . . . thou has acquired') is incorrect and has given rise to centuries of unnecessary exegetical gymnastics. *Wm-ᵓt* is not the common *ûmêᵓēt* 'and from' but the uncommon *wm-* 'and, but' + the indicator of the definite direct object.

Now that we can take the consonantal text exactly as it stands, we can appreciate the dramatic climax of the Scroll of Ruth. Boaz and Ruth had spent a night together secretly in conjugal embrace (Ruth 3:14), thus cementing their union through one of the three ways in which a man acquires an eligible woman in marriage (Mishna, *Qid* 1:1). We can at last appreciate the surprise ending of the romantic scroll, where love triumphs over obstacles and the heroine weds the hero.[1]

When new discoveries reveal something surprising, it often proves to be only the tip of the iceberg. When George Smith pointed out the relationship

[1] I have discussed *wm-* in Ruth 4:5, with additional details, in *Forgotten Scripts: Their Ongoing Discovery and Decipherment* (New York: Basic Books, 1982) 168–71.

between the Flood in the eleventh tablet of the Gilgamesh Epic and the Deluge in Genesis, he was in fact opening up a whole era of discovering cuneiform parallels to the OT. When Sidney Smith observed that Rachel stole her father's household gods in defiance of a prohibition spelled out in Nuzi contracts, he anticipated a spate of Nuzi parallels to the Hebrew Bible, particularly in the Genesis narratives about Abraham, Isaac, and Jacob.

Constance Wallace and Gary Rendsburg were both members of my Ebla Seminar at New York University in 1982–83. Wallace was simultaneously enrolled in my course on Nehemiah. She immediately detected *wm-* on coming across it in Neh 5:11. All sorts of contrived solutions had been proposed for that crux, and all of them were wide of the mark. No scholar, to the best of my knowledge, had ever suspected the correct analysis of *wmʾt* in Neh 5:11. Ebla provided Wallace with the means of solving the crux convincingly (see the article which follows). Next appears Rendsburg's article, with a comprehensive discussion of other examples of *wm-* in the OT.

The significance of this trilogy of articles is not that every example of *wm-* in Hebrew has been ferreted out, but that the phenomenon is firmly established. There is room for others to share in the mopping-up operation.

WM- in Nehemiah 5:11

CONSTANCE WALLACE

Neh 5:11 has a problem which can be addressed afresh, thanks to the recent finds at Ebla. The *crux interpretum* is consonantal *wm*ʾ*t*, pointed as *ûmĕ*ʾ*at* by the Masoretes, but to be revocalized as *ûma*-ʾ*et*. The vocalization of MT suggests 'and a hundred of (the silver),' which makes no sense. It has been rendered as 'the hundred pieces of' (JPSV) and 'the hundredth part' (KJV), both of which require supplying an extra word in the translation. The text is sometimes altered to *wmš*ʾ*t*, 'and the interest of.'[1] The ancient versions, summarized by Edward Neufeld,[2] are no more successful in handling this problem.

Enclitic *-ma* is a particle occurring in various Semitic languages, including Akkadian and Ugaritic. Until the application of Ugaritic to biblical scholarship, it was not recognized in Hebrew. The conjunction *ù-ma* is frequent in Eblaite, occurring five times in one treaty tablet.[3] Recognizing this combination in Neh 5:11 gives us: 'Return to them, even this day, their fields, their vineyards, their olive groves, and their houses, and also the silver, the grain, the wine, and the oil which you exact from them.' The crucial word occurring in the middle of the verse divides real from movable property. The compound conjunction adds force to its simple counterpart. This interpretation is in keeping with the consonantal text and makes good sense of an otherwise difficult word.

[1] See, e.g., J. M. Myers, *Ezra-Nehemiah* (AB; Garden City, NY: Doubleday, 1965) 129.

[2] E. Neufeld, "The Rate of Interest and the Text of Neh. 5:11," *JQR* 44 (1953–54) 198–99. I am indebted to Gary Rendsburg for calling my attention to this article.

[3] E. Sollberger, "The So-Called Treaty Between Ebla and 'Ashur'," *SEb* 3 (1980), pp. 129–55.

Eblaite *Ù-MA* and Hebrew *WM-*

GARY A. RENDSBURG

Eblaite *ù-ma*, the conjunction followed by enclitic *ma*, occurs sporadically in the Tell Mardikh tablets. Of the materials published so far, it is attested seven times in TM.75.G.2420 and once in TM.75.G.2268.[1] During his visit to New York in February, 1983, A. Archi confirmed that it appears in other texts as well.[2]

In light of these occurrences, it is appropriate to resurrect and reinvestigate the suggestion of F. I. Andersen more than a decade ago that a cognate construction occurs in the Hebrew Bible. Writing in the days before the publication of the Ebla tablets, Andersen already proposed that several seemingly inexplicable *wm-* forms be parsed as conjunctive *waw* with *mem* enclitic. He thought *wmmhr* in Gen 41:32, *wmplʾ* in Judg 13:19, *wmsrpw* in Amos 6:10, and *wmʾt* in Ruth 4:5 were sure occurrences of *waw* plus *mem* enclitic, and that possible examples of this construction are present in 2 Sam 16:5, Job 6:22, 7:14, 10:14, 19:26, 21:20.[3]

Before progressing to a discussion of these passages, we should commend Andersen for his ingenuity, having isolated Hebrew *wm-* without the impetus of a cognate language. (One need only compare the method by which most recent advances in Hebrew grammar have been made: usually a usage is clarified in another Semitic language, e.g., Ugaritic, and only then is its appearance in Hebrew revealed.) It should be noted, therefore, that the examples to be presented below can stand on internal analysis alone. If I have adduced the Eblaite evidence first and have included Eblaite *ù-ma* in the title, it is because (a) these attestations have served as the springboard of my research, and (b) they supply the desired Semitic cognate most often sought by Hebrew linguists.

[1] For TM.75.G.2420, see E. Sollberger, "The So-Called Treaty Between Ebla and 'Ashur'," *SEb* 3 (1980) 155, for exact references. For TM.75.G.2268, see the few lines transliterated and translated by A. Archi, "I rapporti tra Ebla e Mari," *SEb* 4 (1981) 154.

[2] In the Ebla texts published so far, enclitic *ma* is never affixed to the conjunction *wa*, only to *ù*. The exact differences between the two Eblaite conjunctions are still to be worked out; cf. D. O. Edzard, "Neue Erwägungen zum Brief des Enna-Dagan von Mari (TM.75.G.2367)," *SEb* 4 (1981) 89–90, n 4.

[3] F. I. Andersen, *The Hebrew Verbless Clause in the Pentateuch* (Nashville, 1970) 48, 124, n 13.

Of the proposed examples, Ruth 4:5 is the most important, for the entire story hinges on this difficult and crucial verse.[4] Andersen suggested that Masoretic *ûmēʾēt rût* should not be read 'from Ruth,' but rather as conjunctive *waw*, enclitic *mem*, the accusative indicator *ʾet*, and then the personal name Ruth. He states that "the field is not to be acquired *from* Ruth as well as from Naomi; rather, when the field is acquired from Naomi, Ruth must be acquired with it, and is the object of the following verb."[5]

C. H. Gordon has recently taken up the problem again, independent of Andersen's work and now with Eblaite *ù-ma* as a Semitic cognate to bolster the proposal for a Hebrew *wm-*.[6] Gordon's analysis of *wmʾt* is the same as Andersen's, though whereas the latter implies reading the Qere *qnyt* (2 m.s. perfect), the former accepts the Ketiv *qnyty* (1 s. perfect). Gordon therefore translates the verse, "Boaz said: 'On the day you acquire the field from the hand of Naomi, (well and good); but I have acquired Ruth the Moabitess, the wife of the deceased, to raise the name of the deceased on his estate.'" Boaz is telling Mr. So-and-So that although he (Mr. So-and-So) may redeem the land, he (Boaz) has already obtained Ruth, a fact known to the reader of the story from the secret tryst in 3:6–14. Gordon invokes the Mishnaic law in Qiddushin 1:1 which states that one of the methods of acquiring a bride is sexual intercourse, and thus Boaz is legally correct in claiming to have acquired Ruth already.

Another clear instance of enclitic *mem* following conjunctive *waw* is Amos 6:10: *ûnĕśāʾô dôdô ûmĕsārĕpô lĕhôṣîʾ ʿăṣāmîm min habbayit*. Commentators have long recognized the difficulties of *wmsrpw*,[7] but the difficulties disappear when the word is parsed as conjunctive *waw*, enclitic *mem*, the root *srp*, and pronominal suffix *ô*. The root *srp* must be a byform of *śrp*, 'burn.'[8] The burning of the deceased's bones, while usually considered a heinous crime in the Bible (see Amos 2:1), can be an honorable act as well (see 1 Sam 31:12–13; cf. *Iliad* 23:208–25, 24:786–87).[9] More important for our present purposes is the observation that Masoretic *ûmĕsārĕpô* is the only Piʿel of *śrp*/*srp* in the Bible. Elsewhere, this root occurs only in the Qal; in Lev 10:16 *śôrāp* should be read as passive Qal.[10] Accordingly, *wmsrpw* in Amos 6:10 should be revocalized as a Qal, most probably as a perfect parallel to *ûnĕśāʾô*, and be read *ûmāsĕrāpô*. If

[4] For a very thorough analysis of the verse, see J. M. Sasson, *Ruth* (Baltimore, 1979) 119–35.

[5] Andersen, p. 124, n 13. E. F. Campbell, *Ruth* (AB; Garden City, NY, 1975) 146, provisionally accepts Andersen's proposal.

[6] C. H. Gordon, *Forgotten Scripts* (New York, 1982) 169–71; and C. H. Gordon, "The 'Waw Conversive': From Eblaite to Hebrew," *Proceedings of the American Academy for Jewish Research* 50 (1983) 90.

[7] See H. W. Wolff, *Joel and Amos* (Hermeneia; Philadelphia, 1977) 280, n h, for a brief discussion.

[8] So, e.g., W. R. Harper, *Amos and Hosea* (ICC; New York, 1910) 158.

[9] See further C. H. Gordon, *The Common Background of Greek and Hebrew Civilizations* (New York, 1965) 18.

[10] See R. J. Williams, "The Passive *Qal* Theme in Hebrew," in J. W. Wevers and D. B. Redford, eds., *Essays on the Ancient Semitic World* (Toronto, 1970) 47–48.

this be the case, then Gordon may be correct in analyzing *wmsrpw* as a *waw* conjunctive with the perfect, with *m* interposed, to be translated 'and he shall burn him.'[11]

Andersen's two other primary examples are not as clear, though in one instance there is enough evidence to defend his analysis. Andersen has carefully classified the independent participial clauses of the Pentateuch and notes that *ûmĕmahēr hâʾĕlôhîm laʿăśōtô* in Gen 41:32 is the only one which begins with *waw* and participle. Since we expect *hinneh* as an auxiliary predicator, Andersen concludes, "The explanation probably lies in the survival (masquerading as the participle) of *wm-mhr*, that is, the conjunction has enclitic *mem*, and the 'perfect' verb is used as a consecutive future—'and God will hasten to do it.'"[12]

The fourth example deduced by Andersen is the famous crux in Judg 13:19, *ûmaplîʾ laʿăśôt*. His argument that this participle is otherwise unknown is correct per se, but faulty in that enough Hiphʿil perfects, imperfects, and infinitives of the root *plʾ* occur to admit the possibility of the form *maplîʾ*. In other words, while this argumentation may have worked for *wmsrpw* in Amos 6:10, it will not work for *wmplʾ* in Judg 13:19. Moreover, G. F. Moore defended the passage on the basis of similar vocabulary in Isa 29:14, Joel 2:26, and 2 Chr 26:15.[13] Perhaps it is best to conclude, then, that the text either should be accepted without difficulty or should be emended according to any number of suggestions.[14]

Turning now to Andersen's secondary list of passages, i.e., where "other examples of enclitic *mem* with *w-* may be present,"[15] only 2 Sam 16:5 deserves serious consideration. The final clause reads *yôṣēʾ yāṣōʾ ûmĕqallēl.* The use of a participle after an infinitive absolute is most extraordinary, for the usual usage calls for a second infinitive absolute or perhaps a finite verb. S. R. Driver commented, "The type is unusual: *yôṣēʾ yāṣōʾ wĕqallēl* would be the ordinary one."[16] Both Driver and P. Joüon[17] noted that Jer 41:6 *hôlēk hālōk ûbôkeh* offers a suitable parallel, but it also must be pointed out that some manuscripts point *wbkh* as the infinitive absolute *ûbākōh.*[18] It is not good linguistic practice to expunge anomalous forms from the corpus, but in light of variant manuscripts for Jer 41:6, we may wish to admit *wmqll* in 2 Sam 16:5 as another example of conjunctive *waw* and enclitic *mem* and read *qallēl* as infinitive absolute. Of the remainder of Andersen's proposals, all from Job, none is compelling, even though *ûmibbĕśārî* in Job 19:26 has elicited much discussion.[19]

[11] Gordon, "The 'Waw Conversive': From Eblaite to Hebrew," 89. See the next example, Gen 41:32, as well.

[12] Andersen, *Hebrew Verbless Clause*, 48.

[13] G. F. Moore, *Judges* (ICC; Edinburgh, 1895) 324–25.

[14] For different solutions, see C. F. Burney, *The Book of Judges* (London, 1920) 349–59.

[15] Andersen, *Hebrew Verbless Clause*, 124, n 13.

[16] S. R. Driver, *Notes on the Hebrew Text of the Books of Samuel* (Oxford, 1890) 247.

[17] P. Joüon, *Grammaire de l'Hébreu biblique* (Rome, 1947) 352, § 123m.

[18] See the apparatus in *BHS.*

[19] See, e.g., S. R. Driver and G. B. Gray, *Job*, vol. 2 (ICC; New York, 1921) 130–32.

But there are still other vocables in the Hebrew Bible which are to be analyzed as conjunctive *waw* with *mem* enclitic. Ps 147:3 reads *hârôpēᵓ lišĕbûrê lēb ûmĕḥabbēš lĕᶜaṣṣĕbôtām*. The expression *ûmĕḥabbēš*, 'and binds,' seems unproblematic at first glance, but since this verb is not used as a Piᶜel in Hebrew,[20] the pointing is suspect. Indeed, in Hos 6:1 and Isa 30:26 *ḥbš* occurs in the Qal parallel to *rpᵓ*, 'heal.' Since these two verbs are also parallel in Ps 147:3, we should read consonantal *wmḥbš* as conjunctive *waw*, enclitic *mem*, and a Qal form of *ḥbš*. Presumably we should read a Qal participle *ḥôbēš*, since *rôpēᵓ* appears in the parallel stich.

In actuality, there is an exception to the above statement that *ḥbš* is not used in the Piᶜel. In addition, there are two instances where the biblical text has *ḥbš* in the Puᶜal. All three require comment. In Ezek 30:21 *ḥubbĕšâh* should be read as passive Qal, especially in light of the Qal infinitive *lĕḥobšâh* earlier in the same verse. In Isa 1:6 *ḥubbāšû* should be similarly interpreted as passive Qal. The only other Piᶜel of this root is *ḥibbēš* in Job 28:11. This word has elicited endless discussion, with all sorts of interpretation being offered. The most common solution is to adduce a *b/p* interchange and to treat the word as akin to *ḥippēš*, 'searches.'[21] Regardless, it seems certain that *ḥibbēš* is not our word 'bind' and therefore we may reaffirm the conclusion that *ḥbš* is only a Qal and should be read as such in Ps 147:3.

Through similar methodology we may recover another *wm-* form. Nah 2:13 reads *ᵓaryēh ṭôrep bĕdê gôrôtāw ûmĕḥannēq lĕlibᵓôtāw*. Elsewhere in the Bible, the root *ḥnq* 'strangle' occurs in the Qal, or in the case of 2 Sam 17:23, the Niphᶜal. In Job 7:15 the nominal form *maḥănāq* occurs, which also implies a Qal form of the verb (cp. *maᵓăkāl* from *ᵓkl* in the Qal). In the cognate languages, this verbal root appears in the corresponding G-stems; note especially Akkadian *ḫanāqu*[22] and Arabic *ḫanaqa* (the root occurs also in derived conjugations with derived meanings).[23] In light of this cumulative evidence, consonantal *wmḥnq* in Nah 2:13 should not be read as a Piᶜel participle, but rather as conjunctive *waw*, enclitic *mem*, and a Qal form of *ḥnq*, presumably the participle *ḥônēq* parallel to *ṭôrēp* in the first stich. Accordingly, in three instances—Amos 6:10, Ps 147:3, Nah 2:13—the received text preserved *wm-* forms followed by Qal verbs, which the Masoretes pointed as Piᶜel participles.

Still another passage where a *wm-* form may be recognized is Num 23:10, *mî mānāh ᶜăpar yaᶜăqōb ûmispār ᵓet rôbaᶜ yiśrāᵓēl*. Exegetes long ago reached

[20] This holds not only for Biblical Hebrew but for Rabbinic Hebrew as well; cf. M. Jastrow, *A Dictionary of the Targumim, the Talmud Babli and Yerushalmi, and the Midrashic Literature* (New York, 1903) 423.

[21] Thus M. H. Pope, *Job* (AB; Garden City, NY, 1973) 203; A. C. M. Blommerde, *Northwest Semitic Grammar and Job* (Rome, 1969) 106–7; and *Textual Notes on the New American Bible* (Paterson, NJ, n.d.) 376. Already the LXX and the Vulgate seem to have interpreted the text in a like fashion. On the entire problem, see L. L. Grabbe, *Comparative Philology and the Text of Job* (Missoula, MT, 1977) 94–98.

[22] *CAD* Ḫ, 77.

[23] H. Wehr and J. M. Cowan, *A Dictionary of Modern Written Arabic* (Ithaca, NY, 1976) 263.

the consensus that Masoretic *ûmispār* is to be emended to *ûmî sāpar* "in agreement with Sam[aritan] and G[reek], to say nothing of the parallelism" with *mî mānāh* in the first stich.[24] However, in light of Eblaite *ù-ma* and with a growing respect for at least the consonantal portion of the Masoretic Text,[25] we may now retain *wmspr* without emendation. This form preserves conjunctive *waw* with enclitic *mem*, followed by the revocalized verb *sāpar*. The meaning of emended *ûmî sāpar* and that of revocalized *ûmāsāpar* are hardly very different, but this example illustrates well how new evidence can always controvert even the most accepted solutions to textual and philological enigmas.

Returning now to prose texts, we may note three *wm-* forms in *wmpʾt* in Ezek 48:16 and *wmʾḥzt* in Ezek 48:22 (*bis*). The Masoretes pointed these words respectively as *ûmippĕʾat* and *ûmêʾăḥuzzat*, i.e., they treated the *mem* in each instance as the preposition 'from.' Most commentators realize the impossibility of this interpretation and simply delete the *mem*s; in the first instance, they at least defend their emendation with the textual support of six variant manuscripts.[26] However, the Masoretic Text may once again be reaffirmed if we analyze these forms as conjunctive *waw*, enclitic *mem*, and construct noun.

Another example of a *wm-* form in prose is consonantal *wmʾt* in Neh 5:11, vocalized *ûmĕʾat* 'and a hundred of' by the Masoretes, but surely to be analyzed as conjunctive *waw*, enclitic *mem*, and the accusative marker *ʾet*, exactly as in Ruth 4:6. This passage is treated elsewhere in this volume by C. Wallace,[27] so there is no need to enter into detailed discussion here.

Finally, we come to 1 Kgs 14:14 with what many consider an intrusive *ûmeh*. A typical solution is that adopted by *NAB* which omits the word based on dittography from the preceding *hayyôm* (note the consonants *hywm wmh*).[28] But the received text, even with its problems,[29] may be accepted if we analyze *ûmeh* as *waw* conjunctive and *mem* enclitic. Most enclitic *mem*s in the Bible are

[24] W. F. Albright, "The Oracles of Balaam," *JBL* 63 (1944) 213. Cf. G. B. Gray, *Numbers* (ICC; New York, 1906) 348; J. H. Greenstone, *Numbers* (Philadelphia, 1939) 255; S. Gevirtz, *Patterns in the Early Poetry of Israel* (Chicago, 1973) 61–63; D. K. Stuart, *Studies in Early Hebrew Meter* (Missoula, MT, 1976) 111; and G. J. Wenham, *Numbers* (TynOT; Leicester, 1981) 174, n 1. It should be noted that C. H. Gordon, "Review of W. von Soden, *Grundriss der akkadischen Grammatik*," *Or* 22 (1953) 229, resisted emending *ûmispār* to the "easier reading" *ûmî sāpar*; his patience has now been rewarded by proper elucidation of the verse and an acceptance of at least the consonants of the Masoretic Text. Similarly, E. Y. Kutscher, "Notes to the Biblical Lexicon," *Leshonenu* 21 (5717) 254–55, rejected the usual emendation and ingeniously explained *mispār* as the Aramaic Peʿal (= Qal) infinitive in the mouth of the Aramean Balaam.

[25] See the fine remarks by D. N. Freedman, "Review of A. R. Ceresko, *Job 29–31 in the Light of Northwest Semitic*," *JBL* 102 (1983) 138–40.

[26] On Ezek 48:16, see *BHS*; G. A. Cooke, *Ezekiel* (ICC; Edinburgh, 1936) 540; G. Fohrer, *Ezechiel* (Tübingen, 1955) 262; W. Zimmerli, *Ezechiel II* (Neukirchen-Vluyn, 1969) 1208; and W. Eichrodt, *Ezekiel* (Philadelphia, 1970) 588–90. On Ezek 48:22, see *BHS*; Fohrer, 262; and Zimmerli, 1209.

[27] C. Wallace, "*wm-* in Nehemiah 5:11."

[28] *Textual Notes on the New American Bible*, 353.

[29] The entire end of the verse is problematic; see the discussion by J. A. Montgomery and H. S. Gehman, *Kings* (ICC; Edinburgh, 1951) 272.

affixed to the preceding word, but occasionally we do have *mh* appearing as enclitic *mem*;[30] *ûmeh* in 1 Kgs 14:14 would be another example.[31]

At this stage it is worthwhile to summarize the evidence, and then to proceed to the question of whether Hebrew *wm-* has any special syntactic function and how it should be translated. Eblaite *ù-ma*, the conjunction and enclitic *ma*, has led to the search for cognate forms in the Hebrew Bible. Our investigation has turned up ample passages, in both poetry and prose, where a consonantal *wm-* in the Masoretic Text should be interpreted as conjunctive *waw* and enclitic *mem*. In poetic texts there are four examples, *wmsrpw* in Amos 6:10, *wmḥbš* in Ps 147:3, *wmḥnq* in Nah 2:13, and *wmspr* in Num 23:10. In prose texts there are seven or eight examples, *wm*ᵓ*t* in Ruth 4:5, *wmmhr* in Gen 41:32, *wmp*ᵓ*t* in Ezek 48:16, *wm*ᵓ*ḥzt* in Ezek 48:22 (*bis*), *wm*ᵓ*t* in Neh 5:11, *wmh* in 1 Kgs 14:14, and possibly *wmqll* in 2 Sam 16:5.

That Hebrew *wm-* has a special syntactic function becomes apparent from a closer look at three of the four poetic examples. In the verses below, *wm-* serves to introduce the second of the parallel stichs:

Ps 147:3	who heals the brokenhearted *wm-* binds their wounds
Nah 2:13	the lion preys for its cubs *wm-* strangles for its lionesses[32]
Num 23:10	who has counted the dust of Jacob *wm-* has numbered the dustcloud of Israel[33]

In view of these examples, I am inclined to consider *wm-* as an emphasizing conjunction and translate it, depending on the context, as 'indeed, even, verily, yea.' In other words, *wm-* cannot and does not occur as a simple conjunction. One would not use it, for example, in a merism (e.g., 'heaven and earth'), in a

[30] E.g., in Num 24:22; cf. Albright, 222; and Wenham, 181, n 2. Oddly, this example is missing from the most thorough treatment of enclitic *mem* to date, namely, D. A. Robertson, *Linguistic Evidence in Dating Early Hebrew Poetry* (Missoula, MT, 1972) 79–110. Two other examples of *mh* as enclitic (Ps 21:2, Prov 30:13) are proposed by D. H. Hummel, "Enclitic *Mem* in Early Northwest Semitic, Especially Hebrew," *JBL* 76 (1957) 99, 102, but neither is particularly compelling; see Robertson, 102–3; and M. Dahood, *Psalms I* (AB; Garden City, NY, 1966) 131.

[31] It is possible that another example of "unattached" *wm-* is to be found in *ûmāh* in Mal 2:15. However, since this passage is "one of the most obscure verses in the entire O.T." (thus R. C. Dentan, "Malachi," *IB* 6 [1956] 1136), I refrain from any detailed discussion. See, however, J. M. P. Smith, *Malachi* (ICC; Edinburgh, 1912) 59, who feels that the entire problem may be cleared up by deleting *ûmāh*.

[32] Parenthetically, one may note that the prophet's knowledge of nature is somewhat deficient; it is the lioness who provides food for her mate and cubs, not the lion who hunts prey. On the other hand, since Nahum intends the king of Assyria, the metaphor of *aryēh* is certainly more apropos than *lābî*ᵓ.

[33] For a complete discussion of *rôba*ᶜ 'dustcloud' see H. R. Cohen, *Biblical Hapax Legomena in the Light of Akkadian and Ugaritic* (Missoula, MT, 1978) 37–39 and 60–63, nn 65–87.

hendiadys (e.g., 'love and mercy'), or in a long list of items, unless there was a special desire by the author to stress a particular point.

This understanding of the function of *wm-* also explains the fourth poetic example, Amos 6:10 *ûnĕśā˒ô dôdô ûmāsĕrāpô* (revocalized *wmsrpw*), 'his kinsman is to carry him, even to burn him.' As discussed earlier, under extraordinary circumstances the burning of the deceased was an honorable act in the biblical world. To accentuate this exceptional situation, the prophet utilizes the emphasizing conjunction *wm-* instead of the simple conjunction *w-*.

We can observe the same syntactic role for *wm-* in the prose texts. In each of the following cases, *wm-* serves to emphasize what follows, coming right after a simple declarative statement or at the end of a lengthy speech.

Ruth 4:5 — Boaz said, "Today you acquire the field from the hand of Naomi, *wm-* I have acquired Ruth the Moabitess, the wife of the deceased, to raise the name of the deceased on his estate."

As alluded to earlier, Boaz has set up this climactic scene in the book and has manipulated Elimelech's closer kinsman brilliantly. He saves his revelation till the end, that no matter what happens to the field, his marriage to Ruth is a *fait accompli*. The author's use of *wm-* to introduce Boaz's disclosure is an effective climax to what is by all accounts a masterly-woven tale. Moreover, the Masoretic accentuation is effective too, since *wm-* follows the *˒atnāḥ*, where Boaz's declaration comes to a momentary rest. Since the second clause of Ruth 4:5 stands adversatively to the first clause, we may add for *wm-* the meanings 'but, however.'

Gen 41:32 — As for Pharaoh having had the same dream twice, it means that the matter has been affirmed by God, *wm-* that God will hasten to carry it out.

In this instance, *wm-* introduces the final clause of Joseph's lengthy interpretation of Pharaoh's dreams[34] and is appropriately used to emphasize the point that the pair of seven-year periods is imminent.

Ezek 48:16 — And these are its dimensions: the north side 4500 cubits and the south side 4500 cubits, *wm-* the east side 4500 cubits and the west side 4500 cubits.

Here *wm-* divides the verse, again coming immediately after the *˒atnāḥ*. The prophet first lists the northern and southern boundaries, then climactically the eastern and western boundaries. Just as the second lines of parallel poetry are introduced by *wm-*, so too the second halves of parallel prose lines.

[34] Joseph's speech actually continues for four more verses, but the dream interpretation ends here. See the paragraph divisions in *NJPSV* and *NAB*.

Ezek 48:[21-]22(*bis*) The sacred portion and the Temple sanctuary shall be in the middle of it; *wm-* the property of the Levites *wm-* the property of the city shall be in the middle of that belonging to the prince.

There are three areas which were geographically located in the middle of the prince's property according to Ezekiel's description of the land. The last two listed are introduced by *wm-*. Whether the prophet intended some special emphasis here is difficult to determine, but it is not unlikely given other usages of *wm-*, including six verses earlier by the same author. It should also be pointed out that the twofold correlative use of *wm-* is paralleled by *ù-ma . . . ù-ma* in Eblaite (TM.75.G.2420 rev. viii 9 [=line 439]).

Neh 5:11 Please return to them this very day their fields, their vineyards, their olive groves, and their houses, *wm-* the money, the grain, the wine, and the oil that you have lent them.

Again *wm-* comes after an *ʾatnāḥ* and again it is prefixed to the final clause of a lengthy speech. Nehemiah ends his plaint to the nobles with the plea to return to the plebians what is rightfully theirs and moreover to cancel the debt of owed money and goods. Accordingly, the use of *wm-* here is most appropriate.

1 Kgs 14:14 this day *wm-* even now

Once again *wm-* follows an *ʾatnāḥ*. The author must certainly have wished to emphasize the imminence of Ahijah's statement that the house of Jeroboam would fall. He not only utilized *wm-* but the emphatic particle *gam* as well.[35]

2 Sam 16:5 As King David approached Bahurim, there came a man from Saul's clan named Shimei ben Gera, cursing as he came.

In the discussion on *wmqll* above, we were unsure on morphological grounds whether to admit the presence of a *wm-* form. On syntactic grounds, the evidence is equally ambiguous; however, the author may have used the emphasizing particle *wm-* to stress the severity of Shimei's sin, namely, cursing the king. If this be the case, then the use of *wm-* here is most fitting.

It is evident that Hebrew *wm-* had a specific syntactic function. This morpheme was an additional item in the arsenal of emphasizing particles available to Hebrew writers both of prose and of poetry. Whether or not its Eblaite cognate *ù-ma* had the same or similar function in the Tell Mardikh tablets is hard to determine due to the difficulty of interpreting the texts. But this is a detail which might be investigated as Ebla research progresses. Finally,

[35] For emphatic *gam*, see R. J. Williams, *Hebrew Syntax* (Toronto, 1976) 63.

another avenue of inquiry which might be pursued is the possible if not probable use of *wm-* in other Northwest Semitic literatures, especially Ugaritic.[36]

[36] M. Dahood, "Additional Notes on the *MRZḤ* Tablet," in L. R. Fisher, ed., *The Claremont Ras Shamra Tablets* (Rome, 1971) 53, has proposed reading *wm* in RS.1957.702 obv. 6 as conjunctive *waw* plus enclitic *mem*. This suggestion was offered independently of Andersen's proposal for Hebrew and, needless to say, several years before the discovery of the Ebla tablets. Dahood has been followed by B. Halpern, "A Landlord-Tenant Dispute at Ugarit?" *Maarav* 2 (1979–80) 138. However, R. E. Friedman, "The *MRZḤ* Tablet from Ugarit," *Maarav* 2 (1979–80) 193–96, is correct in rejecting this interpretation and analyzing *wm* as a dialectal form of *hm*, 'they.' As Friedman astutely notes, there are three such instances in RS.1957.702 where *w* occurs for *h*.

It has not escaped the attention of the writer that more than a millennium separates the attestation of this particle in Eblaite and its appearance in Hebrew. Moreover, a good number of the biblical passages cited are late (e.g., Ezekiel, Nehemiah). But this is not unparalleled, for various Late Biblical Hebrew and Mishnaic Hebrew characteristics find their reflexes not in earlier stages of Hebrew or in Aramaic but in earlier Canaanite and Ugaritic usage. See further E. Y. Kutscher, *A History of the Hebrew Language* (Jerusalem, 1982) 85, 128. The same holds for vocabulary items; cf. B. A. Levine, *Survivals of Ancient Canaanite in the Mishnah*, unpublished dissertation, Brandeis University, 1962.

Ebla and Dilmun

ROBERT R. STIEGLITZ

References to Dilmun, the maritime market in the Persian Gulf so well known from Mesopotamian cuneiform texts of the second millennium B.C., are now found in the administrative documents of Ebla (Tell Mardikh) in northern Syria, dated to the 24th century B.C. While Dilmun is usually identified with the island of Bahrein and the nearby Arabian coast,[1] it has recently been advocated by T. Howard-Carter[2] that before 2,200 B.C. Dilmun is to be located in the Qurna region, north of Basra, and only later in the Bahrein-Failaka region. Although the problem of the precise location of Dilmun in the Early Bronze Age is of great significance, it is quite sufficient for our purpose here to assume only that Dilmun was a coastal and/or island area in the Persian Gulf.[3]

At Ebla, the most frequent occurrence of the term Dilmun (written NI+TUK) is in the expression gín DILMUN 'Dilmun-shekel,' a ubiquitous term in the economic documents. Other uses of the term Dilmun include DILMUN-ku$_5$ '½ mana of Dilmun,' referring to wool,[4] DILMUN.PAD,[5] and a listing of 10 an-na DILMUN '10 (shekels) of tin of Dilmun.'[6] A lexical text, TM.75.G.2000 VII:45–46, has the entry:[7]

GIŠ.DILMUN = *wa-za-nu-um*
= *sa-qí-lum*

Here, an (originally wooden) object of or pertaining to Dilmun is defined by the Eblaite words (1) *wazanum* 'weight,' and (2) *saqilum* 'shekel, weight.' These entries are evidently connected with the use of gín DILMUN in the economic texts and suggest that we read the latter as Eblaite **ṯaqilum* 'shekel.'

[1] See A. L. Oppenheim, "The Seafaring Merchants of Ur," *JAOS* 74 (1954) 6f.

[2] "The Tangible Evidence for the Earliest Dilmun," *JCS* 33 (1981) 210–23.

[3] The ships of Dilmun are already mentioned by Sargon of Akkad, and the lexical series Ḫḫ IV 281 (*MSL* V 174) lists GIŠ.MÁ DILMUN^{ki} = *Til-mu-ni-tum* 'Dilmunite (boat).'

[4] See A. Archi and M. G. Biga, *ARET* 3 (1982) 344.

[5] Ibid. This term is not translated by Archi and Biga.

[6] TM.75.G.1521. See A. Archi, *SEb* 2 (1980) 1.

[7] See D. O. Edzard, *ARET* 2 (1981) 141, *s.v.* Tilmun.

The main problem is how to interpret the significance of the term DILMUN as related to the shekel of Ebla. G. Pettinato[8] suggested two possible explanations, since DILMUN may be understood as either a noun or as an adjective. In the first case, as a toponym, it "would contain a forceful indication that this unit of weight originated in Dilmun, the present-day Islands of Bahrein, famous in antiquity as the source of precious metals."[9] If we take Dilmun as an adjective, it means, according to Pettinato "noble shekel" or a measure standardized by international agreements."[10] D. O. Edzard[11] did not commit himself to an interpretation, stating simply that the "meaning is still unknown." He did, however, note that while understanding the term adjectivally as 'Dilmunite' would be "far-fetched," it does not, therefore, rule out the possibility. In light of the lexical evidence from Ebla, as noted above, we would prefer to interpret the gín DILMUN as the 'DILMUN (standard)-shekel.' This could only mean that other shekel standards were utilized alongside this unit at Ebla.

The weight standards of Dilmun are better known from economic texts of the Ur III period, when Dilmun was the main market for copper.[12] The study of Dilmun metrology at this period by M. Rolf[13] indicates that the Dilmun mina was a weight of ca. 1,350 grams, divided into eight and one hundred, while its multiples were reckoned in thousands.[14] This system is in sharp contrast to the Mesopotamian sexagesimal standard, where, for example, the Old Babylonian Ur mina of ca. 500 grams was utilized. The numerical system at Ebla in the Early Bronze Age was, as at later Dilmun, not sexagesimal but decimal—in spite of the fact that a Sumerian mana divided into 60 shekels was utilized at Ebla.[15]

It is now known that already in the Early Bronze Age there were extensive commercial links between Ebla and major Mesopotamian city-states. Since the Dilmun standard is well attested in Mesopotamia in the Middle Bronze Age (ca. 2000–1550 B.C.), there seems to be little reason not to accept the proposal of Pettinato that the Dilmun shekel at Ebla does indeed indicate trade with Dilmun in the Early Bronze Age. Ebla was a land-locked site, so that any Dilmun-Ebla interconnections would necessarily mean that an intermediary riverine port linked Ebla to Dilmun. The route from Ebla to Dilmun was most

[8] *The Archives of Ebla* (Garden City, NY, 1981) 182.

[9] Ibid.

[10] Ibid.

[11] *ARET* 2 (1981) 141.

[12] See Oppenheim, "Merchants of Ur," 10.

[13] "Weights on the Dilmun Standard," *Iraq* 44 (1982) 137–41.

[14] See, e.g., *UET* V 796 (*JAOS* 75 [1954] 10) for 13,000 minas (!) of copper according to the Dilmun standard.

[15] On the standards and numbers at Ebla, see G. Pettinato, *Archives*, 180ff. Eblaite scribes studied Sumerian numbers (Edzard, *SEb* 3 [1980] 121–27) and even sexagesimal mathematical problems (Archi, *SEb* 3 [1980] 63–64) as part of their bicultural education. But their native numeration was decimal. Eblaite, like Egyptian, even had a separate term for 100,000, which in sexagesimal notation would be written 27,46,40.

likely via the river-ports of Southern Mesopotamia, i.e., Sumer. This link between Ebla and the Persian Gulf, by way of overland and riverine-maritime routes, was probably the port at Mari.[16] The introduction of the Dilmun standard to Ebla may have been connected with extensive metal trade via these riverine-maritime lanes.

In addition to metals, Dilmun was also a source of luxury products in the Old Babylonian period, and if the Dilmun trade can now be extended back into the third millennium B.C., it may well account for the lumps of lapis lazuli found at Ebla. This precious stone, so widely used in the Ancient Near East, most likely originated in Badakhshan (Afghanistan) and reached Mesopotamia by way of riverine-maritime trade via Meluhha (the Indus and Makran Coast), Magan (Oman), and Dilmun.[17] The lapis at Ebla was probably acquired directly at Mari.

In view of our supposed Dilmun-Ebla connections, we can now better appreciate the famous bilingual (Sumerian-Akkadian) royal inscription of Sargon of Akkad (ca. 2350 B.C.), in which he records the establishment of his realm from Meluhha to the Cedar Forest and the Silver Mountain (on the Upper Sea = Mediterranean). In this text,[18] Sargon claims to have moored at the wharf of Akkad the ships of Meluhha, Magan, and Dilmun, as well as capturing the cities of Mari, Yarmuti, and Ebla.

What appears to be outlined in his inscription, in geographical order from southeast to northwest, is a series of major trading centers linked by both riverine-maritime as well as overland routes: Meluhha, Magan, Dilmun, Mari, Yarmuti, Ebla. Sargon thus claims to control this extensive network of commercial centers, forming the backbone of his empire.[19] If we continue this route to its logical end—the Mediterranean coast—it is most tempting to suggest that the maritime outlet for this transit-trade was on the Syrian coast not far from Ebla. Indeed, a geographical list from Ebla (TM.75.G.2231) includes both Ugarit and Arwad,[20] and either or both could have served the merchants of Ebla.

The epigraphic evidence from Ebla suggesting at least close commercial ties between Dilmun and North Syria in the Early Bronze Age should also be

[16] See R. R. Stieglitz, "Notes on Riverine-Maritime Trade at Ebla," *Proceedings of the First International Workshop on Ancient Mediterranean Harbours*, Caesarea Maritima 24–28 June 1983; British Archaeological Report International Series 257 (Oxford, 1985) 7–10.

[17] M. Rolf ("Weights on the Dilmun Standard") found that the same non-sexagesimal weight standards were utilized at Dilmun/Bahrein and in the Indus region. On Meluhha as the main source of carnelian, see J. G. Young, "Semi-Precious Stones in the Aegean," *Archaeological News* 8 (1979) 40–44.

[18] See G. A. Barton, *The Royal Inscriptions of Sumer and Akkad* (New Haven, 1929) 108f. Also see A. K. Grayson, "The Empire of Sargon of Akkad," *AfO* 25 (1974–77) 56–64.

[19] On the foreign trade of Middle Mesopotamia in this period, see G. Pettinato, "Il commercio con l'Estero della Mesopotamia Meridionale nel 3. millennio av. Ch. alla luce delle fonti letterarie e lessicali Sumeriche," *Mesopotamia* 7 (1972) 43–166.

[20] See A. Archi, "Notes on Eblaite Geography," *SEb* 2 (1980) 2.

considered in light of ancient traditions about Canaanite origins. According to both biblical and Greek sources, the Phoenicians originated somewhere along the shores of the Erythraean Sea, i.e., the Red Sea-Persian Gulf region.

In the biblical Table of Nations (Gen 10:6), both Canaan and Egypt are derived from a common ancestor, Ham, implying that the Canaanites were originally connected with the coasts of the Erythraean Sea. Herodotus in two passages (1.1, 7.89) also relates that the Phoenicians by their own accounts migrated from the coasts of the Erythraean Sea to the maritime parts of Syria. The attempt by W. F. Albright[21] simply to dismiss the historical possibility of "the Erythraean theory of Herodotus" can now be seen to have been unwarranted. Justin (18.3) reports that the Phoenicians were settled around the Sea of Galilee during the early periods of their history, before they settled on the Syrian coast. Thus, he too suggests that they were not native to the Levantine coasts.

The publication of additional texts from the archives of Ebla will hopefully shed further light on the suggested relationships between Ebla and Dilmun, and on the historical background of the Canaanites in the Middle Bronze Age.

[21] "The Role of the Canaanites in the History of Civilization," in *The Bible and the Ancient Near East*, ed. by G. E. Wright (Garden City, NY, 1965; reprinted, Winona Lake, 1979) 443.

Reflections on the System of Weights from Ebla*

ALFONSO ARCHI

During the course of the excavations carried out between 1975 and 1978 at Tell Mardikh, some weights were found, all coming from the area of the Royal Palace G in the Mardikh IIB1 phase, dating from the Early Bronze Age IVA. The tables on the following pages summarize the data relative to them and to another group of examples, almost all from the Middle Bronze Age and coming from Palace Q, from houses B, from the temple area N, from Gate A and from Palace E.[1]

Weight no. 21, which weighs 467.5 g. and has a groove in the spherical vault, certainly represents the unit value of the mina. This corresponds (with only one gram difference) to the Ugaritic example in bronze, which weighs 468.5 g. and is cast in the shape of a kneeling bull.[2] There is also a weight from Tell Sweyhat (on the Euphrates, approximately 64 km. south of Karkemiš) in limestone, slightly chipped, weighing 472.2 g., which is inscribed with the value:

*This study was published in Italian in 1980, as a pre-print. It is republished here without any changes, but with an appendix listing weights found during the 1981–1983 seasons.

[1] I thank P. Matthiae for having given me this material for publication. I want to mention that S. Mazzoni supplied all the pertinent archeological data, and that N. Parise was willing to discuss this article with me. For the terminology regarding the phases of Mardikh correlated to a more general classification, see P. Matthiae, *Ebla* (Turin, 1977), 60; and for the identification of excavation sites, see ibid., 34 (Q, begun again in 1978, now extends the entire length of G).

[2] C. F. A. Schaeffer, *Syria* 18 (1937) 147 and table XXIII. The author also recalls (p. 148) "autres exemplaires, dont l'un également en forme de bovidé couche" published in *Syria* 16 (1935), table XXXIII, 5. Two examples of Cypriot weights in bronze in the form of a cow have been published, but without an indication of their weights, by H. W. Catling, *Cypriot Bronzework in the Mycenaean World* (Oxford, 1964), 251ff., and Pl. 44 d–e. The weight of specimen 1896.12–1.64, as Veronica Tatton-Brown of the British Museum has kindly informed me, is 92.824 g.; it represents ⅕ of a mina of 464.12 g., thus equal to the Ugaritic one. Tatton-Brown also informed me of "an unpublished weight in the form of a bull found during R. H. Lang's excavations at Idalion. It is either Late Bronze or Early Iron Age. Its inventory number is 1872.8–16.98, and it weighs 87.052 grams." It thus represents ⅕ of a mina of 435.25 g. Catling had already referred to weights from Tell el-Amarna, in the form of a bull; one of them weights 437 g. and is inscribed with 5 *dbn*; the other, inscribed with one *dbn*, weights 92.9 g.; see J. D. S. Pendlebury, *The City of Akhenaten* (London, 1951), III, 1, pp. 109 and 125; 2, pl. 77:1–2. Regarding the problem, cf. N. Parise, *Dialoghi di Archeologia* 4 (1970–71), 20, n 21.

1 mina. The archeological context seems to place this piece in the Akkadian age ("Late Sargonid [!]" according to M. E. L. Mallowan).[3] Since it is certain from the texts of Ebla that the mina was divided into 60 shekels,[4] that Ebla mina was based on a shekel unit of about 7.80 g. This series of weights is represented by Eblaic examples no. 1: 1/5 of a shekel; no. 2: 1/2 of a shekel; nos. 3 and 4: 1 shekel; no. 11: 2 shekels. This unit, known as "Phoenician standard," was widespread in the Eastern Mediterranean during the Late Bronze and Iron Ages; actually, it was used already not only during the Middle Bronze,[5] but also in the Early Bronze Age.[6] If, therefore, the specimen of one mina—no. 21—is precise, those of 2, 3, 5 minas—nos. 24, 25, 26—represent shekel unit values considerably underweight, that is, respectively, 7.16 g., 7.4 g., and 7.44 g. It must be noted, however, that the entire series from 1 to 5 minas is made up of weights in unpolished stone and thus (especially the piece of 5 minas) is not absolutely precise. For more precious materials, it is probable that other specimens were used.

There is, however, an element which leads one to think that the mina of 467.5 g. was also divided by 50: nos. 22 and 23, in addition to the groove indicating 1 mina, show 5 (no. 22) and 4 (no. 23) incisions perpendicular to it. It is true that these specimens weigh 106.8 g (no. 22) and 198.6 (99.3 × 2) g. (no. 23) more than no. 21, and therefore more than one mina, whose fifth part is equal to 93.5 g. But it is easy to think that the assumed unit values of the shekel are slightly overweight: 9.5716 g. (574.3 ÷ 60) and 9.5157 g. (666.1 ÷ 70). It seems legitimate to deduce that the series represented here was in fact divided into 5 parts of 10 shekels each. Between 1 and 2 minas, the following scale of intermediate values should be set up, fixed through notations which seem to proceed by subtraction from 2 minas:

 = 1 mina

 = 1 mina and 1/5

 = 1 mina and 2/5

[ = 1 mina and 3/5]

[ = 1 mina and 4/5]

 = 2 minas

[3] J. T. H. Holland, *Iraq* 37 (1975) 75ff.

[4] See below.

[5] For Ebla, see below.

[6] For Byblos, see M. Dunand, *Fouilles de Byblos* (Paris, 1939), I, p. 426, no. 6566: 7.4 g. (?); p. 188, no. 2955: 22.1 g.; and see below, n 15. For Tarsus, see H. Goldman, *Excavations at Gözlü Kule, Tarsus* (Princeton, 1950–63), II, p. 275, no. 129: 7 g. (EB III). For Tepe Gawra, see E. A. Speiser, *Excavations at Tepe Gawra* (Philadelphia, 1935), I, p. 92, no. 22: 7.49 g. (Str. VII). Many specimens from Susa, classified as *peyem* by N. T. Belaiew in *MDP* XXV, 146ff., are open to other interpretations; nevertheless, see for the unit values, for example, nos. 188, 193, 199–201. For the spread of this standard in the Sumerian area in general see A. S. Hemmy, *Ancient Egypt* 20 (1935) 89–91.

Therefore, if this is true, then there is also another unit value, that is, a shekel of about 9.4 g. In fact, this series is evidenced in an unequivocal way by specimens nos. 5 and 6: 1 shekel; no. 10: 1.5 shekel; nos. 12, 13, 14, 15, 16: respectively 3, 4, 5, 6, 7 shekels (and it may therefore be presumed that all the values from 1 to 10 are represented); nos. 18 and 20: 15 shekels. Specimens nos. 12, 13, 14, 15, and 16 are slightly underweight, in particular no. 15, which is intact, while for no. 12 it must be kept in mind that a part of the circumference of a base is missing. Certainly these do not constitute a homogeneous group, since they have different shapes; in any case, they cannot belong to the series having as a base 7.80 g., as is inferred by placing in succession the unit values of each weight, calculated according to that standard: from 6.35 g. for no. 12 (damaged), there is a constant rise to 8.02 g. for no. 16.[7]

Although this series is the one proven more completely, and although the division of the mina by 5 seems to be seen in nos. 22 and 23, in any case it is necessary to keep as the basic unit in use in the territory of Ebla a shekel of about 7.80 g. (that is, 1/60 of the mina weighing about 468 g.), since according to innumerable bookkeeping entries, as has already been anticipated, the mina is divisible on a sexagesimal basis. For example, we have: TM.75.G.1226 II 3: 2 ma-na 50 lá 1 bar$_6$:kù '2 minas, 49 (shekels) of silver'; XIII 3: 8 ma-na 50 bar$_6$:kù '8 minas, 50 (shekels) of silver'; TM.75.G.10143 XVI 13: 50 gín DILMUN bar$_6$:kù '50 shekels DILMUN of silver.' However, this division is utilized in a region in which counting by tens was well established (as later in Ugarit), both with regard to solids and textiles. For example: TM.75.G.1331 VI: 2 *mi-at* 3 ma-na ŠA.PI kù-gi '203 minas, 40 (shekels) of gold'; TM.75.G.2349 II 5: 1 *mi-at* 90 gu$_4$-áb '190 bovines'; TM.75.G.10143 XVII 4: 4 *mi-at* 40 íb-3-gùn-túg '440 girdles of three (segments).'[8] For the moment, the unit of the talent is not attested.

This situation is comparable to that of Ugarit in the second millennium. C. F. A. Schaeffer, comparing three weights of 9.9 g., 18.70 g., and 90.9 g. to a mina specimen of 470 g., with 1, 2, and 10 incisions respectively, has determined the division of the Ugaritic mina into 50 shekels of 9.4 g.[9] Actually, beside this series, others have been proven, as N. Parise demonstrated in his systematization of the Ugaritic weights.[10] For the Phoenician standard, even if there is no specimen for the unit value, there are specimens of its multiples by 2, 10, and 15.[11] The shekel of 9.4 g. corresponds to the Egyptian *qdt* weight and constitutes

[7] According to their shape, nos. 1, 4; 3, 9; 13, 18; and 17, 19 may belong to the same series.

[8] The three terms for clothing which appear most frequently in the Ebla texts are *ʾà-da-um*-túg, aktum(A.SU)-túg, and íb-3/4-túg-(sa$_6$-)gùn, always cited in this order, and without anything added. Therefore, these respective equivalents can be temporarily proposed: cape, tunic, girdle/belt (in various sizes, or in 3 or 4 segments). Rather frequent are also gada-túg, túg-NI.NI, *gu-zi-tum*-túg (which sometimes appears in the place of *ʾà-da-um*-túg), and mí-túg (sometimes in the place of aktum-túg).

[9] C. F. A. Schaeffer, *Syria* 18 (1937) 147–49.

[10] N. Parise, *Dialoghi di Archeologia* 4 (1970–71) 3–36.

[11] See specimen nos. 11, 20 and 21, and 25, according to the list of Parise, *Dialoghi di Archeologia* 4 (1970–71) 6.

the point of contact between the Syrian area and Egypt. The Amarna letter *EA* 369 shows this clearly, since the sender, the Pharaoh, makes a *qdt* (a tenth of *dbn*) correspond to a shekel: "A total of 160 *dbn.* A total of 40 women cupbearers. 40 silver (shekels) is the price of (each) woman cupbearer."[12] The fact that this standard is so well attested at Ebla during the Early Bronze Age proves how deeply entrenched it actually was in the Syrian area, and therefore it cannot be solely an Egyptian measure which was spread along the Asiatic coast during the second millennium.[13]

Already during the Early Bronze Age the mina of about 470 g. acted as a linking element, not only between the two systems of weights based respectively on the shekel of 9.4 g. and that of 7.80 g., but also between these two systems and the so-called Anatolian one. The Anatolian standard, of 11.75 g., which was thought to have been spread in Syria by the Hittites only during the Late Bronze Age, now appears to be present there already during the Early Syrian age, and is linked to the series of 7.80 g. shekels and 9.4 g. shekels on the basis of the mina of 470 g.[14] The unit value is represented by nos. 7, 8, and perhaps 9. Furthermore, no. 17, which shows 6 incisions, can be reduced to a unit of 11.45 g. This weight, and no. 19—a chip with 14 incisions which express a

[12] Translation by A. F. Rainey, *El Amarna Tablets 359–379* (Neukirchen-Vluyn, 1970) 37. M. Liverani (*OA* 11 [1972] 196, n 16) has called attention to this passage.

[13] For the attestations of this standard during the Early and Middle Bronze Age, see Parise, *Dialoghi di Archeologia* 4 (1970–71) 25, n 29. In particular, for the Early Bronze, consider Tarsus (cf. Goldman *Tarsus*, II, 267, no. 124: 18.50 g.), Tell Taʾyinat (cf. R. J. Braidwood and L. S. Braidwood, *Excavations in the Plain of Antioch* [Chicago, 1960], I, 482: 19.10 g.), and Tepe Gawra (cf. Speiser, *Tepe Gawra*, 92, no. 23: 9.60 g. [Str. VIII]).

Note that the Ugaritic talent without doubt weighed 3,000 shekels; cf. Parise, *Dialoghi di Archeologia* 4 (1970–71) 13ff. M. Heltzer (*Iraq* 39 [1977] 204, n 10), although accepting the value of the Ugaritic shekel as 9.4 g., instead holds that the mina was made up of 60 shekels, and therefore the talent of 50 minas. This is based on a decree of Ini-Tešup, king of Karkemiš, RS 17.146 (see *PRU* IV, pp. 154–57) in which a fine of 3 minas was to be paid if merchants from Karkemiš were killed by men from Ugarit or if merchants from Ugarit were killed by men from Karkemiš. Instead, in a verdict by the same sovereign, RS 17.158 (see *PRU* IV, pp. 169–71), some inhabitants of Ugarit are condemned to pay 180 shekels for the murder of an Anatolian merchant. It may be, however, that at Karkemiš the shekel of 7.80 g. was mainly used. In any case, since it is certain that the Ugaritic mina was of 470 g., if in fact it must be divided by 60, then the Ugaritic shekel weighed 7.80 g. and not 9.4 g.!

[14] The hypothesis that it was the Hittites who introduced the Anatolian shekel to Syria was proposed by D. Arnaud (*RA* 61 [1967] 167–69). But it has been contested by Parise (*Dialoghi di Archeologia* 4 [1970–71] 27–29), who recalls the equivalent of the double "small mina": ⅔ of the Mesopotamian foot, with half of the Mesopotamian foot. Parise refers to Tarsus, for which see also Goldman, *Tarsus*, II 267 and 275, no. 117: 10.20 g. (EB I); no. 123: 22.50 g. (EB III); no. 125: 20.50 g. (EB III); and consider again no. 132: 44.80 g. (EB III); and also to Byblos, to the weight no. 12548: 84.85 g. (with 4 incisions), and cf. no. 1911: 85.5 g. in Dunand, *Byblos*, II, 2, p. 533, and I, p. 129.

The division of the Hittite mina into 40 shekels was discovered by H. Otten, *AfO* 17 (1954–56) 128ff.; it is attested through the collection of Laws, since the Old Kingdom. See now also a ritual in ancient *ductus*; cf. E. Neu, *Ein althethitisches Gewitterritual* (Wiesbaden, 1970) 16ff., I 49ff.: "The king gives to 20 lancers 5 minas of silver: each one takes 10 shekels of silver."

CHART 1

No. 17	68.7 g.	3 × 3 units of 7.63 g.		2 × 3 units of 11.45 g.
No. 18	141.9 g.	3 × 6 units of 7.883 g.	5 × 3 units of 9.46 g.	2 × 6 units of 11.825 g.
No. 19	[164.5 g.]	3 × 7 units of [7.83 g.]		2 × 7 units of [11.75 g.]

theoretical value of 164.50 g.—constitute links with the 7.80 g. shekel series, for multiples of 2 and 3, respectively. No. 18 shows no incisons, and therefore does not belong to the group of two weights here examined, but links all three series (with a multiple of 5 for the series of 9.4 g.; see Chart 1).

The Mesopotamian standard shekel of 8.41 g. is absent from Ebla during the Early Bronze Age (at least as far as we can now determine); the data relative to Byblos are difficult to evaluate.[15]

Thus we see the autonomy of Syria—in economic relations—with respect to south-central Mesopotamia, or better, Syria's contrast with it. Ebla, then, used the system based on a unit of about 7.80 g. for trade within its territory and for all of northern Syria, as far as Mari, which is cited so often in the texts (in particular for the purchase of wool), and Assur. Mari must have served as a link with the Sumero-Akkadian area. For long-distance trade, which bypassed south-central Mesopotamia, traversed Assyria, and pushed even further east (to Elam, for example), it is precisely this standard which predominated during the Early Bronze Age.[16] The noteworthy quantities of worked and especially unworked lapis lazuli found at Mardikh bear witness to the connections with the Iranian plateau. Also linked to this standard was the unit of 11.75 g. for trade with Anatolia. Relations with Syrian coastal centers, Palestine, and Egypt instead must have made use of the system based on the shekel of 9.4 g., which corresponds precisely to the Egyptian *qdt*, for which is registered a standard of 9.33 g. (I–X Dynasties) and 9.46 g. (XII Dynasty).[17] The importance of the

[15] The Early Bronze weights listed by Dunaud (*Byblos*, I, 35ff.) and by Arnaud (*RA* 61 [1967] 164, n 3) as belonging to the series of the Mesopotamian shekel almost all point to the standard of 7.80 g. or to that of 9.4 g.:

p. 239, no. 3515: 4.05 g., ½ of 8.1 g.
p. 233, no. 3392: 31 g., 4 × 7.75 g.
p. 253, no. 3706: 43.5 g., 6 × 7.25 g.
p. 311, no. 4160: 48.4 g., 5 × 9.68 g.
p. 335, no. 4996: 63.7 g., 8 × 7.965 g., 7 × 9.1 g.
p. 353, no. 5243: 68 g., 9 × 7.555 g.
p. 129, no. 1911: 85.5 g., 9 × 9.5 g.

[16] See Belaiew, *MDP* XXV, 148ff. As an intermediate point, keep in mind Tepe Gawra, with the specimen cited above (n 6) from Stratum VII; but contacts with the culture of Mohenjo-Daro are found especially in Stratum VI. See Speiser, *Tepe Gawra*, 163ff., 175.

[17] See the distribution curve of values established by A. S. Hemmy (*JEA* 23 [1937] 41) on the specimen in the Petrie collection. And more generally, cf. Parise, pp. 9–13. One should bear in

documentation from Ebla is that it represents—in its divisions (even if incomplete) and diverse values—the first system of weights of the third millennium known from an area to the west of the Mesopotamian cultures, and this permits us better to evaluate the sporadic elements previously acquired.

For the Middle Bronze Age, not only does the 7.80 g. series (nos. 33, 34, 35, and 36, for the unit value; 30: two-thirds; 45: double value) persist, but also that of 9.4 g. (nos. 29 [? 1/3], 32 [2/3], 42 [1]). But—as is to be expected because of the radically changed political conditions in northern Syria—the Mesopotamian shekel is also attested. Nos. 40 and 41 constitute two very accurate specimens in different materials of that unit, while nos. 47 and 48 represent 1/6 of the mina. Finally, the Anatolian series is witnessed by nos. 31 (1/2) and 44 (unit value).[18]

A mina of approximately 470 g. is attested in Syria also for the first millennium, for example, at Arslan-Tash. In the buildings attributed to Tiglath-pileser II were found 2 weights representing 1 mina, and another three of 4 minas, 5 minas, and 5 double minas, respectively, whose value is represented by 4, 5, and 5 incisions twice, and the unit weight fluctuates between 438 and 491 g.[19]

---

mind the statement of Hemmy (p. 52) regarding the 7.80 g. shekel: "The evidence for the existence of a standard in the range of the *Peyem* is distinctly uncertain. The curves for the periods of Dyns. I–IV and V–VI show a long level line in that region, and with such inadequate numbers of specimens may be merely a general spread of the Beqa and the Daric. . . . The *Peyem* is definitely absent in Dyn. XVIII, yet in Dyns. XX–XXV there is a clear maximum when inferred specimens are added."

[18] No. 46, which has the same shape as no. 44 but is of different material, could be analyzed as 1/10 of a mina, but it would be a question of a specimen quite below weight. It is more probable to make it equal to 5 shekels of the Phoenician standard.

[19] See F. Thureau-Dangin, *et al.*, *Arslan-Tash* (Paris, 1931) 141ff.

TABLE I

No.	Period	Weight	Divisor	Unit	Shape	Inscr. signs	St. pres.
1	EB IVA	1.4 g.	1/5	7 g.	spherical		scratches
2	EB IVA	3.6 g.	1/2	7.2 g.	cylindrical		scratches
3	EB IVA	7 g.	1	7 g.	cylindrical		abrasions
4	EB IVA	7.9	1	7.9 g.	spherical		intact
5	EB IVA	9.2 g.	1	9.2 g.	cylindrical		intact
6	EB IVA	9.4 g.	1	9.4 g.	ovoidal		scratches
7	EB IVA	10.4 g.	1	10.4 g.	cylindrical		abrasions and scratches
8	EB IVA	11.4 g.	1	11.4 g.	ovoidal		intact
9	EB IVA	12.02 g.	1	12.02 g.	cylindrical		chipped
10	EB IVA	13.8 g.	1.5	9.2 g.	cylindrical		chipped
11	EB IVA (?)	15.5 g.	2	7.75 g.	conical		chipped
12	EB IVA	25.4 g.	3	8.466 g.	trunc. cone		chipped
13	EB IVA	36.5 g.	4	9.125 g.	elong. ovoid		intact
14	EB IVA /MB	45.4 g.	5	9.08 g.	trunc. cone		chipped
15	EB IVA	53.9 g.	6	8.983 g.	cylindrical		abrasions
16	EB IVA	64.2 g.	7	9.171 g.	cylindrical		scratches
17	EB IVA	68.7 g.	9	7.633 g.	ovoidal	6 incisions	abrasions
			6	11.45 g.			
18	EB IVA	141.9 g.	18	7.883 g.			
			15	9.46 g.	ovoidal		abrasions
			12	11.825 g.			
19	EB IVA	[164.5 g.]	21	[7.833 g.]	ovoidal	14 incisions	chip
			14	[11.75 g.]			
20	EB IVA	149.1 g.	15	9.94 g.	ovoidal		chipped
21	EB IVA	467.5 g.	1	467.5 g.	semi-ovoidal	1 groove	abrasions and scratches
22	EB IVA	574.3 g.	1+1/5	478.583 g.	semi-ovoidal	1 groove and 5 incisions	abrasions and scratches
23	EB IVA	666.1 g.	1+2/5	475.785	semi-ovoidal	1 groove and 4 incisions	abrasions and scratches
24	EB IVA	860 g.	2	430 g.	semi-ovoidal	2 grooves	abrasions and scratches
25	EB IVA	1332 g.	3	444 g.	semi-ovoidal	3 grooves	abrasions and scratches
26	EB IVA	2232 g.	5	446.4 g.	ovoidal		scratches
27	EB IVA	1107 g.			pear-shaped	n a_4 *ša-da-su*^{ki}	scratches

TABLE II

No.	Period	Weight	Divisor	Unit	Shape	St. pres.
28	MB				ovoidal	chip
29	MB(?)	3 g.	1/3	9 g.	ovoidal	intact
30	MB	5.4 g.	2/3	8.1 g.	ovoidal	scratches
31	?	5.9 g.	2/3	8.85 g.	cylindrical	scratches
			1/2	11.8 g.		
32	MB	6.1 g.	2/3	9.15 g.	parallelepiped	intact
33	MB	6.8 g.	1	6.8 g.	ovoidal	chipped
34	MB	6.9 g.	1	6.9 g.	trunc. cone	chipped
35	MB/LB	7.7 g.	1	7.7 g.	cylindrical	chipped
36	MB	7.9 g.	1	7.9 g.	ovoidal	scratches
37	MB	8 g.	1	8 g.	triangular	scratches
38	Persian	8 g.	1	8 g.	cylindrical	scratches
39	Persian	8.4 g.	1	8.4 g.	semi-spheric	chipped
40	MB	8.5 g.	1	8.5 g.	spindle-shaped	2 holes
41	MB	8.6 g.	1	8.6 g.	spindle-shaped	scratches
42	MB	9.5 g.	1	9.5 g.	trunc. cone	abrasions
43	MB	10.4 g.	1/5	6.933 g.	spheroid	chipped
			1	10.4 g.		
44	MB	11.9 g.	1	11.9 g.	parallelepiped	2 cavities
45	MB	15.6 g.	2	7.8 g.	ovoidal	scratches
46	MB	40.3 g.	5	8.06 g.	parallelepiped	scratches
			4	10.075 g.		
47	MB	82.1 g.	10	8.21 g.	ovoidal	scratches
48	MB	89.5 g.	10	8.95 g.	ovoidal	chipped

CATALOGUE A

1. Inv.: TM.77.G.374; loc.: D1V2i; lev.: 5; L. 2866
Dim.: diam. 1.6 cm.
Shape: spherical
St. pres.: scratches
Mat.: soft limestone, yellowish in color
Wt.: 1.4 g.
Photo: Fig. 1.1.

2. Inv.: TM.77.G.110; loc.: EAV4iii; lev.: 4; L. 2906
Dim.: h. 0.8; max. diam. 2.2 cm.
Shape: cylindrical with central bulging
St. pres.: scratches on the entire surface
Mat.: basaltic stone, brownish-gray
Wt.: 3.6g.
Photo: Fig. 1.2.

3. Inv.: TM.77.G.109; loc.: EaV4iii, lev.: 4; L. 2906
Dim.: h. 1.6; diam. 1.3 cm.
Shape: irregular cylinder
St. pres.: abrasions
Mat.: basaltic stone, brownish-gray
Wt.: 7 g.
Photo: Fig. 1.3.

4. Inv.: TM.77.G.274; loc.: D1V3ii; lev.: 6; L. 2913
Dim.: diam. 1.6 cm.
Shape: spherical
St. pres.: intact
Mat.: hematite
Wt.: 7.9 g.
Photo: Fig. 1.4.

5. Inv.: TM.77.G.117; loc.: EaV4iii; lev.: 4; L. 2906
Dim.: h. 2.0; diam. 1.3 cm.
Shape: cylindrical
St. pres.: intact
Mat.: brown stone
Wt.: 9.2 g.
Photo: Fig. 1.5.

6. Inv.: TM.77.G.87; loc.: D1V2ii; lev.: 3
Dim.: h. 2.1; diam. 1.4 cm.
Shape: ovoidal with two hemispherical ends
St. pres.: a few scratches
Mat.: hematite
Wt.: 9.4 g.
Photo: Fig. 1.6.

7. Inv.: TM.76.G.482; loc.: EaV5i; lev.: 5; L. 2890
Dim.: h. 2.6; diam. inf. base 1.8; diam. sup. base: 0.8 cm.
Shape: irregular cylinder, tapered at top
St. pres.: many abrasions and scratches
Mat.: hematite
Wt.: 10.4 g.
Photo: Fig. 1.7.

8. Inv.: TM.76.G.339; loc.: DiV3ii+D1V3iii; lev.: 4; L. 2875
Dim.: h. 2.1; diam. 1.6 cm.
Shape: ovoidal with two hemispherical ends
St. pres.: intact with slightly abrased surfaces
Mat.: hematite
Wt.: 11.4 g.
Photo: Fig. 1.8.

9. Inv.: TM.77.G.108; loc.: EaV4iii; lev.: 4; L. 2906
Dim.: h. 1.7; diam. 1.7 cm.
Shape: irregular cylinder
St. pres.: chipped on one of bases
Mat.: basaltic stone
Wt.: 12.02 g.
Photo: Fig. 1.9.

10. Inv.: TM.77.G.208; loc.: EaV4iii; lev.: 5; L. 2917
Dim.: h. 2.6; diam. 1.8 cm.
Shape: cylindrical with semi-spherical ends
St. pres.: chipped on one end
Mat.: hematite
Wt.: 13.8 g.
Photo: Fig. 1.10.

11. Inv.: TM.77.G.855; loc.: EaV3ii; lev.: 3
Dim.: h. 2.8; diam. 2.2 cm. base
Shape: conical
St. pres.: some chips missing
Mat.: gray limestone
Wt.: 15.5 g.
Photo: Fig. 1.11.

12. Inv.: TM.76.G.513; loc.: DiV2i+DiV2iv; lev.: 2/6; L. 2866
Dim.: h. 2.1; diam. inf. base 2.3; diam. sup. base 1.7 cm.
Shape: truncated cone with rounded upper end
St. pres.: upper end chipped, part of circumference of inf. base missing
Mat.: hematite
Wt.: 25.4 g.
Photo: Fig. 1.12.

13. Inv.: TM.75.G.498; loc.: dump.
Dim.: length 6.2; max. diam. 1.5 cm.

	Shape:	ovoidal, very long
	St. pres.:	intact
	Mat.:	hematite
	Wt.:	36.5 g.
	Photo:	Fig. 1.13.
14.	Inv.:	TM.75.G.193; loc.: EaV7ii; lev.: 2
	Dim.:	h. 3.3.; diam. lower base 2.5; diam. upper base 2 cm.
	Shape:	irregular truncated cone, inf. base flat and sup. convex
	St. pres.:	surfaces lightly abrased with scratches and missing a chip near lower base.
	Mat.:	hematite
	Wt.:	45.4 g.
	Photo:	Fig. 1.14.
15.	Inv.:	TM.75.G.426; loc.: EaV5iii; lev.: 11; L. 2877
	Dim.:	h. 5.6; diam. inf. base 2.3; diam. sup. base 1.6 cm.
	Shape:	irregular cylinder, tapered at top, with convex ends and one side slightly flattened as a base.
	St. pres.:	a few abrasions
	Mat.:	veined gray-dark gray stone with large beige veins, shiny
	Wt.:	53.9 g.
	Photo:	Fig. 1.15.
16.	Inv.:	TM.75.G.366; loc.: DIV 5ii; lev.: 3
	Dim.:	h. 6; diam. inf. base: 2.7. diam. sup. base: 1.6 cm.
	Shape:	cylindrical, tapered at top; inf. base convex and sup. base rounded; shallow regular cavity at center of inferior base for rest
	St. pres.:	a few scratches on inf. base
	Mat.:	stone with regular, oblique gray and brown veins
	Wt.:	64.2 g.
	Photo:	Fig. 1.16.
17.	Inv.:	TM.77.G.173; loc.: D1V3ii; lev.: 6; L. 2913
	Dim.:	length 4.5; max. diam. 2.1 cm.
	Shape:	ovoidal with pointed ends
	St. pres.:	few abrasions
	Notes:	6 parallel incisions perpendicular to height
	Mat.:	pyrite
	Wt.:	68.7 g.
	Photo:	Fig. 1.17.
18.	Inv.:	TM.76.G.2098; loc.: EaV4iv; lev.: 9; L. 2764
	Dim.:	length 8.6; max. diam. 2.6 cm.
	Shape:	very elongated ovoidal
	St.pres.:	few abrasions
	Mat.:	hematite
	Wt.:	141.9 g.
	Photo:	Fig. 1.18.

19.	Inv.:	TM.77.G.315; loc.: D1V3ii; lev.: 6; L. 2913
	Dim.:	h. 4.2; width 3.2 cm.
	St. pres.:	chip of an ovoidal weight
	Notes:	14 parallel incisions
	Mat.:	hematite
	Wt.:	20 g.
	Photo:	Fig. 1.19.
20.	Inv.:	TM.87.G.317; loc.: DeV3i/iv; lev.: 6; L. 2913
	Dim.:	length 5.5; max. diam. 3.3 cm.
	Shape:	ovoidal, elongated, with two rounded ends
	St. pres.:	without a chip, and some scratches, even deep ones, due to nature of the stone
	Mat.:	pyrite
	Wt.:	149.1 g.
	Photo:	Fig. 1.20.
21.	Inv.:	TM.75.G.1208; loc.: D1V6ii; lev. 3; L. 2712
	Dim.:	h. 5.6; max. diam. 8.9; min. diam. 7.9 cm.
	Shape:	semi-ovoidal
	St. pres.:	abrasions and scratches
	Notes:	a groove on top
	Mat.:	whitish limestone
	Wt.:	467.5 g.
	Photo:	Fig. 2.21
22.	Inv.:	TM.75.G.1209; loc.: D1V6ii; lev.: 3; L. 2712
	Dim.:	h. 6.2; max. diam. 9.2; min. diam. 8.2 cm.
	Shape:	semi-ovoidal
	St. cons.:	abrasions and scratches
	Notes:	a groove on top and 5 incisions perpendicular to it
	Mat.:	light gray basaltic stone
	Wt.:	574.3 g.
	Photo:	Fig. 2.22.
23.	Inv.:	TM.75.G.1207; loc.: D1V6ii; lev.: 3; L. 2712
	Dim.:	h. 6.2; max. diam. 10.6; min. diam. 7.1 cm.
	Shape:	semi-ovoidal
	St. pres.:	abrasions and scratches
	Note:	a groove on top and 4 incisions perpendicular to it
	Mat.:	light gray basaltic stone.
	Wt.:	666.1 g.
	Photo:	Fig. 2.23ab.
24.	Inv.:	TM.75.G.1206; loc.: D1V6ii; lev.: 3; L. 2712
	Dim.:	h. 6.5; max. diam. 10.4; min. diam. 9.7 cm.
	Shape:	semi-ovoidal
	St. pres.:	abrasions and scratches
	Note:	2 grooves on top
	Mat.:	light gray basaltic stone

	Wt.:	860 g.
	Photo:	Fig. 2.24.
25.	Inv.:	TM.75.G.1210; loc.: D1V6ii; lev. 3; L. 2712
	Dim.:	h. 6.5 max. diam. 12.8; min. diam. 10.8 cm.
	St. pres.:	abrasions and scratches
	Note:	3 grooves on top
	Mat.:	grayish basaltic stone
	Wt.:	1332 g.
	Photo:	Fig. 2.25.
26.	Inv.:	TM.75.G.1211; loc.: D1V6ii; lev.: 3; L. 2712
	Dim.:	length 18; diam. 10.6 cm.
	Shape:	ovoidal with one end flattened
	St. pres.:	scratches over entire surface
	Mat.:	whitish limestone; partially burned
	Wt.:	2232 g.
	Photo:	Fig. 3.26.
27.	Inv.:	TM.77.G.640; loc.: EaV3liv; lev.: 7; L. 2906
	Dim.:	h. 12.7; max. diam. 8.6 cm.
	Shape:	pear-shaped, with hole through upper end
	St. pres.:	scratches
	Note:	inscription of 3 lines, vertical: (1) na$_4$; (2) *ša-da-* (3) *su*^{ki}
	Mat.:	whitish limestone
	Wt.:	1107 g.
	Photo:	Fig. 3.27ab.
28.	Inv.:	TM.78.Q.298; loc.: DfV10iii; lev.: 6; L. 2988
	Dim.:	h. 2.5; width 3.6 cm.
	Shape:	ovoidal with one side as base
	St. pres.:	thin transversal chip
	Mat.:	granitic stone
	Photo:	Fig. 3.28.
29.	Inv.:	TM.70.B.461; loc.: DhIV8ii; lev.: 2
	Dim.:	length 2.1; diam. 0.7 cm.
	Shape:	ovoidal, elongated, with flattened ends
	St. pres.:	intact
	Mat.:	hematite
	Wt.:	3 g.
	Photo:	Fig. 3.29.
30.	Inv.:	TM.69.G.459; loc.: square III
	Dim.:	h. 1.7; diam. 1.1 cm.
	Shape:	cylindrical
	St. pres.:	scratches; some chips missing
	Mat.:	basaltic stone, dark gray
	Wt.:	5.4 g.
	Photo:	Fig. 3.30.

31.	Inv.:	TM.72.N.383; loc.: FcVII4i; lev.: 3
	Dim.:	h. 2.9; diam. 0.9 cm.
	Shape:	irregular cylinder
	St. pres.:	numerous scratches
	Mat.:	basaltic stone, very dark brown
	Wt.:	5.9 g.
	Photo:	Fig. 3.31.
32.	Inv.:	TM.67.A.96
	Dim.:	h. 0.7; length 2.4; width 1 cm.
	Shape:	parallelepiped with tapered ends
	St. pres.:	intact
	Mat.:	hematite
	Wt.:	6.1 g.
	Photo:	Fig. 4.32.
33.	Inv.:	TM.72.N.463; loc.: FfVII2i
	Dim.:	length 2.3; width max. 1.4 cm.
	Shape:	elongated ovoidal with ends and one side flattened
	St. pres.	missing part of lateral flat base
	Mat.:	hematite
	Wt.:	6.8 g.
	Photo:	Fig. 4.33.
34.	Inv.:	TM.69.E.O.733; loc.: square XIV; L. 761
	Dim.:	h. 1.1; diam. inf. base 1.6; diam. sup. base 1.4 cm.
	Shape:	truncated cone
	St. pres.:	missing chips; scratches
	Mat.:	basaltic stone, dark brown
	Wt.:	6.9 g.
	Photo:	Fig. 4.34.
35.	Inv.:	TM.74.E.342; loc.: EgVI3ii; lev.: 7; trench αη
	Dim.:	h. 2.6; diam. 1.1 cm.
	Shape:	rather irregular cylinder
	St. pres.:	irregular surface
	Mat.:	basaltic stone, dark brown
	Wt.:	7.7 g.
	Photo:	Fig. 4.35.
36.	Inv.:	TM.70.B.414; loc.: DhIV8ii; lev.: 2
	Dim.:	length 2.9; width 0.8 cm.
	Shape:	elongated ovoid with flattened ends and one side
	St. pres.:	a scratch on edge of one end
	Mat.:	hematite
	Wt.:	7.9 g.
	Photo:	Fig. 4.36.
37.	Inv.:	TM.69.E.772; loc.: square XIV; L. 761
	Dim.:	h. 0.9; length 2; width max. 1.8 cm.

	Shape:	triangular, with rounded points, flat base
	St. pres.:	a few scratches
	Mat.:	hematite
	Wt.:	8 g.
	Photo:	Fig. 4.37ab.
38.	Inv.:	TM.70.E.636; loc.: FaVIliii; lev.: 3
	Dim.:	h. 1.9; diam. 1.3 cm.
	Shape:	cylindrical
	St. pres.:	scratches and abrasions
	Mat.:	basaltic stone, dark brown
	Wt.:	8 g.
	Photo:	Fig. 4.38.
39.	Inv.:	TM.69.E.O.726; loc.: square IX; L. 1334
	Dim.:	h. 1.2; diam. 2 cm.
	Shape:	irregular hemisphere
	St. pres.:	missing a chip; some scratches
	Mat.:	basaltic stone, dark gray
	Wt.:	8.4 g.
	Photo:	Fig. 4.39.
40.	Inv.:	TM.78.Q.406; DfV8iv; lev.: 5; L. 2945
	Dim.:	length 2.8; width 1.1 cm.
	Shape:	spindle-shaped with flattened ends and base
	St. pres.:	two opposing holes near one of the two ends
	Mat.:	hematite
	Wt.:	8.5 g.
	Photo:	cf. no. 41
41.	Inv.:	TM.78.Q.228; loc.: DfV10iii; lev.: 5; L. 2988
	Dim.:	length 2.9; width 1.2 cm.
	Shape:	spindle-shaped, with flattened ends and base
	St. pres.:	one small scratch
	Mat.:	pyrite
	Wt.:	8.6 g.
	Photo:	Fig. 4.41.
42.	Inv.:	TM.69.B.O.226
	Dim.:	h. 1.5; inf. base diam. 2; diam. sup. base 1.6 cm.
	Shape:	irregular truncated cone
	St. pres.:	abrasions and scratches
	Mat.:	basaltic stone, gray
	Wt.:	9.5 g.
	Photo:	Fig. 4.42.
43.	Inv.:	TM.78.Q.259; loc.: DeV10iii; lev.: 4; L. 3005
	Dim.:	1.8 cm. diam.
	Shape:	spheroid
	St. pres.:	missing various large chips

	Mat.:	basaltic stone
	Wt.:	10.4 g.
	Photo:	Fig. 4.43.
44.	Inv.:	TM.70.E.557; loc.: EiVI4iii; lev.: 5
	Dim.:	h. 1.5; length 2.3; width 1.5 cm.
	Shape:	parallelepiped with a rounded face
	St. pres.:	two deep cavities in base; abrasions
	Mat.:	brown basaltic stone
	Wt.:	11.9 g.
	Photo:	Fig. 4.44.
45.	Inv.:	TM.72.N.437; loc.: FfVII2iii; lev.: 3; L. 2500
	Dim.:	length 3; width 2 cm.
	Shape:	elongated ovoidal with flattened ends and side
	St. pres.:	some scratches
	Mat.:	hematite
	Wt.:	15.6 g.
	Photo:	Fig. 4.45.
46.	Inv.:	TM.70.B.741; loc.: DIIV7iv; lev.: 4; L. 1562
	Dim.:	h. 1.8; length 3.3; width 2.1 cm.
	Shape:	parallelepiped with a rounded face
	St. pres.:	scratches and abrasions
	Mat.:	pyrite
	Wt.:	40.3 g.
	Photo:	Fig. 4.46.
47.	Inv.:	TM.78.Q.157; loc.: DeV9i; lev.: 4; L. 2975
	Dim.:	length 5.6; max. diam. 2.4 cm.
	Shape:	very elongated ovoidal with one end flattened, the other rounded; one side slightly flattened
	St. pres.:	some scratches, a few deep, due to nature of the stone
	Mat.:	pyrite
	Wt.:	82.1 g.
	Photo:	Fig. 4.47.
48.	Inv.:	TM.78.Q.297; loc.: DfV10iii; lev.: 6; L. 2988
	Dim.:	length 5.1; width 2.9 cm.
	Shape:	elongated ovoidal with flattened ends and base side slightly flattened
	St. pres.:	missing a chip, some abrasions
	Mat.:	hematite
	Wt.:	89.5 g.
	Photo:	Fig. 4.48.

Figure 1

21

22

23a

23b

24

25

Figure 2

26

27a

27b

28

29

30

31

32

Figure 3

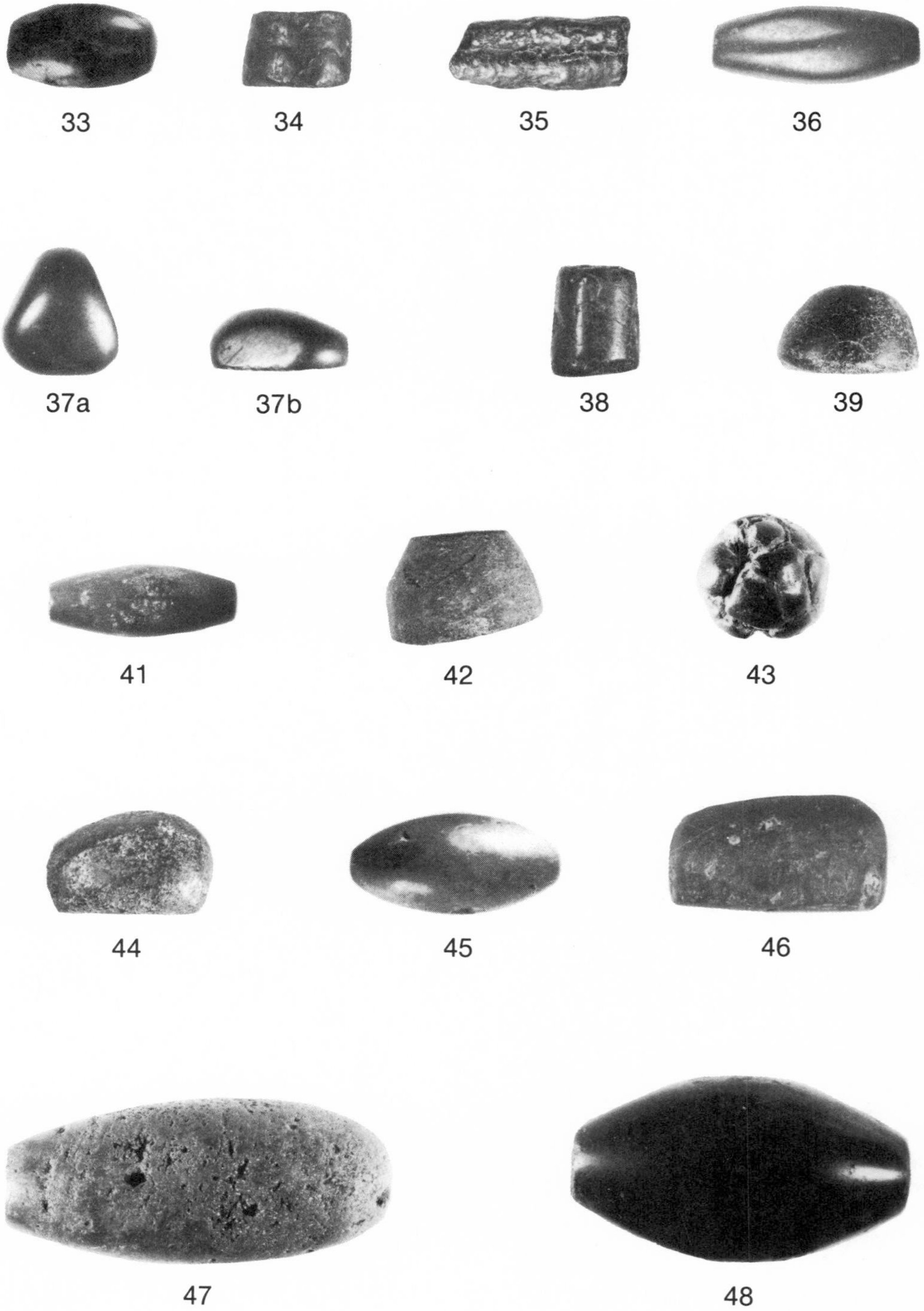

Figure 4

Appendix I

Determination of Value of Signs Indicating Fractions of the Mina**

In the texts from Ebla, three signs appear which indicate fractions of the mina. The first sign resembles GUR_8 (see *LAK* 382), but at the end of the rhombus there is both a "Winkelhaken" and a "Senkrechter." The value of this sign is ⅓, that is, 20 shekels, as is shown by TM.75.G.1293 (Fig. 5), where the sign appears in III, 2, and is indicated in the transcription with x_1:

[1]

obv.	I	1	5 ma-na bar_6:kù	5 minas silver:
		2	mu-túm	delivery
		3	*ig-na-da-mu*[20]	(of) Igna-Damu
		4	UL.KI	. . .
		5	1 *gú-li-lum*[21] [kù-]gi	1 gold cup
	II	1	TAR 5 gín DILMUN kù-gi	(of) 35 shekels D. gold:
		2	mu-túm	delivery
		3	*ti-ir*[22]	(of) Tir;
		4	è	issue:
		5	níg-ba	gift
		6	*en-na-*^{d}*da-gan*	(for) Enna-Dagan,
		7	lugal[23]	the lord;

**I am grateful to D. O. Edzard and E. Sollberger, both of whom provided me with information.

[20] At Ugarit there is attested a PN *ia-*AG*-ni*, which F. Gröndahl (*Die Personennamen der Texte aus Ugarit* [Rome, 1967] 176) derives from *qnī* 'to create', rather than from *knū* 'to cure', attested in Akkadian, Hebrew, and Aramaic only in the D stem, but in Arabic in both G and D stems. This person, qualified as UL.KI, appears not only in TM.75.G.1267 V 4ff. (see below), but also, for example in TM.75.G.1296 II 3ff. Without any qualification he is attested in TM.75.G.1226 I 6 and *passim*.

[21] *gú-li-lum*, cf. Akk. *gullu*(*m*), Ug. *gl*, in general in gold, is among the objects in precious metal most frequently mentioned at Ebla. In TM.75.G.1290 I 1ff., an example weighs 155 g.: 20 kù-gi / *gú-li-lum*. For a specimen in an alloy of lead and gold, cf. TM.75.G.11700: 2 *gú-li-lum* a-gar_x(GÚG.GÚG) kù-gi. The frequency with which this object in metal occurs in the texts (only gír is more common) favors this identification, even if in theory the identification with *kulīlum* 'little crown' could also be proposed.

[22] Cf. *ti-ra-il*, the scribe of the letter of Hamazi, TM.75.G.2342 VI 4; cf. G. Pettinato, *RBI* 25 (1977) 240.

[23] In the Ebla texts it is necessary to translate en = *ma-li-ku-um* as 'king', whereas for lugal a generic term such as 'lord' is preferable. This Enna-Dagan is perhaps to be identified with the commander who conquered Mari and then became its king; cf. G. Pettinato, *Akkadica* 2 (1977), 23ff. *Malikum* for en is attested, for example, in TM.75.G.1933 obv. VIII 3: *ma-lik i-za-rí-lum*^{ki}.

obv.

rev.

Figure 5. Text 1: TM.75.G.1293.

III	1	2 šu mu-dúb[24]	one has *registered* (it) twice;
	2	x$_1$ gín DILMUN bar$_6$:kù	20 shekels D. silver:
	3	dumu-nita-*sù*	his son.
	4	10 gín DILMUN bar$_6$:kù	10 shekels D. silver:
	5	gal:sukkal	(for) the chief of the messengers.
	6	10 gín DILMUN bar$_6$:kù	10 shekels D. silver:
	7	lugal	(for) the lord,
IV	1	kas$_4$-kas$_4$[25]	(to) the messengers.
	2	10 gín DILMUN bar$_6$:kù	10 shekels D. silver:
	3	gàraš (RAŠ:GA)	(for) the trader.
	4	*iš*$_{11}$(LAM×KUR)-*ki*	. . .
	5	*ma-rí*^{ki}	Mari.
	6	10 gín DILMUN bar$_6$:kù	10 shekels D. silver:
	7	sagi	(for) the cup-bearer.
	8	10 gín DILMUN bar$_6$:kù	10 shekels D. silver:

[24] Šu mu-dúb indicates a bureaucratic operation. TM.75.G.10143 I 18: 1 ma-na an-na / (II 1) *ar-ra-du-núm* / 20 gín DILMUN bar$_6$:kù 2 *bu-di* / dam-sù / *iš-ma-ga-lu* / šu mu-dúb. Evidently here Išma-galu supervises the passage of tin to Arra-dunum and 20 shekels of silver to make some *bu-di* (see below) for the wife of the latter. Therefore, we may provisionally propose the meaning 'to record'. Similarly, TM.75.G.1325 II 9–III 3: 1 *ʾà-da-um*-túg-II 1 aktum-túg 1 íb-III-ša$_6$-gùn-túg / *na-ka-ù* / *ib-al*^{ki} / *en-na-ma-lik* / šu-mu-dúb '1 *cloak* of 2nd (quality), a tunic, a fine girdle of three (measures, *scil.* turns around the body?), multicolored, (for) Nakau (from) Ibal; Enna-Malik *recorded.*' A briefer formulation is that in TM.75.G.1325 VIII 3–6: 1 aktum-túg 1 íb-III-gùn-túg / *en-na-ma-lik* / *ì-ra-ar*^{ki} / šu mu-dúb 'a tunic, a girdle of three (measures?), multicolored (for) Enna-Malik (from) Irar, *was recorded.*'

For *bu-di*, cf. Akk. *būdu*, *buʾdu*. According to *CAD* B, s.v.: "The meaning may be narrowed down to a spatula or a spoon." It is attested already in OAkk.: 2 *bu-tum* kù-gi; cf. I. J. Gelb, *MAD* 3, p. 86. At Ebla this term appears almost exclusively in pairs (an exception is TM.75.G.1765 obv. VIII 4: 1 *bu-di* NI kù-gi). Accordingly, P. Fronzaroli suggests to me 'earring', but perhaps better 'pendant', to be worn on either side of the face, but not directly attached to the ear lobe, since, for example, in text [3] below each *buʾdu* weighs 15 shekels, or 116 grams. Note the following passages:

[1] TM.75.G.1303: 2 *bu-di* 15 bar$_6$:kù
[2] TM.75.11688 II 1: 2 *bu-di* 20 bar$_6$:kù
[3] TM.75.G.12040 I 3′: 2 *bu-di* TAR bar$_6$:kù
[4] TM.75.G.1962 obv. IV 4: 2 *bu-di* 10 kù-gi
[5] TM.76.G.788 obv. I–II (rev. unwritten): 60 *bu-di* zabar / *si-gi* / simug / ì-na-sum / (II 1) 30 *bu-di* / *al-sù* '60 bronze pendants; Sigi, the smith, gave; 30 pendents, for him' (see Fig. 8.5).

Therefore, these objects are in silver (weighing, respectively, 58 g. [1], 77.5 g. [2], 116 g. [3], in gold (39 g. [4],) and in bronze ([5]).

[25] In TM.75.G.427 (see G. Pettinato, *AfO* 25 [1974–77] 2–23) distinction is made between níg-kas$_4$ 'journey' (constructed with *in* ì-ti), cf. obv. I 11, IV 25 and *passim*, and kas$_4$ 'messenger', cf. obv. III 29: kú / SA+X^{ki} / *wa* / kas$_4$ (in rev. XIII 7: kas$_4$-kas$_4$). For sheep destined for kas$_4$, see TM.75.G.2096; cf. G. Pettinato, *OA* 16 (1977) 263–71.

	V	1	níg-sám	price
		2	ba-ba	(for) turtles,
		3	*i-ti*	Iti.
		4	1 ma-na bar$_6$:kù	1 mina silver:
		5	mu-túm	delivery
		6	*ig-na-da-mu*	(of) Igna-Damu;
		7	è	issue
		8	MÁ.ḪU[26]	(for) the MÁ.ḪU,
	VI	1	*u*$_9$(EZEN×AN)*-ra-na-an*^{ki}[27]	(of) Uranan,
		2	*ib-dur-i-sar*	Ibdur-Isar,
		3	LAM-*da-mu*	LAM-Damu,
		4	lú	man
		5	BAD.É	(of) . . .
		6	šu mu-dúb	one has registered.
		7	iti MA×*ganatenû*-sag	VII month.
rev.	VII	1	4 ma-na bar$_6$:kù	4 minas silver,
		2	1 ma-na kù-gi	1 mina gold,
		3	3 gín DILMUN zabar	3 shekels D. bronze,
		4	3 ma-na zabar	3 minas bronze,
	VIII	1	3 gín zabar	3 shekels bronze
		2	1 ma-na TAR zabar	1 mina 30 (shekels) bronze,
		3	3 dub nagar[28] zabar	3 bronze carpenter's tablets
		4	1 ma-na zabar	1 mina bronze
		5	1 gír-zu[29]	1 toothed dagger,

[26] For Ebla, cf. further TM.75.G.10274 rev. IV 4: *a-zi-bu* / MÁ.ḪU / *ì-ra-ar*^{ki}. G. Pettinato (*Or* 44 [1975] 365, n 16 [cf. p. 369]) translates this term as 'weight', also giving the context of the passage cited. It is necessary to distinguish this term from the profession name. Pettinato probably was referring to this when he stated various times that ecstatic priests are attested in the documents from Ebla. This was picked up by M. Dahood in *La Civiltà Cattolica* 129 (1978), p. 547: "The institution of prophecy at Ebla can be deduced from the expression *makhkhu wa-nabiʾutu* found in one of the tablets. The first term refers to so-called 'ecstatic' prophets. . . ." *Maḫḫu* is already attested in OAkk.: *a-na* LÚ *maḫ-im*; cf. *CAD* M/1, p. 90b; and Gelb, *MAD* 3, p. 171. However, it must be demonstrated that this is the same as MÁ.ḪU, about whose function in the Mesopotamian juridical procedure of the third millennium see D. O. Edzard, *Sumerische Rechtsurkunden* (Munich, 1968) 46.

[27] At Ebla EZENxAN also probably has the same value as EZENxBE (about which see I. J. Gelb, *MAD* 2, p̄. 72); see below, n. 29. *LAK* 614 corresponds to EZENxAN, cf. *ib-LAK* 614-*mu-ut* in TM.75.G.1226 III 1 and XIII 4, and *ib*-EZEN-AN-*mu-ut* in TM.75.G.1267 II 1 and TM.75.G.1219 II 3 (see below).

[28] DUB.NAGAR at Ebla is also the writing for tibira; cf., TM.75.G.1488 III (G. Pettinato, *OA* 15 [1976] 173).

[29] For this term, cf. the list published by O. R. Gurney, *Iraq* 31 (1969) 5: VI 6. Often attested is simply gír or also gír-tur, 'sword, dagger'; TM.75.G.1641 I 1f.: 40 gír / 2 gír-tur. But very frequent, and certainly one of the most frequently cited objects in the administrative texts concerning metal products, is gír mar-tu, for which it is possible to propose the tentative interpretation: 'sword of Amorite shape'. The abbreviated spelling is mar, TM.75.G.10132 obv. I 7: 1 gír mar kù-gi; whereas mar-tu TI or also mar TI would seem to be a plural (not used very

	6 1 gada-sa$_6$	1 good linen:
	7 níg-ba	gift
IX	1 *i-ku-wa-an*	(for) Ikuwan.
	2 1 kaskal	One expedition,
	3 *in* u$_4$	when
	4 šu mu-dúb	one registered
	5 níg-ba	the gift
	6 *ḫir-du-ud*	(for) Ḫirdud
	7 É×PAP	. . .
	8 5 ma-na 10 gín DILMUN bar$_6$:kù	5 minas 10 shekels D. silver:

often), TM.75.G.5515 III 4: 2 gír mar-tu TI kù-gi; obv. I 1ff.: 3 gír mar TI / 1 gír mar kù-gi KA.LU / 1 gír mar-tu KA.AK. See. however, TM.75.G.1422 obv. I 6: 1 gír mar-tu TI kù-gi! These swords also could have been in precious materials, and therefore their value varied:

a) 1 shekel, TM.75.G.10201 obv. X 26f.: 11 gín bar$_6$:ku / níg-sám 11 gír mar-tu.
b) 25 shekels, TM.75.5515 III 3f.: 50 bar$_6$:kù / níg-sám 2 gír mar-tu TI kù-gi.
c) 30 shekels, TM.75.G.10201 obv. IX 28f.: TAR bar$_6$:kù / níg-sám 1 gír mar-tu kù-gi.
d) 40 shekels (very often, cf., e.g., TM.75.G.10149 rev. 12ff.; 10201 obv. IX 31f.; 11695 IV 9f.), TM.75.G.10143 obv. X 15-XI 1: ŠA.PI gín DILMUN bar$_6$:kù / níg-sám / 1 gír mar-tu kù-gi / *ba-da-lum* / (XI 1) *ḫa-ra-an*[ki] '40 shekels DILMUN of silver: price of an Amorite gold sword for the merchant from Harran' (this *badalum* seems to be the highest authority of Harran, which is significant for the commercial importance which the city enjoyed in subsequent millennia).
e) 1 mina, TM.75.G.5639 III 4–6: 3 ma-na bar$_6$:kù / níg-sám / 3 gír mar-tu kù-gi.

Swords of this kind in gold and silver occasionally receive another qualifying term the meaning of which is for the moment unknown: *ba-du-ud.* TM.75.G.1234 (see fig. 8; rev. unwritten), which records a delivery in the presence of a "commissary," lists some of those swords together with others called GIŠ.MÍ, a quantity of bronze and 10 *ma-ḫa-bí-lum*:

obv. I 1 1gír mar-tu *ba-du-ud* kù-gi
2 1 gír mar-tu *ba-du-ud* bar$_6$:kù-gi
3 5 gír mar-tu *ba-du-ud* bar$_6$:kù
4 3 gír mar-tu GIŠ.MÍ bar$_6$:kù
II 1 10 lá-3 ma-na 30 zabar
2 10 *ma-ḫa-bí-lum* x (=20) 5
3 maškim
4 *ir-ʾà-ak-da-mu*

In TM.75.G.12036 I 1f., the value of such a sword is 10 shekels: 10 gín DILMUN bar$_6$:kù / níg-sám 1 gír mar-tu *ba-du-ud* kù-gi; or also 5 shekels, TM.75.G.10148 IX 2: 5 gín DILMUN bar$_6$:kù / níg-sám 1 gír mar-tu *ba-du-ud* bar$_6$:kù. The swords may also be made from an alloy of gold and silver: *ba-du-ud* bar$_6$:kù-gi. This reading is ensured by TM.75.G.1447 obv. II 5 (see fig. 8).

obv. I 1 1 gír mar-tu kù-gi
2 4 gír mar-tu TI ku-gi
3 2 gír mar-tu *bu-du-ud* kù-gi
4 5 gír mar-tu *ba-du* bar$_6$:kù-gi
II 1 1 gír mar-tu *ba-du-ud* bar$_6$:kù
2 1 gír mar-tu KA.SUG

X	1	maškim-sù	his agent.
	2	10 gín DILMUN bar$_6$:kù	10 shekels D. silver:
	3	UR$_4$	(for) . . .
	4	10 gín DILMUN bar$_6$:kù	10 shekels D. silver:
	5	lugal	(for) the lord,
	6	kas$_4$-kas$_4$	(to his) messengers.
	7	10 gín DILMUN bar$_6$:kù	10 shekels D. silver:
XI	1	AB×ÁŠ maškim-*sù*	(for) the Elder, (to) his agent.
	2	1 kaskal	One expedition.
	3	*áš-du*	From
	4	*en-na-*^{d}*da-gan*	Enna-Dagan,
	5	lugal	the lord.
XII	1	AN.ŠÈ.GÚ 16 ma-na 50 gín DILMUN bar$_6$:kù	Total: 16 minas, 50 shekels D. silver;
	2	[1] ma-na TAR 5 gín DILMUN kù-gi	[1] mina, 36 shekels D. gold.
	3	1 mu	One year.

---

3 10 lá-2 gír mar-tu *ga-me-ù* bar$_6$:kù
4 *ᵓà-a-ki-al*
5 1 gír mar-tu *ba-du-ud* bar$_6$:kù-gi
6 1 gír mar-tu *ba-du-ud* bar$_6$:kù
III 1 [x gír mar-tu] *g[a-me-ù]* bar$_6$:kù
2 5 gír mar-tu KA.AK
3 É x x[b]
4 gír mar-tu IGI+ŠÈ
5 *LAK* 425 GABA
6 SU$_7$X[c]
rev. IV 1 *wa*
2 1 gír mar-tu kù-gi
3 2 gír mar-tu *ᵓà-lum*
4 20 gír mar-tu GIŠ.MÍ
5 20 gír mar-t[u] *ga[me-ù]* bar$_6$[:kù]
V 1 *iš$_{11}$-gi-li-im*
2 šu-ba$_4$-ti
(then unwritten)
VI (unwritten)
b, c: see fig. 1.

The term is also abbreviated *ba-du*: TM.75.G.12433 IV 7: 20 lá-1 gír mar-tu *ba-du* bar$_6$:kù; V 3: 20 gír mar *ba-du* bar$_6$:ku. Further, the following spellings are noted in TM.75.G.12154 rev. II 2′: 3 gír mar-tu *ba-du-*EZEN×AN kù-gi; and in TM.75.G.1422 obv. V 2: 1 gír *ba-du-*EZEN×AN bar$_6$:kù-gi. Here, however, a value u_9 (see above, n. 27), or ud_x for EZEN×AN can be proposed. For the term *ᵓà-lum* (IV 3), see again TM.75.G.12433 obv. II 6: 20 gir mar *ᵓà-lum*. To be kept in mind also is the qualification NAM-*lum*; TM.75.G.1812 obv. I 1–II 1 (rev. unwritten; see fig. 8): 1 gír mar NAM-*lum* kù-gi / lú mu-túm / *i-bí-zi-kir* / (II 1) en "an Amorite sword . . . of gold, which is a delivery (for) Ibbi-Zikir, the king."

For *ga-me-ù* (II 3, III 1) TM.75.G.1422 alternates this spelling with *ga-mi-ù*. An abbreviation is *ga-ù*; cf. TM.75.G.12154 rev. III 1. See further these other qualifications: gír-kun MAŠ.MAŠ kù-gi; cf. TM.75.G.1849 I 1; 1 gír nídba / 1 gír *ma-ga-zu* / 1 gír-tur: TM.75.G.2302 obv. I 1–3.

Recapitulation of gold and silver:

kù-gi			
(II 1)		TAR	5
(VII 2)	1		
	1 mina	TAR	5 shekels

bar$_6$:kù			
(I 1)	5		
(III 2)		x_1	
(III 4)			10
(III 6)			10
(IV 2)			10
(IV 6)			10
(IV 8)			10
(V 4)	1		
(VII 1)	4		
(IX 8)	5		10
(X 2)			10
(X 4)			10
(X 7)			10
	15 minas	x_1	90 shekels (= 1 mina 30 shekels)

That is:

15; x_1; 90 = 16 mana 50 gín
x_1; 90 = 1 mana 50 gín
x_1; 30 = 50 gín
x_1; = 50 minus 30 = 20 gín

Therefore, to arrive at the total, shown as 16 minas and 50 shekels, it is necessary to give x_1 the value of 20 shekels. The sign TAR, which means to cut, to divide, must be given the value of one-half a mina, that is, 30 shekels. But in TM.75.G.1222 II 3 is found MAŠ (which is generally used for a half-shekel): MAŠ 5 bar$_6$:ku '35 (shekels) of silver.' It is also thus, for example, in TM.75.G.1226 XIII 7.[30] The third sign, written ŠA.PI (but sometimes the final "Waagerechter" of PI missing) means ⅔, therefore 40 shekels, and is to be considered the abbreviation of ša-na-bi / bì(PI).[31] These values are obtained from the six quantities of silver recorded in TM.75.G.1267 (Fig. 6). Each amount is always followed by a personal name, and only in two cases is a function name added; V 4 sg.: Igna-Damu UL.KI, Vii 3 sg.: Enna-ia di-ku$_5$ 'judge.'

[30] See below.
[31] As Edzard points out to me.

obv.

rev.

Figure 6. Text 2: TM.75.G.1226.

[2]

obv.	I	1	1 ma-na ŠA.PI gín DILMUN bar_6:kù
		2	*i-bí-zi-kir*
		3	1 ma-na ŠA.PI gín DILMUN bar_6:kù
	II	1	*ib-u_9*(EZEN×AN)*-mu-ut*
		2	1 ma-na ŠA.PI gín DILMUN bar_6:kù
		3	*gi-gi*
		4	1 ma-na ŠA.PI gín DILMUN bar_6:kù
	III	1	*la-da-at*
		2	1 ma-na 10 gín DILMUN bar_6:kù
		3	*ìr-kab-ar*
		4	1 ma-na 10 gín DILMUN bar_6:kù
	IV	1	*íl-zi-da-mu*
		2	1 ma-na bar_6:kù
		3	*i-ti-^{d}ga-mi-iš*
		4	2 ma-na bar_6:kù
		5	*íl-zi*[32]
	V	1	1 ma-na 10 gín DILMUN bar_6:kù
		2	*a-da-mu*[33]
		3	1 ma-na x_1 gín DILMUN bar_6:kù
		4	*ig-na-da-mu*
rev.	VI	1	UL.KI
		2	TAR bar_6:kù
		3	ŠUBUR
		4	1 ma-na bar_6:kù
		5	*dar-mi-a*
		6	ŠA.PI gín DILMUN bar_6:kù
	VII	1	*i-rí-gú-nu*
		2	3 ma-na bar_6:kù
		3	*en-na-ià*
		4	di-ku_5
		5	x_1 gín DILMUN bar_6:kù
	VIII	1	*a-bu*
		2	2 ma-na TAR bar_6:kù
		3	*ti-ir*
		4	2 ma-na TAR bar_6:kù
		5	*ar-*EN*-núm*
			(uninscribed)

[32] It is surely a question of a PN (cf. in IV I: *íl-zi-da-mu*), and not of a functionary, as is maintained by G. Pettinato, *RSO* 50 (1976) 5: VI 7; see also G. Pettinato, *AfO* 25 (1974–77) 11, XII 3.

[33] This PN is also attested in OAkk.; see Gelb, *MAD* 3, p. 19.

IX	1	in-na-sum	It was given.
	2	2 mu	Two years.
		(uninscribed)	
X	1	AN.ŠÈ.GÚ	Total:
	2	25 ma-na bar_6:kù	25 minas silver,
	3	šu bal-ak	exchange
	4	5 ma-na kù-gi	(for) 5 minas gold;
	5	lugal-lugal	(concerning) the lords.

Recapitulation of gold and silver:

(I 1)	1	ŠA.PI	
(I 3)	1	ŠA.PI	
(II 2)	1	ŠA.PI	
(II 4)	1	ŠA.PI	
(III 2)	1		10
(III 4)	1		10
(IV 2)	1		
(IV 4)	2		
(V 1)	1		10
(V 3)	1	x_1	
(VI 2)		TAR	
(VI 4)	1		
(VI 6)		ŠA.PI	
(VII 2)	3		
(VII 5)		x_1	
(VIII 2)	2	TAR	
(VIII 4)	2	TAR	
	19 minas	330 shekels	30 shekels

If the section regarding the total is interpreted correctly, then there is a ratio of 1 to 5 between gold and silver. See, for example, TM.75.G.10143 II 23-III 4: 2 ma-na ŠA.PI gín DILMUN bar_6:kù šu-bal-ak TAR 2 gín DILMUN kù-gi/šer-za 2 giš-x '160 shekels DILMUN of silver, exchange (for) 32 shekels DILMUN of gold: (as) . . . two . . . '; VII 7-9: 15 gín DILMUN bar_6ku/šu-bal-ak/ 3 gín DILMUN kù-gi; VII 18–21 and VIII 13–17: 50 gín DILMUN bar_6:ku/šu-bal-ak/10 gín DILMUN kù-gi/šer-za agrig-*sù*. It is not always easy to distinguish the types of economic operations recorded in these texts. In TM.75.G.1219 (Fig. 7) (where more quantities of silver are recorded), some of the personages named in the first two tablets recur. Only in the first case (I 1-3) is it specified that it is a matter of a "delivery," mu-túm: "4 minas of silver: delivery (from) LAM-Damu." In the total, however, mu-túm reappears, thus establishing that it is always a matter of "deliveries."

obv.

rev.

Figure 7. Text 3: TM.75.G.1267.

[3]

obv.	I	1	14 ma-na bar$_6$:kù
		2	mu-túm LAM-*da-mu*
		3	8 ma-na bar$_6$:kù
	II	1	*ig-na-da-mu*
		2	9 ma-na bar$_6$:kù
		3	*ib-u*$_9$(EZEN×AN)-*mu-ut*
		4	2 ma-na bar$_6$:kù
	III	1	*i-ti-ga-mi-iš*
		2	1 ma-na bar$_6$:kù
		3	*i-rí-gu-um*[34]
		4	8 ma-na bar$_6$:kù
	IV	1	*a*-KA?-*lum*
		2	12 ma-na bar$_6$:kù
		3	DI-*gu-si*
		4	6 ma-na bar$_6$:kù
		5	*ìr*-[*ka*]*b*-[*ar*]
	V	1	5 ma-na bar$_6$:kù
		2	LAM-*zi-da-mu*
		3	9 ma-na bar$_6$:kù
		4	*i-bí-zi-kir*
rev.	VI	1	5 ma-na bar$_6$:kù
		2	LAM-*zi*
		3	4 ma-na bar$_6$:kù
		4	*za*[-x-x]-*mu*
	VII	1	4 ma-na bar$_6$:kù
		2	*en-bù-uš-li-im*
		3	80 ma-na bar$_6$:kù *ti-ir*
	VIII	1	93 ma-na bar$_6$:kù
		2	*dar-mi-lu*
		3	60?+20?+6? ma-na 10? bar$_6$:kù
	IX	1	10 ma-na 10 bar$_6$:kù *du-ti*-x[a]-*tum*
		2	60?+10?+1? ma-na 10 bar$_6$:kù na$_4$ máḫ(AL)
	X	1	AN.ŠÈ.GÚ 2 *mi-at* 57 ma-na bar$_6$:kù
		2	mu-túm
lower edge			mu-túm 97

a: see fig. 1.

[34] Cf. *i-rí-ig-da-mu*, TM.75.G.1345 XV 9.

The minas counted up to VIII 1 are 260, and therefore already are more than the total recorded in X 1. The numbers in VIII 3–IX 2 are written in an anomalous way, and if correctly read, exceed the total increased by the 97 minas marked on the lower edge.

An error in calculation worth pointing out is noted in TM.75.G.1226, where again deliveries mu-túm of the lords lugal-lugal are recorded. Twice the sum of silver is in error, for a deficit of 4 shekels. Therefore, in both cases ŠA.PI and two times the sign determined above as ⅓ mina would add up to not 80 but 76 shekels; in fact: 24, 80, 104 = 24; 184 = 27; 04 (instead of 27; 00!).

[4]

obv.	I	1	1 ma-na		7 bar$_6$:kù	
		2				*a-da-mu*
		3		ŠA.PI	5 bar$_6$:kù	
		4				*la-ti-at*
		5	3 ma-na		12 bar$_6$:kù	
		6				*ig-na-da-mu*
		7	2 ma-na		11 bar$_6$:kù	
		8				*en-bù-ma-lik*
	II	1	1 ma-na	x$_1$	2 bar$_6$:kù	
		2				*ìr-kab-ar*
		3	2 ma-na		50 lá-1 bar$_6$:kù	
		4				LAM-*zi-da-mu*
		5				lugal-lugal
		6				*ig-du-ra*^{ki}
		7	10 ma-na	x$_1$	3 bar$_6$:kù	
	III	1				[*ib*]-*u*$_9$(*LAK* 614)-*mu-ut*
		2	5 ma-na		15 bar$_6$:kù	
		3				DI-*gu-si*
		4				šu-nígin 27 ma-na bar$_6$:kù
		5				lugal na$_4$ *i-ra-sum*[35]
			24 minas	x	104 shekels	

Therefore, the 27 minas in the total would mean that x equals 76 shekels. Similarly, in a subsequent section, we have: 20; 110; 132 = 23; 50; 12 = 24; 02 (instead of 23; 58).

rev.	XII	1	1 ma-na		50 bar$_6$:kù	
		2				*en-bù-ma-lik*
		3	2 ma-na	ŠA.PI	5 bar$_6$:kù	

[35] Cf. Gelb, *MAD* 3, p. 66, *sub* ʾ$_3$RS.

TM.75.G.1447 (obv.)

TM.75.G.1447 (rev.)

TM.75.G.1234 (obv.)

TM.75.G.1812 (obv.)

TM.76.G.788 (obv.)

Figure 8

	4				*ig-na-da-mu*
	5	2 ma-na	x$_1$	5 bar$_6$:kù	
	6				LAM-*zi-da-mu*
	7	1 ma-na		10 lá-1 bar$_6$:kù	
					ìr-kab-ar
XIII	1	4 ma-na	x$_1$	5 bar$_6$:kù	
	2				DI-*gu-si*
	3	8 ma-na		50 bar$_6$:kù	
	4				*ib-u*$_9$(*LAK* 614)-*mu-ut*
	5	1 ma-na		bar$_6$:kù	
	6				*a-da-mu*
	7		½	bar$_6$:kù	
	8				*la-ti-at*
	9	1 ma-na		bar$_6$:kù	
	10				*i-rí-ú-gu*
XIV	1				na$_4$ en
	2				mu-túm
	3				šu-nígin 24 lá-2 ma-na bar$_6$:kù
		20 minas	x	132 shekels	

Therefore, the 23 minas and 58 shekels of the total should result from 22 minas + 12 shekels + x (= 30 + 76 shekels). The grand total amounts to 137 minas of silver: AN.ŠÈ.GÚ 1 *mi-at* 37 ma-na bar$_6$:kù.

If the circulation of such quantities of precious metals is surprising, it is only because at Ebla it is necessary to become accustomed to the very large quantities of gold and silver recorded in texts such as the three texts examined above. However, the structure of these texts does not permit us to consider the silver in them to be a standard of value for other merchandise. In general, the lack of chronological references prevents a precise evaluation of the data. Even if the number of a year is sometimes indicated, there are no further details enabling us to attribute the text to one sovereign rather than to another.

Here are other totals, chosen at random. TM.75.G.1218: AN.ŠÈ.GÚ 87 ma-na bar$_6$:ku. TM.75.G.1219 (transcribed above): AN.ŠÈ.GÚ 2 *mi-at* 57 ma-na bar$_6$:kù/mu-túm. TM.75.G.1222: AN.ŠÉ.GÚ 66 ma-na 16 bar$_6$:ku/2 ma-na ŠA.PI kù-gi (it is mostly a question of gifts,níg-ba, to functionaries). TM.75.G.1260 rev. 13: 11 ma-na kù-gi/6 *mi-at* ma-na bar$_6$:kù. TM.75. G.1261: AN.ŠÈ.GÚ 8 *mi-at* 80 ma-na 10 bar$_6$:kù/5 *mi-at* 71 *ʾà-da-um*-túg-2/ . . . TM.75.G.1270: AN.ŠÈ.GÚ 12 ma-na TAR 5 2 NI[36] gín DILMUN kù-gi/dub-gar/ mu-túm/en/4 mu. TM.75.G.1296: AN.ŠÈ.GÚ 2 *mi-at* ma-na

[36] NI seems to correspond to ¼ shekel. This is deduced from TM.75.G.10143 XII 13–15: 3 gín DILMUN 3 NI bar$_6$:kù / šu-bal-ak / 3 NI gín DILMUN kù-gi. Keeping in mind that the

bar$_6$:kù/mu-túm/lugal-lugal/3 mu. TM.75.G.1299: AN.ŠÈ.GÚ 74 ma-na ŠA.PI 5 gín DILMUN bar$_6$:kù/3 ma-na 20 gín DILMUN kù-gi (predominantly gifts, níg-ba, to various persons: 1 mu). And finally, the tribute of the conquered Mari is recalled, TM.75.G.1953: AN.ŠÈ.GÚ 2 *li-im* 1 *mi-at* 93 ma-na bar$_6$:kù/ 1 *mi-at* 34 ma-na 26 kù-gi. Total: '2,193 minas of silver, 134 minas and 26 (shekels) of gold, which means 1,031 kilograms of silver and 63 kilograms of gold.'[37]

---

ratio between gold and silver is 1 to 5 (see above), the passage must be understood as 'three shekels DILMUN and $3/4$ shekel, exchange (for) $3/4$ shekel DILMUN of gold', that is $15/4$ of silver = $3/4$ of gold.

[37] Cf., for the text in general, G. Pettinato, *Akkadica* 2 (1977) 27.

INDEX

(a) Glossary

AB×ÁŠ 'Elder' [1] XI, 1
AN.ŠÈ.GÚ 'total' [1] XII, 1; [2] X, 1; [3] X, 1
áš-du 'from' [1] V, 2
ba 'turtle' [1] V, 2
BAD.É [1] VI, 5
bar$_6$kù 'silver' *passim*
bu-di 'pendant' (see n. 24)
di-ku$_5$ 'judge' [2] VII, 4
DILMUN (qualification of the shekel) *passim*
dub 'tablet' [1] VIII, 3 (dub-nagar)
dumu-nita 'son' [1] III, 3
è 'issue' [1] II, 4, V 7
É×PAP [1] IX, 7
en 'king' [4] XIV, 1
gada 'linen' [1] VIII, 6 (gada-sa$_6$)
gal:sukkal 'chief of the messengers' [1] III, 5
gàraš(RAŠ:GA) 'trader' [1] IV, 3
gín 'shekel' *passim*
gír mar-tu 'dagger . . .' (see n. 29)
gír-zú 'toothed dagger' [1] VII I, 5
gú-li-lum 'cup' [1] I, 5 (see n. 21)
in 'in' [1] IX, 3
iti 'month' [1] VI, 7 (MA×*ganatenû*-sag)
kas$_4$ 'messenger' [1] IV, 1, IX, 2, X, 6, XI, 2
kù-gi 'gold' *passim*
lú 'man; who' [1] VI, 4
lugal 'lord' [1] II, 7, III, 7, X, 5, XI, 5; [2] X, 5 (lugal-lugal); [4] II 5 (lugal-lugal), III, 5
MA×*ganatenû*-sag, see iti
MÁ.ḪU (name of a profession) [1] V,8
ma-na 'mina' *passim*
máḫ 'big' [3] IX,2
maškim 'agent' [1] X,1, XI,1
mu 'year' [1] XII,3 (1 mu); [2] IX,2 (2 mu)
mu-túm 'delivery' [1] I,2, II,2, V,5; [3] I,2, X,2, lower edge; [4] XIV,2
na$_4$ 'stone(-weight)' [3] IX,2 (na$_4$ máḫ); [4] III,5 (na$_4$ *i-ri-sum*), XIV,1 (na$_4$ en)
nagar 'carpenter', see dub
níg-ba 'gift' [1] II,5, VIII,7, IX,5
níg-sám 'price' [1] V,1
sagi 'cup-bearer' [1] IV,7
-sù 'his' [1] III,3
sukkal see gal
sum 'to give' [2] IX,1 (in-na-sum)
ša$_6$ 'fine', see gada
ŠA.PI '$2/3$ (of a mina)' *passim*
šu bal-ak 'to change' [2] X,3
šu dúb 'to register' (šu mu-dúb) [1] III,1, VI,6, IX,4
šu-nígin 'grand total' [4] III,4, XIV,3
TAR 'half (of a mina = 30 shekels)' *passim*
UL.KI (name of a profession) [1] I,4
UR$_4$ [1] X,3
zabar 'bronze' *passim*

(b) Personal Names

a-bu [2] VIII,1 (lugal)
a-da-mu [2] V,2 (lugal); [4] I,2 (lugal), XIII,6
a-KA?-*lum* [3] IV,1
ar-EN-*núm* [2] VIII,5 (lugal)
dar-mi-a [2] VI,5 (lugal)
dar-mi-lu [3] VIII,2
DI-*gu-si* [3] IV,3; [4] III,3, XIII,2
du-ti-x-*tum* [3] IX,1
en-na-^{d}*da-gan* [1] II,6 (lugal), XI,4 (lugal)
en-na-ià [2] VII,3 (di-ku$_5$, lugal)
en-bù-ma-lik [4] I,8, XII,2
en-bù-uš-li-im [3] VII,2; [4] I,8
gi-gi [2] II,3 (lugal)
ḫir-du-ud [1] IX,6
i-bí-zi-kir [2] I,2 (lugal); [3] V,4
i-ku-wa-an [1] IX,1
i-ra-sum [4] III,5
i-rí-gu-um [3] III,3
i-rí-gú-nu [2] VII,1 (lugal)
i-rí-ú-gu [4] XIII,10
i-ti [1] V,3
i-ti-^{d}*ga-mi-iš* [2] IV,3 (lugal); [3] III,1 (*i-ti-ga-mi-iš*)
ib-u$_9$ (EZEN×AN)-*mu-ut* [2] II,1 (lugal); [3] II,3; [4] III,1, XIII,4
ib-dur-i-sar [1] VI,2
ig-na-da-mu [1] I,3 (UL.KI), V,6; [2] V,4 (UL.KI, lugal); [3] II,1; [4] I,6 (lugal), XII,4
íl-zi [2] IV,5 (lugal)
íl-zi-da-mu [2] IV,1 (lugal)
ìr-kab-ar [2] III,3 (lugal); [3] IV,5; [4] II,2 (lugal), XII,8
la-da-at [2] III,1 (lugal)
la-ti-a-at [4] I,4 (lugal), XIII,8
LAM-*da-mu* [1] VI,3; [3] I,2
LAM-*zi* [3] VI,2
LAM-*zi-da-mu* [3] V,2; [4] II,4 (lugal), XII,6
ŠUBUR [2] VI,3 (lugal)
ti-ir [1] II,3; [2] VIII,3 (lugal); [3] VII,3
za[-x-x-]*mu* [3] VI,4

c) Geographical Names

ig-du-ra^{ki} [4] II,6
ma-rí^{ki} [1] IV,5
u$_9$(EZEN×AN)-*ra-na-an*^{ki} [1] VI,1

Appendix II

Weights Found during 1981–1983 Seasons

Renewed examination of the finds coming from Royal Palace G, dating from the third millennium B.C., has allowed the identification of yet another weight, TM.75.G.6052, coming from L.2712, the room in which was found the so-called "small archive" during the 1975 excavations. Weighing 95.67 g., it represents ⅕ of a mina of 478.35 g., that is, a Syrian mina the theoretical weight of which has been established as 470 g. (whereas the Mesopotamian mina weighs 504 g.).

This weight may be analyzed as a piece of 12 "Phoenician" shekels of 7.792 g. This is suggested by the fact that this was the shekel in use at Ebla; according to the Eblaite economic texts, the mina was divided into 60 shekels, and therefore the theoretical weight of the shekel corresponding to 1/60 of 470 g. is 7.833 g.

But using an even more simple divisor, it is also plausible to analyze the weight as a piece of 10 shekels of 9.567 g. This is the "Syrian" shekel, well known at Ugarit during the second millennium B.C., where the mina of 470 g. was divided into 50 shekels. The theoretical weight of the "Syrian" shekel therefore is 9.4 g. The author believes that it is possible to demonstrate that this shekel was also used at Ebla, as early as the third millennium.[38]

The "connecting" point between the two series—which have a reciprocal relationship of 6 : 5—is therefore the mina weighing about 470 g. But there certainly must have also existed "intermediate" links of fractional values valid for both series. And this is precisely the case represented by the new weight from Ebla, which represents 12 shekels in one series and 10 shekels in the other.

It is necessary to emphasize the fact that this weight comes from the same room in which weights nos. 21–26 were also recovered. Whereas the values of nos. 21, 24–25 (1, 2, and 3 minas) are determined unquestionably by grooves carved in their surfaces, on nos. 22–23 incisions are added to the groove for 1 mina, indicating a fractional value. Since the Eblaite mina, as has been noted, is always divided into 60 shekels in the economic operations recorded on the tablets, it would have been legitimate to think that the signs incised on these weights indicate a division by 60. But in this case, no. 22, weighing 574.3 g., could only have been assigned the value of 1 mina + ⅙ (70 shekels), obtaining a unit of 8.204 g., and no. 23, weighing 666.1 g., a value of 1 mina + ⅓ (80 shekels), having a unit of 8.326 g. These two units, however, proved to be too much above the theoretical value of 7.833 g. Therefore, I preferred to interpret nos. 22–23 as 1 mina + ⅕ and 1 mina + ⅖ respectively, dividing the mina by 50, and to attribute to nos. 22–23 the values of 60 and 70 "Syrian" shekels respectively. The unit values obtained in this way (9.571 g. and 9.515 g., close

[38] On the entire problem, see the first part of this article.

enough to the theoretical one of 9.4 g.), seem to be rather more credible. They now coincide perfectly with that of the new weight, no. 55, if we assume it represents 10 shekels of 9.567 g.

It may seem unusual that in these examples the mina is divided into 5 parts instead of 6. But it is necessary to keep in mind the function of room L. 2712. It is located in the northeast corner of the Audience Hall, a few meters from the royal dais.[39] In this hall ceremonies were held and diplomatic missions were received. Not only was there preserved in L. 2712 an archive with entries of the goods relating to the court and messengers, but also a rich supply of cups and small-sized vases surely meant for entertaining. It is therefore plausible to think that in this same room was also kept a series of weights cut according to the shekel of 9.4 g. (which in any case had a 5 : 6 relationship with the Eblaite one) in order to be able to verify on the spot the weight of goods coming from the coast, where that standard was widespread. In fact, Ebla was situated at the center of a complex system of exchange which involved not only the coastal cities, but also Anatolia and the eastern regions beyond the Euphrates, It is obvious that it was necessary to adjust its own weighing system to those of other countries.[40]

How true this is is demonstrated by the fact that recently some weights dating from the Early Bronze Age were found, and they can only be analyzed as examples of the standard of 9.4 g. They all come from room L. 3532, that is, from one of the Palace warehouses on the south side of the Acropolis. Four are spherical in form and, even if they are of different materials, belong to the same group. But the other two weights, though of different shapes and materials, are also to be linked to the same standard. Let us consider nos. 51–52, both spherical and of the same material (pyrite?). The first, weighing 19.45 g., and the second, weighing, 27.3 g., can only be examples of a 2-shekel weight (unit value: 9.72 g.), and a 3-shekel weight (unit value: 9.1 g.), respectively. Then, no. 49, also spherical but of hematite, weights 6.7 g. and represents ⅔ of a shekel of 10.05 g., which slightly exceeds the theoretical value of 9.4 g. Yet another example weighing 2 shekels is no. 50, of limestone and ovoidal in shape; its weight of 18.8 g. is divisible exactly into two shekels of 9.4 g. No. 53, despite its irregular shape, must be a weight (39.45 g.) which represents 5 "Phoenician" shekels of 7.89 g. and also 4 "Syrian" shekels of 9.862 g. Finally, no. 54, of basalt, spherical in shape and weighing 60.25 g., can be considered a connecting point between the two series. But if its unit value is exact enough with respect to the standard of 7.833 g. (8 shekels of 7.531 g.), it is over-weight with respect to the 9.4 g. standard (6 shekels of 10.04 g.), in contrast to the other weights of similar shape.

[39] Matthiae, *Ebla*, p. 65, n 1.

[40] A general evaluation of the use of the various standards in Syria from the third to the first millennium is now offered by N. F. Parise, "Unità ponderali e rapporti di cambio nella Siria del Nord," in A. Archi, ed., *Circulation of Goods in Non-Palatial Context in the Ancient Near East* (Rome, 1984) 125–38.

TABLE III

No.	Period	Weight	Divisor	Unit	Shape	St. pres.
49	EB IVA	6.7 g.	⅔	10.05 g.	spherical	scratches
50	EB IVA	18.8 g.	2	9.4 g.	ovoidal	scratches
51	EB IVA	19.45 g.	2	9.725 g.	spherical	scratches
52	EB IVA	27.3 g.	3	9.1 g.	irreg. sph.	scratches
53	EB IVA	39.45 g.	4	9.862 g.	irreg.	scratches
			5	7.89 g.		
54	EB IVA	60.25 g.	6	10.041 g.	spherical	scratches
			8	7.531 g.		
55	EB IVA	95.67 g.	10	9.567 g.	ovoidal	intact
			12	7.792 g.		
56	MB	4.55 g.	½	9.1 g.	spherical	scratches
57	MB	6.75 g.	⅔	10.125 g.	irreg. cyl.	scratches
58	MB	9.15 g.	1	9.15 g.	spindle	intact
59	Iron	47.7 g.	6	7.95 g.	ovoidal	abrasions
60	MB	66.1 g.	7	9.442 g.	ovoidal	not polished
			9	7.344 g.		
61	Iron	79.1 g.	10	7.91 g.	ovoidal	scratches

Of the later weights, four date from the Middle Bronze Age. No. 58, weighing 9.15 g., of hematite, intact, represents—although it is slightly under-weight—a certain example of the "Syrian" shekel. No. 57 comes from the same location, but from a different level. It is also of hematite and, weighing 6.75 g., represents ⅔ of the same shekel (the unit value here is slightly over-weight). No. 56, of 4.55 g., corresponds to ½ of the "Syrian" shekel (9.1 g.). Finally, no. 60 can be interpreted both as an example of 9 shekels of 7.344 g. and of 7 shekels of 9.442 g. Therefore, in this epoch, too, the "Syrian" shekel is better represented.

Finally, two weights, nos. 59 and 61, come from Iron Age levels of Tell Tugan. Of the same shape and material, they represent 6 and 10 "Phoenician" shekels (unit value of 7.95 g. and 7.91 g.), respectively. In fact, it seems that during the Iron Age, in inner Syria, this shekel was more used than the so-called "Syrian" one.[41]

[41] For the use of the "Phoenician" shekel in Syria during the first millennium B.C., see A. Archi and E. Klengel-Brandt, "I pesi provenienti da Zincirli," *SMEA* 24 (1984) 245–61.

CATALOGUE B

49.	Inv.:	TM.83.G.329; loc.: EgIV10IV; lev.: 11; L. 3532
	Dim.:	diam. 1.5 cm.
	Shape:	spherical
	St. pres.:	few scratches
	Mat.:	hematite
	Wt.:	6.7 g.
	Photo:	Fig. 9.49.
50.	Inv.:	TM.83.G.328; loc.: EgIV10IV; lev.: 11; L. 3532
	Dim.:	h. 3; diam. 2.4 cm.
	Shape:	ovoidal, one side flat
	St. pres.:	scratches
	Mat.:	dark brown limestone
	Wt.:	18.8 g.
	Photo:	Fig. 9.50.
51.	Inv.	TM.83.G.335; loc.: EgIV10IV; lev.: 11; L. 3532
	Dim.:	diam. 2.3 cm.
	Shape:	spherical
	St. pres.:	scratches
	Mat.:	pyrite(?)
	Wt.:	19.45 g.
	Photo:	Fig. 9.51.
52.	Inv.:	TM.83.G.334; loc.: EgIV10IV; lev.: 11; L. 3532
	Dim.:	diam. 2.6 cm.
	Shape:	irregular sphere
	St. pres.:	scratches
	Mat.:	pyrite(?)
	Wt.:	27.3 g.
	Photo:	Fig. 9.52.
53.	Inv.:	TM.83.G.414; loc.: EgIV10IV: lev.: 11; L. 3532
	Dim.:	h. 9.8; diam. 5 cm.
	Shape:	irregular, one side flat
	St. pres.:	scratches
	Mat.:	gray limestone
	Wt.:	39.45 g.
54.	Inv.:	TM.83.G.396; loc.: Eg.IV10IV; lev.: 11; L. 3532
	Dim.:	diam. 3.3 cm.
	Shape:	spherical, one side flat
	St. pres.:	few scratches
	Mat.:	basalt
	Wt.:	60.25 g.
	Photo:	Fig. 9.54.
55.	Inv.:	TM.75.G.6052; L. 2712
	Dim.:	h. 6.2; diam. 3.3 cm.

	Shape:	irregular elongated ovoid
	St. pres.:	intact
	Mat.:	gray limestone with brown veins
	Wt.:	95.67 g.
	Photo:	Fig. 9.55.
56.	Inv.:	TM.81.Q.67; loc.: DdV7I/II; lev.: 1
	Dim.:	diam. 1.3 cm.
	Shape:	spherical
	St. pres.:	scratches
	Mat.:	black limestone
	Wt.:	4.55 g.
	Photo:	Fig. 9.56.
57.	Inv.:	TM.83.G.300; loc.: EaIV9I/EbIV9IV; lev.: 5; L. 3462
	Dim.:	h. 2.4; diam. 0.8 cm.
	Shape:	irregular cylinder, tapered at top
	St. pres.:	scratches
	Mat.:	hematite
	Wt.:	6.75 g.
	Photo:	Fig. 9.57.
58.	Inv.:	TM.82.G.87; loc.: EbIV9IV; lev.: 7
	Dim.:	length 4; width 0.8 cm.
	Shape:	spindle-shaped, with flattened ends and base
	St. pres.:	intact
	Mat.:	hematite
	Wt.:	9.15 g.
	Photo:	Fig. 9.58.
59.	Inv.:	TT.81.D.11; loc.: CIIV7; lev.: 4
	Dim.:	length 4.2; width 2.6 cm.
	Shape:	elongated ovoidal
	St. pres.:	few abrasions
	Mat.:	gray limestone
	Wt.:	47.7 g.
	Photo:	Fig. 9.59.
60.	Inv.:	TM.83.G.242; loc.: EaIV9I+IV; lev.: 4/5
	Dim.:	length 5.5; width 3.1 cm.
	Shape:	ovoidal, one side flat
	St. pres.:	not polished
	Wt.:	66.1 g.
	Photo:	Fig. 9.60.
61.	Inv.:	TT.81.E.81; loc.: CdIV9; lev.: 3
	Dim.:	length 5.6; width 3.4 cm.
	Shape:	ovoidal
	St. pres.:	some scratches at the ends
	Mat.:	gray limestone
	Wt.:	79.1 g.
	Photo:	Fig. 9.61.

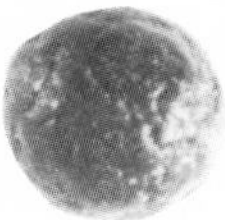
49

50

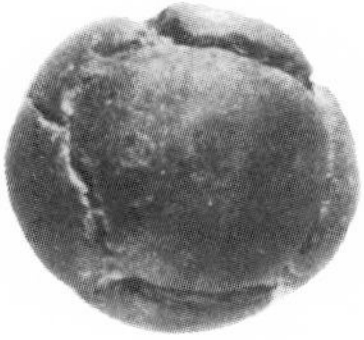
51

52

54

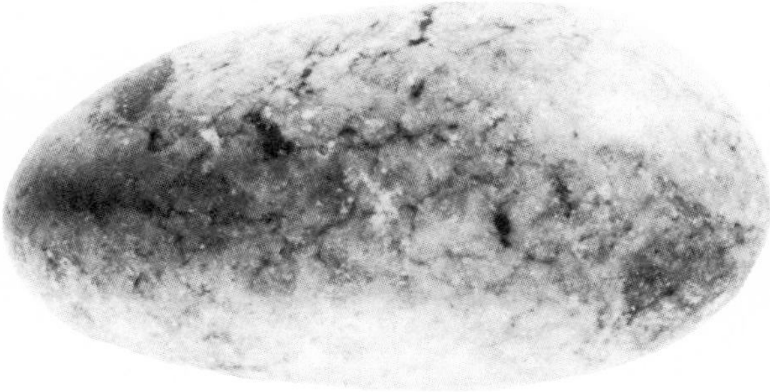
55

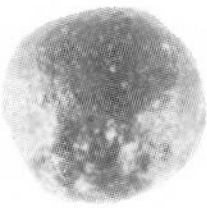

57

58

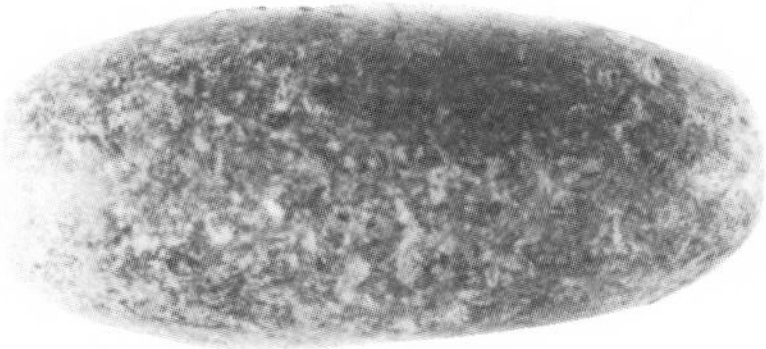
59

60

61

Figure 9

The "Sign-list" from Ebla

ALFONSO ARCHI

Of the two texts presented here, *A* (TM.75.G.1385) is a list of 122 signs. *B* (TM.75.G.1907+12680) reproduces the same signs, as well as others, making a total of 150.[1] In addition, *B* generally adds to each sign its name.[2] Perhaps in only one regard do the two lists differ: *B* (in contrast to *A*) probably gives precedence to ÁB (no. 99) over UL (no. 98).[3]

Evidently it is a question of two school-texts compiled at Ebla by two different, but both expert, scribes. The fact that *A* stops at no. 122 despite there being room for more cases demonstrates that we have an "open" list. It is certainly significant that the other cuneiform "Sign-list" known to us from the third millennium also comes from Syria, specifically from Byblos.[4]

The sign names are "semitized" with -um.[5] Often, however, -LUM appears, with the first consonant lacking a correspondent in Sumerian. In these cases, I have transliterated -núm, even without being able to justify this reading with respect to -lum; šita$_x$: ti-iš-da-núm (1); RAD : me-si-za-núm (6); búr : bí-rí-núm (37); géme : gi-me-núm (84); murgu : gur-gi-núm (89); gudu$_4$: gu-du-

[1] The copies and a first transcription of the texts were prepared in the autumn of 1980. Other commitments, however, prevented my completing the work of publication. At the end of 1981, G. Pettinato included the two tablets in his volume, *Testi lessicali monolingui della Biblioteca L.2769* (Naples, 1981) 187–207. Nevertheless, it does not seem useless to me to offer a new edition here. In fact, Pettinato was not familiar with the fragment TM.75.G.12680, which now makes it possible to complete almost all of the reverse side of *B*.

Just a short time before presenting this article for publication, M. Civil placed at my disposal a work of his in manuscript: *Bilingualism in Logographically Written Languages: Sumerian in Ebla* (henceforth *Bilingualism*). As seen in the text, this enabled me to correct some of my readings. [M. Civil's article is now published in L. Cagni, ed., *Il bilinguismo a Ebla* (Naples, 1984) 75ff.]

[2] As is known, the names of cuneiform signs have been studied by V. Christian, *Die Namen der assyrisch-babylonischen Keilschriftzeichen* (Leipzig, 1913). Cf. S. Lieberman in *Essays on the Ancient Near East in Memory of J. J. Finkelstein*, ed. M. de J. Ellis (Hamden, CT, 1977) 147–54.

[3] Note that in no. 112, *B* has KAD$_4$, whereas *A* has ÍL(= KAD$_4$+SAG). Additionally, the last lines of *B* were only lightly incised, probably after the tablet had already dried; and no. 150 repeats no. 141: LAḪTAN.

[4] G. Dossin, *MUSJ* 45 (1969) (*Mélanges offerts à M. Dunand*) 245–48. The text dates from the Ur III Dynasty or earlier.

[5] Note, however, ub-bí-sa-ga-im (16).

núm (92).[6] But in two cases the ending is -tum: dùn : [du-]wu-tum (22); du_6 : [d]u-tum (23).

It is useless to insist on /r/ being rendered l here, since this is a phenomenon well-known at Ebla; ugar : ù-ga-lum (24); lagar : nu-gú-lum (38).

/l/ can be rendered by n; laḫar : na-ḫi-ru_{12}-um (64); kalam : gi-ne-mu-um (45). But the inverse phenomenon is also possible; nisag : li-sa-gúm (10).

The initial /m/ may be dropped; mùnsub : en-ša-bù (35); munsub : ù-sum (61). Or it may pass to b; muš : bù-sum (47); minbulug : bí-ba-la-ga-um (53); but sometimes /b/ may pass to m; bal : ma-la-ga-um (128). /m/ before a consonant is assimilated; umbisag : ub-bi-sa-ga-im; nimgir : ne-gi-ru_{12}-um (28).[7]

The initial /n/ is rendered l in nisag : li-sa-gúm (10). It is dropped in nínda : en-da-um (80). Before consonants, /n/ is assimilated; munsub : ù-sum (61).

An initial guttural seems to develop a nasalization: gidim : nu-ga-ti-mu-um (97); kul : nu-gú-lum (127). The initial /g̃/ is rendered by n; guruš : nu-rí-sum (46); or by m; gešnu : mu-ša-na-um (79).[8] For /g̃/ in final position, the gloss bar-ga-um for pirig in TM.75.G.10018+ obv. V 3, shows how in pirig : ba-rí-LUM (87) -gúm must be read. Finally, note that for zum we have gi-zu-um (83).

The signs are more or less placed in order according to the analogies suggested by their forms, but in any case not in a systematic way. Easily recognized are these associations: 7–9; 10–12; 14–16; 24–25; 27–28; 32–33; 43–44; 51–52; 54–55; 56–58; 59–61; 62–63; 65–66; 69–70; 75–77; 78–79; 83–84; 85–87; 98–99; 106–107; 108–110; 119–120; 127–128; 143–144. Note that often the similarity is found in the final part of the sign (ŠÁR×DIŠ with respect to GIG, 69–70), or in the sign inscribed inside another sign (TIL in *LAK* 770 and *LAK* 225, 106–107). But other quite similar signs are not associated: dùn (22) and GÍN (41); ERIM (101) and ERIM.X (113); ŠÁR×DIŠ (69) and TE (117); sum (114) and zar (91).

It has been recognized recently that the first part of this collection of signs (1–56) was made keeping in mind the professions list ED Lu A (more complete manuscript: *IAS* 1), omitting, however, some signs.[9] Thus, for the first line of ED Lu A: $ŠITA_x$GIŠ.NÁM, the "Sign-list" gives $šita_x$ and umuš(NÁM) (1–2); then from the second line: NÁM.TUK, the "Sign-list" includes tuk (3); and then—skipping signs like DI, URU, $ŠEŠ_4$ and ŠUBUR—selects apin from line 8. Often, instead, it is the "Sign-list" which adds some signs on the basis of similarity between forms, such as šilig (14), which is placed before gišgal. At other times, the additions of the "Sign-list" are made on the basis of phonetic

[6] It is uncertain whether the case of bal is pertinent here: ma-la-gu-um (128).

[7] For umun : nu-u_9-mu-un, see Civil, *Bilingualism*, Appendix.

[8] Civil, *Bilingualism*, 4.4.

[9] E. Arcari, *OA* 22 (1983), 167–78.

similarity, such as du$_6$ to dùn (22–23). These two principles may also be combined. After umbisag (16) comes KUM, since it is considered similar; then, because they are phonetically similar, follow kam$_4$ and GAN; and finally—because it is similar to the latter—comes il. Only with mes (21) does a sign appear from list ED Lu A.

	A			*B*		
1	obv. I	1	šita$_x$(*LAK* 503)	obv. I	1	⸢šita$_x$⸣
					2	ti-iš-da-núm
2		2	umuš(NÁM)		3	umuš
					4	⸢ù⸣-mu-[šu]m
3		3	tuk		5	[tu]k
					6	[tu$^?$-gú$^?$-u]m$^!$
4		4	uru$_4$(APIN)		7	[uru$_4$]
					8	[ù-r]u$_{12}$-um
5		5	[ŠE+]NÁM		9	[ŠE+NÁM]
					10	su-šum
6		6	RAD		11	RAD
					12	me-si-za-núm
7		7	[gá]ra		13	gára(*LAK* 727)
					14	ga-ru$_{12}$-um
8		8	kisal	II	1	[kisal]
					2	gi-za-lum
9		9	sila$_4$		3	sila$_4$
					4	sa-la-um
10		10	nisag(MURUB$_4$)		5	nisag
					6	li-sa-gúm
11		11	šilam		7	šilam
					8	si-la-mu-um
12	II	1	úmun(*LAK* 155)		9	úmun
					10	nu-u$_9$-⸢mu⸣-um
13		2	adkin$_x$(*LAK* 668)		11	adkin$_x$
					12	a-ti-gi-núm
14		3	šilig$^!$		13	šilig
					14	si-la-ga-um
15		4	gišgal		15	gišgal
					16	giš-ga[l-lum]
16		5	umbisag(ŠID)	III	1	umbisag
					2	⸢ub⸣-bí-sa-ga-im
17		6	KUM		3	KUM
18		7	kam$_4$(*LAK* 29)		4	kam$_4$
					5	ga-mu-um
19		8	GAN		6	GAN
20		9	il		7	il

	A	*B*
21	10 ⌜mes⌝	8 mes
		9 me-šum
22	11 ⌜dùn⌝	10 [d]ùn
		11 [du-]wu-tum
23	12 du$_{6}$	12 du$_{6}$
		13 [d]u-tum
24	III 1 ugar(SIG$_{7}$)	14 ugar
		15 ù-ga-lum
25	2 argab(*LAK* 296)	16 argab
		17 àr-ga-bù-um
26	3 mùš	18 [mù]š
		IV 1 mu-š[a-um]
27	4 šaga$_{x}$(*LAK* 175)	2 ⌜šaga$_{x}$⌝
		3 ša-ga-um
28	5 nimgir	4 nimgir
		5 ne-gi-ru$_{12}$-um
29	6 ezen	6 ezen
		7 ì-zi-núm
30	7 uruš(SAL+TÚG)	8 uruš
		9 ù-ru$_{12}$-sum
31	8 šuḫur(*LAK* 227)	10 šuḫur
		11 šu-ḫu-ru$_{12}$-um
32	9 nun	12 nun
		13 nu-núm
33	10 šir$_{x}$(HAŠḪUR×KÍD)	14 šir$_{x}$
		15 si-ru$_{12}$-um
34	11 idigina	16 idigina
		17 ì-ti-gi-ra-um
35	12 mùnsub(USAN)	V 1 [mùnsu]b
		2 en-ša-bù
36	13 KU$_{7}$	3 KU$_{7}$
		4 ga-ga-LUM
37	IV 1 búr	5 búr
		6 bí-rí-ñúm
38	2 lagar	7 lagar
		8 nu-gú-lum
39	3 súmun(GUL)	9 súmun
		10 su-me-núm
40	4 nagar	11 nagar
		12 na-ga-lum
41	5 àga(GÍN)	13 ága
		14 a-ga-um

		A			*B*	
42		6	ašgab		15	ašgab
						áš-ga-bù
43		7	zadim		16	zadim
					17	za-ti-núm
44		8	dim		18	dim
					19	ti-mu-um
45		9	kalam	VI	1	kalam
					2	gi-ne-mu-um
46		10	[g]uruš		3	guruš
					4	nu-rí-sum
47		11	⸢muš⸣		5	muš
					6	bù-sum
48		12	gána		7	gána
					8	ga-na-um
49		13	DÙL		9	DÙL
					10	lu-ma-ʾà-sum
50	V	1	laḫšu(*LAK* 442)		11	laḫšu
					12	la-ḫa-šu-um
51		2	KÍD		13	KÍD
					14	šu-wu-um AŠ(obliq.)
52		3	alan$_x$(KÍD.ALAM)		15	alan$_x$
					16	la-ʾà-núm
53		4	minbulug(URUDU)		17	minbulug
					18	bí-ba-la-ga-um
54		5	báḫar(*LAK* 742)	VII	1	báḫar
					2	ba-ḫa-ru$_{12}$-um
55		6	eden(*LAK* 747)		3	eden
					4	ì-ti-núm
56		7	kid		5	kid
					6	gi-i-tum
57		8	ùr		7	ùr
					8	u$_9$-ru$_{12}$-um
58		9	*LAK* 670		9	*LAK* 670
					10	NE-rí-LUM
59		10	kun		11	kun
					12	gú-gú-um
60		11	sudu$_x$		13	sudu$_x$
					14	su-du-u$_9$-um
61	rev. I	1	munsub(*LAK* 672)	rev. I	1	munsub
					2	ù-sum
62		2	mun		3	mun
					4	mu-nu-um

		A		*B*
63		3 naga		5 naga
				6 na-ga-um
64		4 laḫar		7 laḫar
				8 na-ḫi-ru$_{12}$-um
65		5 ùmun(AḪ)		9 ùmun
				10 ù-[ma-núm]
66		6 šur$_x$(ŠÁR×MAŠ)		11 [šur$_x$]
				12 su-ru$_{12}$-um
67		7 ÙZ		13 ÙZ
				14 a-ʾà-tum
68		8 AMA	II	1 AMA
				2 [. . .]
69		9 ašar(ŠÁR×DIŠ)		3 [ašar]
				4 [. . .]
70		10 GIG		5 [GI]G
				6 [. . . -]x̣
71	II	1 asud(GAM)		7 asud
				8 a-zu-tum
72		2 NÁ		9 NÁ
				10 ŠÈ-tum
73		3 šudun		11 šudun
				12 uš-ti-núm
74		4 amar		13 [a]mar
				14 ma-ʾà-ru$_{12}$-um
75		5 tir		15 tir
				16 ti-i-ru$_{12}$-um
76		6 ḫuduš(TU)		17 ⌜ḫuduš⌝
				18 ḫu-du-šum
77		7 asal$_x$(*LAK* 212)	III	1 asal$_x$
				2 a-s[a-lum]
78		8 gur$_8$		3 gur$_8$
				4 mar-⌜u$_9$⌝-um
79		9 gešnu(*LAK* 24)		5 gešnu
				6 mu-ša-na-um
80		10 nínda		7 nínda
				8 en-da-um
81		11 šim		9 šim
				10 šè-mu-um
82		12 sig		11 sig
				12 si-gúm
83		13 zum		13 zum
				14 gi-zu-um

		A		B
84		14 géme		15 géme
				16 gi-me-núm
85	III	1 anšu		17 anšu
				18 ù-šu-wu-um
86		2 péš		19 péš
				20 b[í]-sum
87		3 pirig		21 [pirig]
			IV	1 ba-rí-gúm
88		4 LÚ-šeššig(?)		2 LÚ-šeššig(?)
				3 ⸢mu⸣-x̣-[tu]m
89		5 murgu(SIG$_4$)		4 murgu
				5 gur-gi-núm
90		6 sukkal		6 sukkal
				7 su-gal-lu[m]
91		7 zàr		8 zàr
				9 za-ru$_{12}$-um
92		8 gudu$_4$		10 gudu$_4$
				11 gú-du-núm
93		9 šinig		12 šinig
				13 ša-na-gúm
94		10 dím		14 dím
				15 ʾà-ti-núm
95		11 šeg$_9$		16 šeg$_9$
				17 šè-gu-um
96		12 esir$_x$(GI$_4$×GI$_4$)		18 esir$_x$
				19 ù-su-ru$_{12}$-um
97	IV	1 gidim		20 gidim
				21 nu-ga-t[i-]mu-u[m]
98		2 áb	V	3 [áb](?)
99		3 ul		1 ul
				2 ù-lu-um
100		4 *LAK* 228(?)		4 ⸢*LAK* 228(?)⸣
				5 gú-šè-LUM
101		5 ERIM		6 ERIM
				7 [. . . -u]m
102		6 DAG		8 DAG
103		7 ŠÀ		9 ŠÀ
104		8 TAR		10 TAR
105		9 ZÉ		11 ZÉ
106		10 túl(*LAK* 770!)		12 túl
				13 du-lu-tum
107		11 *LAK* 225		14 *LAK* 225

	A	B
108	12 KU	15 KU
109	13 LAGAB	16 LAGAB
110	14 RU	17 RU
111	15 ú	18 ú
112	16 ÍL(*LAK* 172)	19 KAD$_4$(*LAK* 171)
113	V 1 ERIM.X	20 ERIM.X
114	2 SUM	21 SUM
115	3 a	22 e
116	4 GI$_4$	23 GI$_4$
117	5 TE	24 TE
118	6 BALAG	VI 1 [BALAG]
119	7 UNKEN	2 [UNKEN]
120	8 X	3 [X]
121	9 ŠEŠ	4 [ŠEŠ]
122	10 DUG	5 [DUG]
123	11 (uninscribed)	[. . .](?)
	VI (uninscribed)	x+1′ da-l[i-um$^?$]
124		2′ sur
		3′ su-ra-um
125		4′ KUR
126		5′ gur
		6′ gú-ru$_{12}$-um
127		7′ kul
		8′ nu-gú-lum
128		9′ bal
		10′ ma-la-gu-um
129		11′ AZU$_X$(AZU.A)
130		12′ MUNU$_4$
131		13′ taka$_x$(*LAK* 492)
		14′ da-ga-um
132		15′ GAG
133		16′ PAP
134		17′ LAM
135		18′ ⌜ša⌝(?)
		19′ [sa$^?$-]⌜ʾà⌝-um
136		VII 1 [. . .]
		2 x̣[- . . .]
137		3 [. . .]
		4 [. . .]
138		5 [. . .]
139$^?$		6$^?$ [š]ir
		7 [s]i-ru$_{12}$-wu-um

	A	*B*
140		8 [rí]g(?)
		9 [rí$^{?}$-]m[u-]mu
141		10 laḫtan
		11 ⌜la⌝-⌜ḫa⌝-da-mu-mu
142		12 gisal(*LAK* 589)
		13 mu-ša-lum
143		14 GUKKAL
144		15 ḪÚL
145		16 X
		17 sa-ga-tum
146		VIII 1 ut[ua](*LAK* 777?)
		2 ù-[x-]LU[M]
147		3 š[en]
		4 š[a-]n[u-um]
148		5 [. . .]
		6 [. . .]
149		7 [. . .]
		8 x̣-⌜ù⌝$^{?}$-LUM
150		9 laḫtan
		10 la-ḫa-da-mu-mu

Commentary

2. Here NÁM is not tall and slender as at Abū Ṣalābīkh, but the two horizontals cross it completely.

4. Civil, *Bilingualism*, Appendix: " . . . a restoration [en-ga-r]u$_{12}$-um, or even [a-bí-e]n-um, would also be possible."

6. Civil, ibid., proposes, "with some reservation": /g̃eš-šitan/ = (g̃eš) šìta-n.

7. In *A*, the sign is closed by a vertical, as in TM.75.G.1312 obv. II 9 (ED Lu A): TÚG.GÁRA.

14. In *A*, the element ŠI is missing.

15. The form of the sign differs in some way from the Mesopotamian form; cf. *LAK* 648, *RSP* 269.

16. In *B*, the first part of the sign has several verticals.

25. Pettinato notices that in the Ebla manuscripts of ED Lu A, no. 55, 56, the sign *LAK* 296 is written as no. 25 of the "Sign-list." One has to remember that at Ebla BA also has two verticals, the second one being crossed by a horizontal.

34. In *A* the horizontal crossing the last vertical is missing.

51. According to Civil, *apud* Pettinato, it is not correct to equate ŠU with KÍD.

53. Reading according to Civil.

55. The edge of cases VII 3 and 4 in *B* is now missing, but see pl. 5*c*, where a photograph from 1975 is published.

57. The sign is GIŠ×KID, and not *LAK* 679: GÁ×NIR.

60. This sign is very similar to MUNSUB. It is attested in *Fara* II 81 II 3, III 14, V 6, but in dupl. *IAS* 25 obv. II 1, it seems to be replaced by MUNSUB.

61. This is the sign-form in use at Ebla for *LAK* 672; cf. MUNSUB.GA^{mušen} in *Fara* II 58 X 16, and TM.75.G.1415 obv. VI 13, Ebla "Bird List," photograph in *OA* 17 (1978), pl. XIV. For the reading of MUNSUB: sub < (m)u(n)sub, su$_x$, cf. M. Civil, *RA* 54 (1960) 71, n 4; and J. J. van Dijk, *Acta Orientalia* 28 (1964) 38, n 106.

64. For the edge of *B* rev. I 10–11, now missing, see the photograph from 1975, pl. 5*d*.

67. The tablet has a-É-tum, but Civil proposes to read a-sa$^!$-tum.

73. Reading according to Civil.

79. Civil, *Bilingualism*, Appendix: "/ĝuš-na/ = ĝeš-nu$_{11}$, is a well-known value of *LAK* 24."

86. The form of the sign in *B* is the same as the sign wrongly read ḪUŠ by Pettinato, *MEE* II, passim, and A. Archi and M. Biga, *ARET* III, passim (see there Table I).

87. In TM.75.G.10018+11303+12686 obv. V 3, the sign glossed bar-ga-um is like "Sign-list" no. 86!

91. Notice that the sign is clearly different from SUM, no. 114.

96. For the reading of GI$_4$×GI$_4$, see P. Steinkeller, *AfO* 28 (1981/82) 140f. Civil reminds me of ^{e}GI$_4$×GI$_4$ = *sa-na* of the Ebla Vocabulary; Babylonian Lists: e-sir GILIM(GI×GI)/KAD$_5$.KAD$_5$ = *še-e-nu* 'sandals', see Steinkeller, ibid.

97. The sign, both at Abū Ṣalābīkh (ED Lu C, E): *MSL* XII, 15, and at Lagaš, *VS* XIV 163 VI 1, cf. P. Talon, *RA* 68 (1974) 167f., begins as the Mesopotamian BA. The first wedge of the Ebla sign is instead oriented from the top to the left.

98. It is unlikely that ÁB in *B* was written at the end of col. IV.

105. This sign (and others similar) begins at Ebla with a horizontal.

106. In Mesopotamia it is LAGAB×U, to be read túl, cf. *MSL* XIV 32, 37: du-ul.

107. The sign is very similar to *LAK* 225 at *Fara* II 10 I 9, while in dupl. 9 I 9 it is slightly different. Although in *UET* II 234 (another manuscript of the "Fish List") I 9, one reads: nun-sumaš instead of *LAK* 225-ku$_6$, SUMAŠ and *LAK* 225 are two different signs, because in *Fara* II 10 II 8 also sumaš-ku$_6$ is attested.

114. See no. 91.

120. At Ebla this sign is used as a measure for wool; see *ARET* III, 395: x$_1$.

122. In the economic texts, this sign has above two horizontals an oblique wedge.

123. It is uncertain if a sign is really missing here.

127. Civil prefers to read numun: nu-gú-num.

128. This form for BAL is also attested in the bilingual lexical texts, see TM.75.G.2000+ obv. XIII 15f.: GIŠ-bala GIŠ-numun. For the form of the sign in the economic texts, see *ARET* II, 148.

129. At the beginning, there is a horizontal, missing in the Mesopotamian form.

131. This is the sign read DÚB previously in the editions of Ebla texts; see *ARET* II, 150. But J. Krecher suggested privately to me that: "das angebliche DÚB (ist) ein Ebla-Zeichen, das für babylonisches KÍD = taka 'lassen'. . . verwendet wird." Now the "Sign-list" shows that the correct reading of sign no. 131, with KÍD = taka inscribed, is in fact taka$_x$.

135. Or TA?

140. Reading according to a suggestion of Civil.

141. The form of the sign is in some way different from *LAK* 450 and 451.

142. The last two horizontals are crossed by an oblique wedge, contrary to *LAK* 589 (Civil: GUD+GIŠ later BI.GIŠ).

146. For the form of the sign in the economic texts, see *ARET* III, 407.

147. For the reading of this sign, see P. Steinkeller, *OA* 20 (1981), 243–49.

INDEX A: THE SIGNS

a (115; *A* rev. V 3; *B* rev. V 22: e).
áb (98; *A* rev. IV 2).
LÚ-šeššig(?) : mu-x-[tu]m (88; *A* rev. III 4; *B* rev. IV 2).
adkin$_x$(*LAK* 668) : a-ti-gi-núm (13; *A* obv. II 2; *B* obv. II 11).
àga(GÍN) : a-ga-um (41; *A* obv. IV 5; *B* obv. IV 13).
AḪ see ùmun.
alan$_x$(KÍD.ALAM) : la-ˀà-núm (52; *A* obv. V 3; *B* obv. VI 15).
AMA (68; *A* rev. I 8; *B* rev. II 1).
amar : ma-ˀà-ru$_{12}$-um (74; *A* rev. II 4; *B* rev. II 13).
anše : ù-šu-wu-um (85; *A* rev. III 1; *B* rev. III 17).
APIN see uru$_4$
argab(*LAK* 296) : àr-ga-bù-um (25; *A* obv. III 2; *B* obv. III 16).
asal$_x$(*LAK* 212) : a-s[a-LUM] (77; *A* rev. II 7; *B* rev. III 1).
asud : a-zu-tum (71; *A* rev. II 1; *B* rev. II 7).
ašar(ŠÁR×DIŠ) (69; *A* rev. I 9).
ašgab : áš-ga-bù (42; *A* obv. IV 6; *B* obv. V 15).
AZU$_x$(AZU.A) 129 (*A* rev. VI 11).
báḫar : ba-ḫa-ru$_{12}$-um (54; *A* obv. V 5; *B* obv. VII 1).
bal : ma-la-gu-um (128; *A* rev. VI 9).
BALAG (118; *A* rev. V 6).
búr : bí-rí-núm (37; *A* obv. IV 1; *B* obv. V 5).
DAG (102; *A* rev. IV 6; *B* rev. V 8).
dim : ti-mu-um (44; *A* obv. IV 8; *B* obv. IV 18).
dím : ˀà-ti-núm (94; *A* rev. III 10; *B* rev. IV 14).
du$_6$: [d]u-tum (23; *A* obv. II 23; *B* obv. III 12).
DUG (122; *A* rev. V 10).
DÙL : lu-ma-ˀà-sum (49; *A* obv. IV 13; *B* obv. VI 9).
dùn : [du-]wu-tum (22; *A* obv. II 11; *B* obv. III 10).
e (115; *B* rev. V 22; *A* rev. V 3: a).
eden : ì-ti-núm (55; *A* obv. V 6; *B* obv. VII 3).
ERIM (101; *A* rev. IV 5; *B* rev. V 6).
ERIM.X (113; *A* rev. V 1; *B* rev. V 20).
esir$_x$(GI$_4$×GI$_4$) : ù-su-ru$_{12}$-um (96; *A* rev. III 12; *B* rev. IV 18).
ezen : ì-zi-núm (29; *A* obv. III 6; *B* obv. IV 6).
GAG (132; *B* rev. VI 15′).
GAM see asud.
gan (19; *A* obv. II 8; *B* obv. III 6).
gána : ga-na-um (48; *A* obv. IV 12; *B* obv. VI 7).

gára(*LAK* 727) : ga-ru$_{12}$-um (7; *A* obv. I 7; *B* obv. I 13).
géme : gi-me-núm (84; *A* rev. II 14; *B* rev. III 15).
gešnu(*LAK* 24) : mu-ša-na-um (79; *A* rev. II 9; *B* rev. III 5).
GI$_4$ (116; *A* rev. V 4; *B* rev. V 23).
gidim : nu-ga-t[i-]mu-u[m] (97; *A* rev. IV 1; *B* rev. IV 20).
GIG (70; *A* rev. I 10; *B* rev. II 5).
GÍN see àga.
gisal(*LAK* 589) : mu-ša-lum (142; *B* rev. VII 13).
gišgal : giš-ga[l-lum] (15; *A* obv. II 4; *B* obv. II 15).
gudu$_4$: gú-du-núm (92; *A* rev. III 8; *B* rev. IV 10).
GUKKAL (143; *B* rev. VII 143).
GUL see sún.
gur : gú-ru$_{12}$-um (126; *B* rev. VI 5′).
gur$_8$: mar-u$_9$-um (78; *A* rev. II 8; *B* rev. III 3).
guruš : nu-rí-sum (46; *A* obv. IV 10; *B* obv. VI 3).
ḪAŠḪUR×KÍD see šir$_x$.
ḫuduš(TU) : ḫu-du-šum (76; *A* rev. II 6; *B* rev. II 17).
ḪÚL (144; *B* rev. VII 15).
idigna : ì-ti-gi-ra-um (34; *A* obv. III 11; *B* obv. IV 16).
il (20; *A* obv. II 9; *B* obv. III 7).
ÍL (112; *A* rev. IV 16; *B* rev. V 19: KAD$_4$).
KAD$_4$ (112; *B* rev. V 19; *A* rev. IV 16: ÍL).
kalam : gi-ne-mu-um (45; *A* obv. IV 9; *B* obv. VI 1).
kam$_4$(*LAK* 29) : ga-mu-um (18; *A* obv. II 7; *B* obv. III 4).
kid : gi-i-tum (56; *A* obv. V 7; *B* obv. VII 5).
KÍD : šu-wu-um (51; *A* obv. V 2; *B* obv. VI 13).
KÍD.ALAM see alan$_x$.
kisal : gi-za-lum (8; *A* obv. I 8).
KU (108; *A* rev. IV 12; *B* rev. V 15).
kul : nu-gú-lum (127; *B* rev. VI 7′).
KUM (17; *A* obv. II 6; *B* obv. III 3).
kun : gú-gú-um (59; *A* obv. V 10; *B* obv. VII 11).
KUR (125; *B* rev. VI 4′).
KU$_7$: ga-ga-LUM (36; *A* obv. III 13; *B* obv. V 3).
LAGAB (109; *A* rev. IV 13; *B* rev. V 16).
lagar : nu-gú-lum (38; *A* obv. IV 2; *B* obv. V 7).
laḫar : na-ḫi-ru$_{12}$-um (64; *A* rev. I 4; *B* rev. I 7).
laḫšu(*LAK* 442) : la-ḫa-šu-um (50; *A* obv. V 1; *B* obv. VI 11).
laḫtan : la-ḫa-da-mu-mu (141 and 150; *B* rev. VII 10, VIII 9).
LAM (134; *B* rev. VI 17′).
mes : me-šum (21; *A* obv. II 10; *B* obv. III 8).
minbulug(URUDU) : bí-ba-la-ga-um (53; *A* obv. V 4; *B* obv. VI 17).
mun : mu-nu-um (62; *A* rev. I 2; *B* rev. I 3).
munsub(*LAK* 672) : ù-sum (61; *A* rev. I 1; *B* rev. I 1).
mùnsub(USAN) : en-ša-bù (35; *A* obv. III 12; *B* obv. V 1).
MUNU$_4$ (130; *A* rev. VI 12′).
murgu(SIG$_4$) : gur-gi-núm (89; *A* rev. III 5; *B* rev. IV 4).
MURUB$_4$ see nisag.

muš : bù-sum (47; *A* obv. IV 11; *B* obv. VI 6).
mùš : mu-š[a-um] (26; *A* obv. III 3; *B* obv. III 18).
NÁ : ŠÈ-tum (72; *A* rev. II 2; *B* rev. II 9).
naga : na-ga-um (63; *A* rev. I 3; *B* rev. I 5).
nagar : na-ga-lum (40; *A* obv. IV 40; *B* obv. V 11).
NÁM see umuš.
nimgir : ne-gi-ru$_{12}$-um (28; *A* obv. III 5; *B* obv. IV 4).
nínda : en-da-um (80; *A* rev. II 10; *B* rev. III 7).
nisag : li-sa-gúm (10; *A* obv. I 10; *B* obv. II 5).
nun : nu-núm (32; *A* obv. III 9; *B* obv. IV 12).
PAP (133; *B* rev. VI 16′).
pés : b[í-]sum (86; *A* rev. III 2; *B* rev. III 19).
pirig : ba-rí-gúm (87; *A* rev. III 3).
RAD : me-si-za-núm (6; *A* obv. I 6; *B* obv. I 11).
[rí]g(?) : [rí$^{?}$-]mu-mu (140; *B* rev. VII 8).
RU (110; *A* rev. IV 14; *B* rev. V 18).
SAL.TÚG see uruš.
sig : si-gúm (82; *A* rev. II 12; *B* rev. III 11).
SIG$_5$ see murgu.
SIG$_7$ ugar.
sila$_4$: sa-la-um (9; *A* obv. I 9; *B* obv. II 3).
sudu$_x$: su-du-u$_9$-um (60; *A* obv. V 11; *B* obv. VII 13).
sukkal : su-gal-lu[m] (90; *A* rev. III 6; *B* rev. IV 6).
SUM (114; *A* rev. V 2; *B* rev. V 21).
súmun : su-me-núm (39; *A* obv. IV 3; *B* obv. V 9).
sur : su-ra-um (124; *B* rev. VI 2′).
⌜ša⌝(?) : [sa$^{?}$-]⌜ʾà⌝-um (135; *B* rev. VI 18′).
ŠÀ (103; *A* rev. IV 7; *B* rev. V 9).
šaga$_x$(*LAK* 175) : ša-ga-um (27; *A* obv. III 4; *B* obv. IV 2).
šeg$_9$: šè-ga-um (95; *A* rev. III 11; *B* rev. IV 16).
š[en] : š[a-]n[u-um] (147; *B* rev. VIII 4).
[ŠE+]NÁM : su-šum (5; *A* obv. I 5).
ŠEŠ (121; *A* rev. V 9).
ŠID see umbisag.
šilam : si-la-mu-um (11; *A* obv. I 11; *B* obv. II 7).
šilig : si-la-ga-um (14; *A* obv. II 3!; *B* obv. II 13).
šim : šè-mu-um (81; *A* rev. II 11; *B* rev. III 9).
šinig : ša-na-gúm (93; *A* rev. III 9; *B* rev. IV 12).
[š]ir : [s]i-ru$_{12}$-wu-um (139; *B* rev. VII 6).
šir$_x$(HAŠḪUR×KÍD) : si-ru$_{12}$-um (33; *A* obv. III 10; *B* obv. IV 14).
šita$_x$: ti-iš-da-núm (1; *A* obv. I 1; *B* obv. I 1).
šudun : uš-ti-núm (73; *A* rev. II 3; *B* rev. II 11).
šuḫur(*LAK* 227) : su-ḫu-ru$_{12}$-um (31; *A* obv. III 8; *B* obv. IV 10).
šur$_x$ (ŠÁR × MAŠ) : su-ru$_{12}$-um (66; *A* rev. I 6; *B* rev. I 11).
taka$_x$(*LAK* 492) : da-ga-um (131; *B* rev. VI 13′).
TAR (104; *A* rev. IV 8; *B* rev. V 10).
TE (117; *A* rev. V 5; *B* rev. V 24).
tir : ti-i-ru$_{12}$-um (75; *A* rev. II 5; *B* rev. II 15).

TU see ḫuduš.
tuk : [tu$^?$-gú$^?$-u]m (3; *A* obv. I 3; *B* obv. I 5).
túl(*LAK* 770!) : du-lu-tum (106; *A* rev. IV 10; *B* rev. V 13).
TÙR see šilam.
ú (111; *A* rev. IV 15; *B* rev. V 18).
U$_8$ see laḫar.
ugar(SIG$_7$) : ù-ga-lum (24; *A* obv. III 1; *B* obv. III 14).
ul : ù-lu-um (99; *A* rev. IV 3; *B* rev. V 1).
umbisag(ŠID) : ub-bí-sa-ga-im (16; *A* obv. II 5; *B* obv. III 1).
úmun : nu-u$_9$-mu-um (12; *A* obv. II 1; *B* obv. II 9).
ùmun(AḪ) : ù-ma-núm (65; *A* rev. I 5; *B* rev. I 9).
umuš : ù-mu-[šu]m (2; *A* obv. I 2; *B* obv. I 3).
UNKEN (119; *A* rev. V 7).
ùr : u$_9$-ru$_{12}$-um (57; *A* obv. V 8; *B* obv. VII 7).
uru$_4$: [ù-r]u$_{12}$-um (4; *A* obv. I 4).
URUDU see minbulug.
uruš(SAL+TÚG) : ù-ru$_{12}$-sum (30; *A* obv. III 7; *B* obv. IV 8).
USAN see mùnsub.
ut[ua](*LAK* 777?) : ù-[x-]LU[M] (146; *B* obv. VIII 1).
ÙZ : a-ᵓà-tum (67; *A* rev. I 7; *B* rev. I 13).
zadim : za-ti-núm (43; *A* obv. IV 7; *B* obv. V 16).
zàr : za-ru$_{12}$-um (91; *A* rev. III 7; *B* rev. IV 8).
ZÉ (105; *A* rev. IV 9; *B* rev. V 11).
zum : gi-zu-um (83; *A* rev. II 13; *B* rev. III 13).
LAK 225 (107; *A* rev. IV 11; *B* rev. V 14).
LAK 228 : gú-šè-LUM (100; *A* rev. IV 4; *B* rev. V 4).
LAK 670 : NE-rí-LUM (58; *A* obv. V 9; *B* obv. VII 9).

INDEX B: THE SIGN NAMES

a-ᵓà-tum : ÙZ (67).
a-ga-um : àga (41).
àr-ga-bù-um : argab (25).
a-s[a-lum] : asal$_x$ (77).
áš-ga-bù : ašgab (42).
a-ti-gi-núm : adkin$_x$(*LAK* 668) (13).
ᵓà-ti-núm : dím (94).
a-zu-tum : asud (71).
ba-ḫa-ru$_{12}$-um : báḫar (54).
ba-rí-gúm : pirig (87).
bí-ba-la-ga-um : minbulug (53).
bí-rí-núm : búr (37).
b[í-]sum : péš (86).
bù-sum : muš (47).
da-ga-um : taka$_x$(*LAK* 492) (131).
da-l[i-um] : [. . .] (123).
du-lu-tum : túl (106).
[d]u-tum : du$_6$ (23).
[du-]wu-tum : dùn (22).
en-da-um : nínda (80).
en-ša-bù : mùnsub(USAN) (35).
ga-ga-LUM : KU$_7$ (36).
ga-mu-um : kam$_4$ (18).
ga-na-um : gána (48).
ga-ru$_{12}$-um : gára (7).
gi-i-tum : kid (56).
gi-me-núm : géme (84).
gi-ne-mu-um : kalam (45).
giš-ga[l-lum] : gišgal (15).
gi-za-lum : kisal (8).
gi-zu-um : zum (83).
gú-du-núm : gudu$_4$ (92).

gú-gú-um : kun (59).
gur-gi-núm : murgu(SIG$_{5}$) (89).
gú-ru$_{12}$-um : gur (126).
gú-šè-LUM : *LAK* 228(?) (100).
ḫu-du-šum : ḫuduš(TU) (76).
ì-zi-núm : ezen (29).
ì-ti-gi-ra-um : idigina (34).
ì-ti-núm : eden (55).
la-ʾà-núm : alan$_{x}$(KÍD.ALAM) (52).
la-ḫa-da-mu-um : laḫtan (141 and 150).
la-ḫa-šu-um : laḫšu(*LAK* 442) (50).
lu-ma-ʾà-sum : DÙL (49).
ma-ʾà-ru$_{12}$-um : amar (74).
mar-u$_{9}$-um : gur$_{8}$ (78).
me-si-za-núm : RAD (6).
me-šum : mes (21).
mu-nu-um : mun (62).
mu-ša-na-um : gešnu (79).
mu-š[a-um] : mùš (26).
mu-ša-lum : gisal(*LAK* 589) (142).
mu-x̣-[tu]m : LÚ-šeššig(?) (88).
na-ga-lum : nagar (40).
na-ga-um : naga (63).
na-ḫi-ru$_{12}$-um : laḫar (64).
ne-gi-ru$_{12}$-um : nimgir (28).
NE-rí-LUM : *LAK* 670 (58).
nu-ga-t[i-]mu-u[m] : gidim (97).
nu-gú-lum : lagar (38); KUL (127).
nu-núm : nun (32).
nu-rí-sum : guruš (46).
nu-u$_{9}$-mu-um : úmun (12).
[rí?-]mu-um : [rí]g(?) (140).
[sa?-]⸢ʾà⸣-um : ⸢ša⸣(?) (135).
sa-ga-tum : X (145).
sa-la-um : sila$_{4}$ (9).
si-gúm : sig (82).
si-la-ga-um : šilig (14).
si-la-mu-um : šilam (11).
si-ru$_{12}$-um : šir$_{x}$(HAŠḪUR×KÍD) (33).
[s]i-ru$_{12}$-wu-um : [š]ir (139).
su-du-u$_{9}$-um : sudu$_{x}$ (60).
su-gal-lu[m] : sukkal (90).
su-me-núm : súmun (39).
su-ra-um : sur (124).
su-šum : [ŠE+]NÁM (5).
ša-ga-um : šaga$_{x}$(*LAK* 175) (27).
ša-na-gúm : šinig (93).
š[a-]n[u-um] : š[en] (147).
šè-gu-um : šeg$_{9}$ (95).
šè-mu-um : šim (81).
ŠÈ-tum : NÁ (72).
šu-ḫu-ru$_{12}$-um : šuḫur(*LAK* 227) (31).
šu-wu-um : KÍD (51).
ti-i-ru$_{12}$-um : tir (75).
ti-mu-um : dim (44).
ti-iš-da-núm : šita$_{x}$ (1).
[tu?-gú?-u]m : tuk (3).
ub-bí-sa-ga-im : umbisag (16).
ù-ga-lum : ugar(SIG$_{7}$) (24).
ù-lu-um : ul (99).
ù-ma-núm : ùmun (65).
ù-ru$_{12}$-sum : uruš(SAL+TÚG) (30).
[ù-r]u$_{12}$-um : uru$_{4}$ (4).
u$_{9}$-ru$_{12}$-um : ùr (57).
ù-sum : munsab(*LAK* 672) (61).
ù-su-ru$_{12}$-um : esir$_{x}$ (96).
uš-ti-núm : uštil (73).
ù-šu-wu-um : anše (85).
ù-[X-]LU[M] : ut[ua] (146).
za-ru$_{12}$-um : zàr (91).
za-ti-núm : zadim (43).

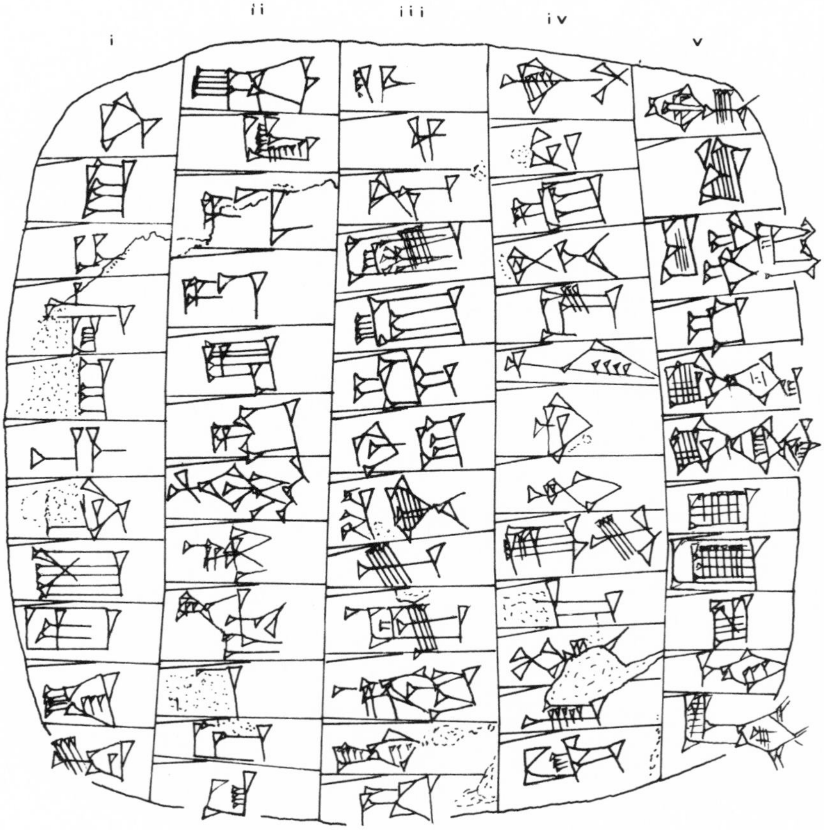

Figure 1. Text *A*, obverse. TM.75.G.1385.

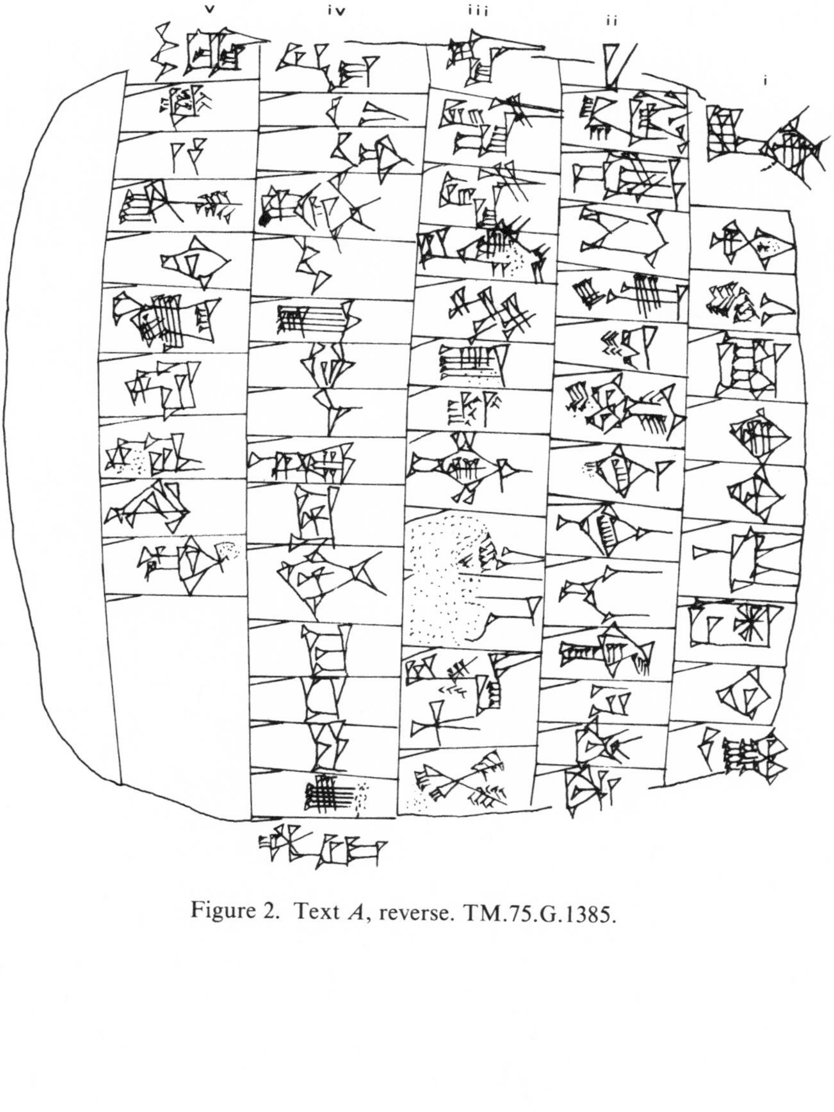

Figure 2. Text *A*, reverse. TM.75.G.1385.

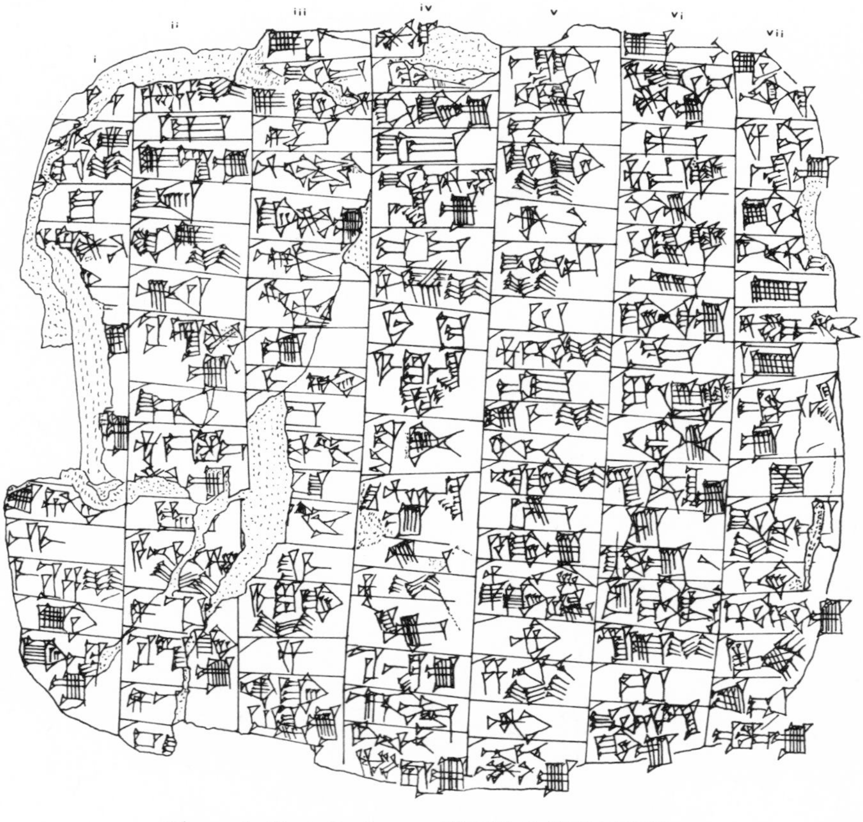

Figure 3. Text *B*, obverse. TM.75.G.1907+12680.

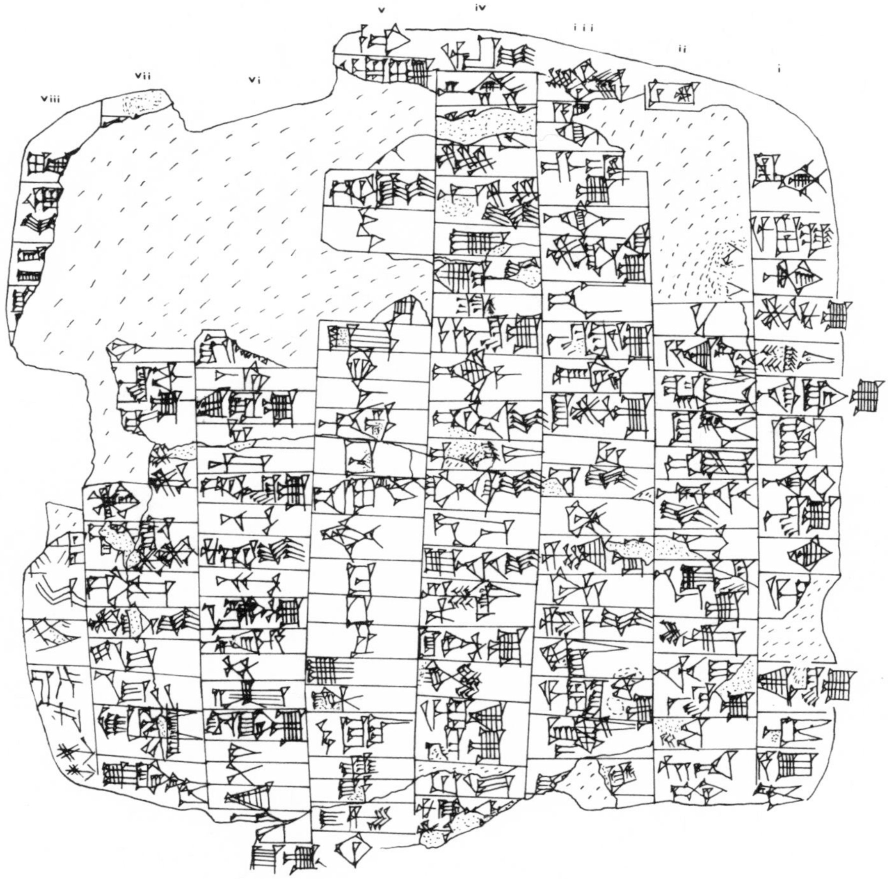

Figure 4. Text *B*, reverse. TM.75.G.1907+12680.

Figure 5. Photo, Text *A*, obverse. TM.75.G.1385.

Figure 6. Photo, Text *A*, reverse. TM.75.G.1385.

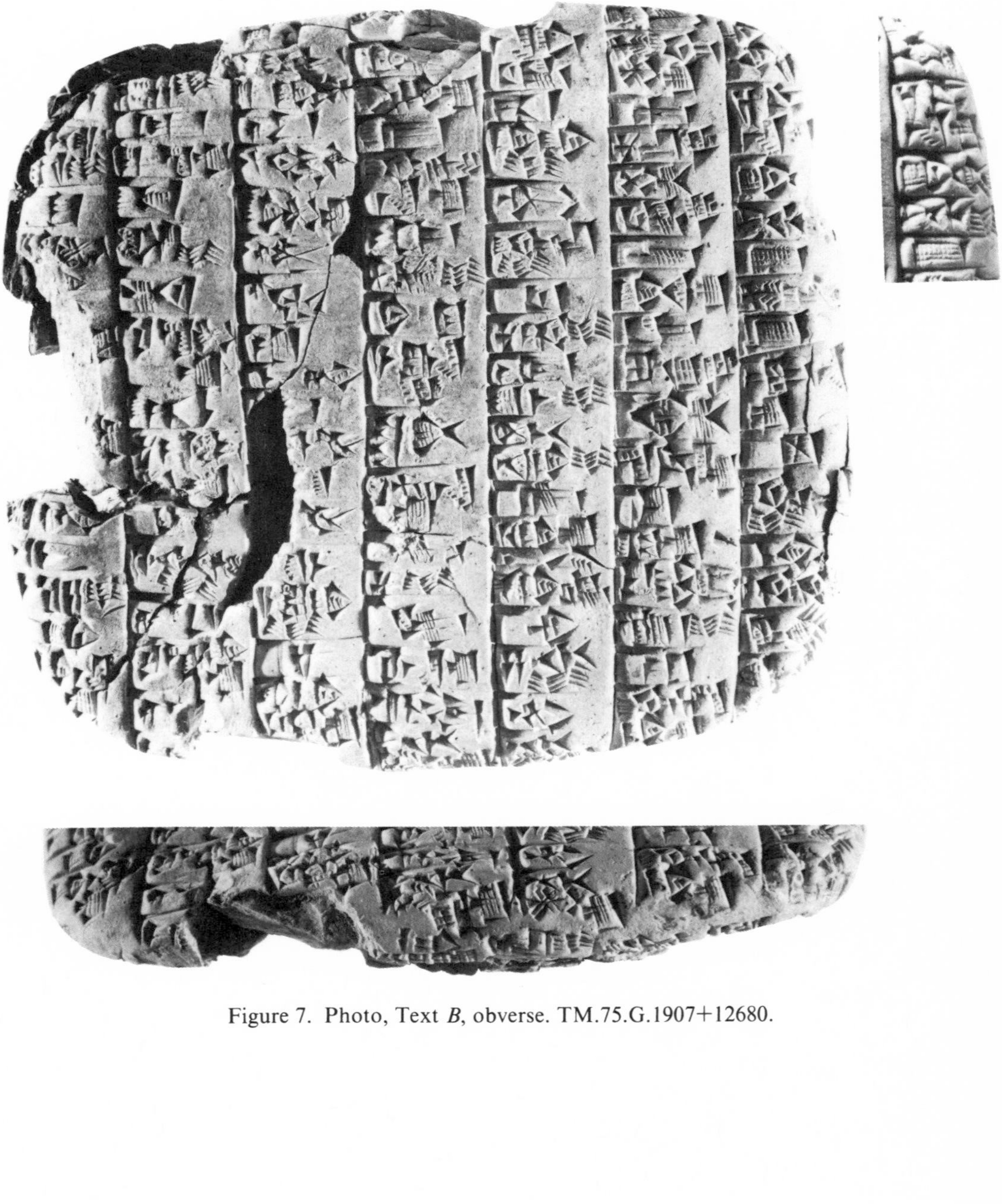

Figure 7. Photo, Text *B*, obverse. TM.75.G.1907+12680.

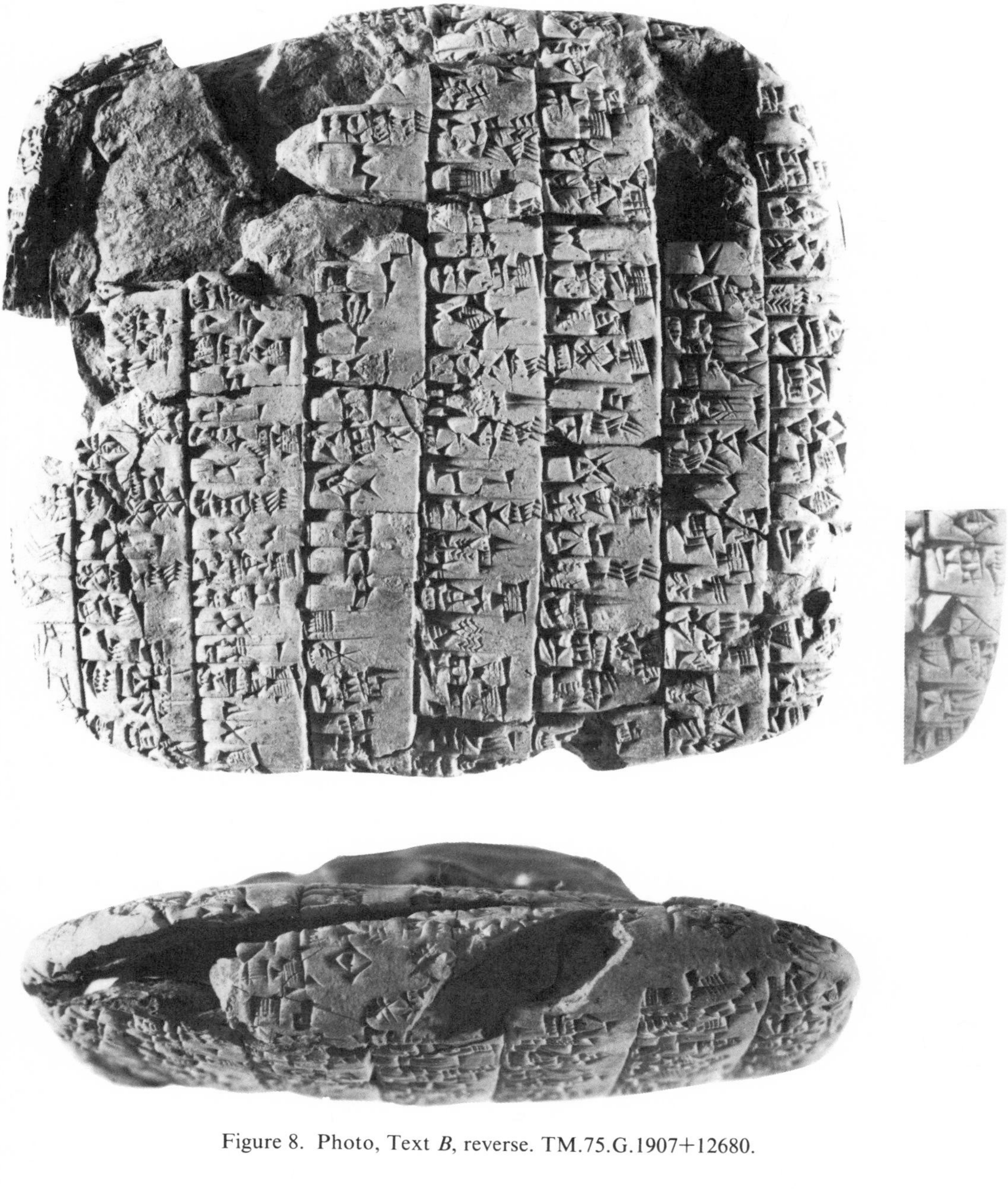

Figure 8. Photo, Text *B*, reverse. TM.75.G.1907+12680.

Gifts for a Princess

ALFONSO ARCHI

Text A (TM.75.G.2022) is defined in the colophon (section 19) as "document for the departure of Sanib-Dulum, priestess (bride of the deity), daughter of the king, for Luban."[1]

There is no doubt that d a m - d i n g i r designated a sacerdotal office at Ebla.[2] And Luban, a city located on the Plain of Antioch, along with Arugadu, was the most important center for the worship of NI-*dakul*, one of the principal deities of the Eblaic pantheon.[3] Another text, *ARET* IV 11 rev. III 4–11, mentions Sanib-Dulum when she had already become a priestess: (1 garment) n í g - b a ^{d}BAD.MÍ l ú *Lu-ba-an*^{ki} *Sá-ne-íb-Du-lum* i n - n a - s u m *in* u_4 m u - TÚG-*sù* '(1 garment) gift for the Lady of Luban, was given to S. on the day of her. . . .' The title "lady" surely means that she was the female companion of NI-*dakul*, as is shown by TM.75.G.1541 obv. II 8–III 1: ^{d}BAD.MÍ ^{d}NI-*da-kul* *Lu-ba-an*^{ki}. Thus, it is now clear that at Ebla princesses of the royal house became priestesses of deities connected with the dynasty and the exercise of power. It is sufficient to recall here Enḫeduanna, the daughter of Sargon of

[1] The name of the priestess is also written *Sá-ni-íb-Du-lum* in TM.76.G.138 I 2, whereas in *ARET* I 12 (= *MEE* II 21) obv. IX 2 and TM.75.G.2359 rev. XIII 5 it appears with *-ne-*. G. Pettinato, *MEE* II, 157, reads *Sá-bí-íb-du-lum* (the commentary, p. 159, is in part contradictory and in part in error; it is not true that the princess went to Luban to marry the king!). Now, if NI can also be read bu_y (*ARET* III, 401), it seems more appropriate to read instead *Sa-ni/ne-íb-Du-lum*. Note names such as *Za/Sa-ni-bu-um*, *Za-na-ba-an*, from the root *ḎNB*, documented during the second millennium; see I. J. Gelb, *Computer-aided Analysis of Amorite* (Chicago, 1980) 298.

For the element *-du-lum*, cf. the following PNs: Tar_x(BAN)*-kab-Du-lum* (*ARET* III, 286), *Gi-dar-Du-lum* (king of the city of Dulu: TM.75.G.2274 obv. III 7), *Ar-ra-du-lum* (very widespread name for Dulu, *ARET* III, 261), which alternates with *Ar-ra-ti-lu* (cf. *ARET* I and IV, Indices). It is not impossible that this element represents the name of the city of Dulu; in TM.75.G.1319 obv. V 9 the name of *Du-lu* is attested for a person from the city of Dulu. That names of cities form elements of PNs is demonstrated, for example, by *Za-ne/ni-ḫi-Ma-rí* (*ARET* III, 303).

With regard to d u - d u '(for) the departure', keep in mind that Sumerian verb forms are used by Eblaite scribes also as substantives: š u ba_4 - t i 'he has received', and also 'receipt' (š u ba_4 - t i - s ù); see *ARET* II, 139; *ARET* III, 386ff.

[2] A. Archi, *SEb* 1 (1979) 109, n. 8.

[3] Ibid., pp. 105–9; cf. *ARET* III, 311.

Akkad, and almost a contemporary of Sanib-Dulum, who became the high priestess (en) of the moon-god Nanna or Ur.[4]

The eighteen sections which make up the document (if the colophon is excluded) are all similar: eighteen personages have consigned or must still consign the same goods. Above all, it is a matter of silver pendants or earrings, *bu*-DI, weighing 78 gr. each (sections 1–11) or 39 gr. each (sections 12–18).[5]

Sections 1–4:	2 pairs	40 shekels of silver	(ša-pi bar_6:kù)
Sections 5–11:	1 pair	20 shekels of silver	($ŠU_4$ + ŠA bar_6:kù)
Sections 12–18:	1 pair	10 shekels of silver	(10 bar_6:kù)

Added to this are 'fine textiles', gíd-TÚG (in the Ebla Vocabulary gíd-TÚG is translated *gu-da-núm*/*nu-um*, Akk. *qutānum*), another cloth or piece of clothing rather frequent at Ebla: $zara_6$-TÚG,[6] and an unidentifiable object: TUR.SAL.[7]

The term which qualifies these consignments is ì-na-sum 'has given'; and if the consignments are incomplete, what is missing is stated by giving the negative form, nu-ì-na-sum 'has not (yet) given'. Instead, when the consignment has been completed, it is defined with zà-me 'has assigned'.[8]

It may be surprising that all these gifts are of the same type (22 pairs of earrings!). But in making up this dowry, what was obviously important was the intrinsic value of the goods, not their usefulness. Earrings of a standardized weight were no more than one of the ways during that epoch for storing up the precious metal.[9]

What is worthy of note is that this patrimony for a princess going to Luban as priestess of one of the principal deities of the state religion is not cumulatively

[4] See W. Hallo and J. J. A. van Dijk, *The Exaltation of Inanna* (New Haven, 1968) 1–11.

[5] 40 shekels are 313 gr. (1 shekel = 7.83 gr.).

[6] Cf. *ARET* III, 395.

[7] "Small SAL," where SAL may be the abbreviation for kù-sal; cf. *ARET* III, 365.

[8] F. Pomponio (*Vicino Oriente* 5 [1983] 211–13), referring to this same text, translates "(la merce è) pervenuta," since he derives *wa-ti-um*, which is the equivalent of zà-me in the Ebla Vocabulary, from a root *WTH*, which would be a secondary form of *ᵓTW* 'come, go', attested in Ug., Hebr. and Aram. However, much more plausible is M. Krebernik's etymology (*ZA* 73 [1983] 41), which interprets this word as /wadihum(?)/ "im Sinne von 'gepreisen' zu hebr. *ydh* (Hifil), 'preisen'."

But it seems better to start from *wadûm* 'to know' and to consider *wa-ti-um* a *paris* form of it. The D form of this verb means, according to *AHw*, 1455: "kennzeichen; für jmd. kennzeichen, zuteilen, zuweisen." And this is precisely the meaning of zà-me in the economic texts of Ebla. In *ARET* II 58 (Pomponio, *Vicino Oriente*, points out that obv. I 1–III 2 makes up only one section!) there are two lists of fabrics followed by PN šu-ba_4-ti 'has received' (sections 1 and 2). The third section has (1 fabric) nu-zà-me, which can only mean 'not assigned'. The meaning 'praise' for zà-me seems to be secondary.

[9] Already in *ARET* III, 342, this standardization of weights was noticed: "(the earrings) usually in silver, weigh 20 shekels a pair (c. 78 gr. each), but a passage mentions a pair weighing 30 shekels. Those for the daughter of the king of Mari weigh 10 shekels, whereas to a deity . . . is destined a pair weighing 6 shekels."

consigned from the palace treasury. Instead, the individual functionaries who must contribute the gifts are listed, so that the economic burden in making up the dowry appears to involve the various sectors of the palace administration.

Among the persons mentioned in the seventeen sections (in section 14 instead of a PN the name of a craft is given: 'preparer of felts', túg-du_8), ten—although they are given no title—are easily identifiable as 'lords', lugal-lugal (which means functionaries of higher rank), on the basis of the lists which register deliveries, mu-DU pertinent to them. And of them, *Ìr*-NI-*ba* (10) and *Iš*$_x$(LAM)-*gi-ba-ir* (13) appear as 'lords' in the lists which date from the time when Ibrium was king; GABA-*Da-mu* (16), GIBIL-*Ma-lik* (9), *Ḫa-ra-ì* (1), *Il-gú-uš-ti* (11), *Ìr-an-Ma-lik* (8) are found in documents both of Ibrium and Ibbi-Zikir; *En-na-ì* lú *Zi-ba-da* (5), *Iš*$_{11}$-*gi-bar-zú* (7) and *Ù-ti* (3), instead, are attested in documents of Ibbi-Zikir. Then there are two 'overseers', ugula, of cities or villages: *Iš*$_{11}$-*ru-ut* of *A-da-ás*^{ki} (6) and *Iš*$_{11}$-*ru-ut* of *Ḫu-za-an*^{ki} (15).

Keeping in mind that the tradition relative to the texts is in some way disturbed, our document probably dates from the last years of Ibrium. *ARET* IV 11 (cited at the beginning), which already mentions Sanib-Dulum in her functions as priestess, dates from Ibrium (rev. VIII 12–16: *in* u_4 *Ib-rí-um* du-du *si-in* GN). But Sanib-Dulum was not a daughter of Ibrium, even though she has the title of 'daughter of the king', dumu-mí en, in Text A (as was stated). This is demonstrated by two documents which can be dated to Ibrium with certainty. The first is TM.75.G.2359 rev. XIII 4′–9′: 3 ma-na 50 gín DILMUN bar_6:kù *Sá-ne-íb-Du-Lum* dam-dingir nin-ni en šu ba_4-ti '3 minas 50 shekels D. of silver (1806 gr.): S., the priestess, sister of the king, has received' (obv. IX 8–10 and rev. IV 7–9: *Ib-rí-um in* u_4 è . . .). The second is *ARET* I 12 obv. IX 1–4: '(2 tunics) for S., sister of the king (nin-ni en)' (obv. VIII 1–2: GIŠ.DUG.DU *Ib-rí-um*). Sanib-Dulum was therefore the sister of Ibrium and not his daughter; and the title of dumu-mí en is to be understood as 'princess'.

Text A (TM.75.G.2022)

(1)

obv. I 1 ša-pi bar_6:kù
4 *bu*-DI
3 1 gíd-TÚG 1 $zara_6$-TÚG
1 TUR.SAL
5 *Ḫa-ra-ì*
ì-na-sum
7 1 TUR.SAL
nu-ì-na-sum

(2)

9 ša-pi bar_6:kù

II 1 4 *bu*-DI
1 gíd-TÚG 1 zara$_6$-TÚG
3 2 TUR.SAL
Ki-ti-ir
5 zà-me
(3)
ša-pi bar$_6$:kù
7 4 *bu*-DI
1 gíd-TÚG 1 zara$_6$-TÚG
9 2 TUR.SAL
Ù-ti
III 1 zà-me
(4)
ša-pi bar$_6$:kù
3 4 *bu*-DI
1 gíd-TÚG 1 zara$_6$-TÚG
5 2 TUR.SAL
A-mur-Da-mu
7 zà-me
(5)
ŠU$_4$ + ŠA bar$_6$:kù
9 2 *bu*-DI
1 gíd-TÚG 1 zara$_6$-TÚG
IV 1 *En-na-ì*
[l]ú *Zi-ba-da*
3 ⸢i⸣-na-sum
1 TUR.SAL
5 [n]u-ì-na-sum
(6)
ŠU$_4$ + ŠA bar$_6$:kù
7 2 *bu*-DI
1 gíd-TÚG 1 zara$_6$-TÚG
9 1 TUR.SAL
Iš$_{11}$-ru-ut
11 ugula *A-da-áš*^{ki}
V 1 zà-me
(7)
ŠU$_4$ + ŠA bar$_6$:kù
3 2 *bu*-DI
Iš$_{11}$-gi-bar-zú
5 ì-na-sum
1 gíd-TÚG 1 zara$_6$-TÚG
7 1 TUR.SAL
nu-ì-na-sum

(8)
9 ŠU$_4$ + ŠA bar$_6$:kù
2 *bu*-DI
11 1 gíd-TÚG
VI 1 1 zara$_6$-TÚG
1 TUR.SAL
3 *Ìr-an-Ma-lik*
zà-me
(9)
5 ŠU$_4$ + ŠA bar$_6$:kù
2 *bu*-DI
7 1 gíd-TÚG 1 zara$_6$-TÚG
1 TUR.SAL
9 GIBIL-*Ma-lik*
zà-me
(10)
VII 1 ŠU$_4$ + ŠA bar$_6$:kù
2 *bu*-DI
3 1 gíd-TÚG 1 zara$_6$-TÚG
1 TUR.SAL
5 *Ìr*-NI-*Ba*
zà-me
(11)
7 ŠU$_4$ + ŠA bar$_6$:kù
2 *bu*-DI
9 1 gíd-TÚG 1 zara$_6$-TÚG
rev. I 1 *Il-gú-uš-ti*
ì-na-sum
3 3 1 TUR.SAL
nu-ì-na-sum
(12)
5 10 bar$_6$:kù
1 TUR.SAL
7 *Gi-ra-Ma-lik*
ì-na-sum
9 1 gíd-TÚG 1 zara$_6$-TÚG
II 1 nu-ì-na-sum
(13)
10 bar$_6$:kù
3 2 *bu*-DI
1 gíd-TÚG 1 zara$_6$-TÚG
5 1 TUR.SAL
Iš$_x$-gi-ba-ir
7 zà-me

(14)
10 bar$_6$:kù
9 2 *bu*-DI
túg-du$_8$
11 ì-na-sum
1 gíd-TÚG
III 1 1 zara$_6$-TÚG
1 TUR.SAL
3 nu-ì-na-sum
(uninscribed)
(15)
IV 1 10 bar$_6$:kù 2 *bu*-DI
1 gíd-TÚG 1 zara$_6$-TÚG
3 1 TUR.SAL
Iš$_{11}$-*ru-ut*
5 ugula *Ḫu-za-an*^{ki}
nu-ì-na-sum
(16)
7 10 bar$_6$:kù 2 *bu*-DI
1 gíd-TÚG 1 zara$_6$-TÚG
9 1 TUR.SAL
GABA-*Da-mu*
11 nu-ì-na-sum
(17)
V 1 10 bar$_6$:kù 2 *bu*-DI
1 gíd-TÚG 1 zara$_6$-TÚG
3 1 TUR.SAL
Ḫa-zu-um
5 nu-ì-na-sum
(18)
10 bar$_6$:kù 2 *bu*-DI
7 1 gíd-TÚG 1 zara$_6$-TÚG
1 TUR.SAL
9 *In-ti*
nu-ì-na-sum
(19)
VI 1 dub
du-du
3 *Sá-ni-íb-Du-lum*
dam-dingir
5 dumu-mí
en
7 *si-in*
Lu-ba-an^{ki}
9 (uninscribed)

Even more difficult to determine is the movement of the goods on the occasion of the marriage. The term níg-mu-sá is surely the Ebla writing for Sum. níg-munus$^{\acute{u}s}$-sá, which is translated by B. Landsberger "Verschwägerung."[10] This meaning is also valid at Ebla, since in some documents there is mention of a ceremony in which a woman's head is anointed (níg-dé ì-giš *si-in* sag), precisely on that occasion: *in* u_4 níg-mu-sá 'on the day of (her) wedding'.[11] Often, níg-mu-sá is followed by the unknown term bur-KAK (often preceded by 1), as in *ARET* I 3 rev. VII 6–10: *in* u_4 níg-mu-sá bur-KAK PN dumu-mí-en.

In *ARET* III 682 obv. II 4–8, three oxen are consigned (by the palace?) for the marriage of the daughter of an unknown person: 3 gu_4 níg-mu-sá *I-rí-ik-ì* dumu-mí *Ga-si-da*. In TM.75.G.1690, the recipients of the gifts on the occasion of the marriage of Zaʾaše (a daughter of Ibbi-Zikir)[12] are instead the "women" who probably made up her retinue: '30 garments . . . 21 fine fabrics: gifts for the female subordinates in GN, Ibbi-Zikir has given for the marriage . . . of Zaʾaše' 30 $zara_6$-TÚG 21 gíd-TÚG níg-ba-níg-ba dam-dam *in Da-ra-um*^{ki} *I-bí-Zi-kir* ì-na-sum *in* níg-mu-sá 1 bur-KAK *Za-a-šè*.[13]

Therefore, the marriage ceremony caused a redistribution of wealth, even if it is not easy to understand who was receiving and often even who was giving. Text B (TM.75.G.2283) is rather enigmatic. It records the "delivery (for) the marriage of KÉŠ-dut, the daughter of the king," that is, a daughter of Ibrium, as may be deduced from *ARET* IV 1 obv. VIII 5–13: (5 fabrics) KÉŠ-*du-ut Dar-kab-Da-mu Dag-rí-iš-Da-mu Da-ḫi-du* dumu-mí en *Zi-me-ḫa-du* dumu-mí *I-bí-Zi-kir*.[14] This wedding must have been a very important event, since it served to give its name to that year, TM.75.G.2612 rev. III 1–4: DIŠ mu níg-mu-sá bur-KAK KÉŠ-*du-ut*. And in fact, from TM.75.G.2327 obv. IX 6–21, it seems very probable that KÉŠ-*du-ut* married a king of Kish.[15]

What makes this document unique is that it only concerns animals, and a very large number of head, without their origin being given. In particular, there is a comparison between the total of livestock, 3,290 head, with that in TM.82.G.266, which represents an annual balance of the king's patrimony, that is, 9,741 head of livestock, whose value is estimated as 389 minas of silver (1.198

[10] B. Landsberger in *Symbolae M. David* (Leiden, 1968) 94–97. The Ebla writing seems to confirm the reading -munus$^{\acute{u}s}$- of -SAL.UŠ-, proposed by Landsberger. A. Falkenstein, *Die neusumerischen Gerichtsurkunden* I (Munich, 1955) 103–5, instead states, "die consumptubilia, die der Bräutigam (oder dessen Eltern) für das Hochzeitsmahl zu stellen hatte." As both authors observe, the Sumerian term does not agree exactly with the Akk. *terḫatum*.

[11] Cf. A. Archi, *SEb* 2 (1980) 20ff., where TM.75.G.1321 rev. III 15–IV 6 and TM.75.G.1935 obv. VIII 1–10 are cited.

[12] See TM.75.G.2447 obv. III 10; 2449 obv. XI 17.

[13] Similarly TM.75.G.1699. The two texts will be published in *ARET* VII.

[14] KÉŠ-dut, always with the title of dumu-mí en, is cited in TM.75.G.2649 rev. V 22 ff.; 2653 obv. II 12ff. In TM.76.G.521 rev. IV 7–9 we find *Ìr-kab-ar* a-zu_x KÉŠ-*du-ut* 'I., physician of K'. And in TM.75.G.1293 rev. III 2–7 we read: 1 kaskal *in* u_4 šu mu-DÚB níg-ba KÉŠ-*du-ut* É×PAP 'one expedition; when the gift for K. . . . was handed over'.

[15] See in this volume A. Archi, "More on Ebla and Kish."

shekels per head; 182.83 kg. of silver; 9.38 gr. per head), in addition to 760 cows in calf (peš-áb) and 700 bulls (gu_4-máḫ). Instead, the total of sheep is 64,515 head, plus 52,200 more, in comparison to the 1,680 sheep attributed to KÉŠ-dut. But for another princess, Tiša-Lim, a noteworthy patrimony of land distributed in various villages (ki-ki: TM.75.G.2396; 1986+) is set up by Irkab-Damu.

Text B (TM.75.G.2283)

obv. I 1	AN.ŠÈ.GÚ 9 *mi-at* 72 gu_4-máḫ	Total: 972 bulls,
	9 *mi-at* 35 peš-áb-máḫ	935 mature cows in calf,
II 1	7 *mi-at* 70 lá-2 niga:gu_4	768 fattened oxen,
	3 *mi-at* 40 lá-2 gu_4-GÍD	338 draught-oxen,
3	2 *mi-at* 41 amar-máḫ	241 mature calves,
III 1	36 amar-GÍD	36 draught-calves.
	AN.ŠÈ.GÚ 1 *li-im* 6 *mi-at* 80 udu	Total: 1680 sheep,
3	1 *mi-at* 60 lá-1 BAR.AN	159 onagers,
rev. I 1	1 IGI.NITA	1 *horse*,
	5 šaḫ	5 pigs,
3	20 lá-1 alim	19 wisens,
	14 az	14 bears.
III 1	ŠU.NÍGIN 3 *li-im* 2 *mi-at* 90 gu_4	General total: 3290 bovines
	mu-DU	Delivery
3	níg-mu-sá	(for) the marriage
	KÉŠ-*du-ut*	of KÉŠ-dut,
5	dumu-mí en	the king's daughter.
II 1	iti *ḫa-li-du*	Month: I.
	(uninscribed)	

Textual Notes

obv. III 3: BAR.AN 'onager' is the writing used in Ebla economic texts for ANŠE.BAR.AN; see *ARET* III, 341. K. Maekawa (*Acta Sumerologica* 1 [1979] 35–38) has provided some good arguments against the prevailing interpretation, which describes this animal as a mule.

rev. I 1: IGI.NITA (an equid) is the Eblaic writing for ANŠE.LIBIR(.NITA/SAL) = dúsu; see *ARET* III, 360. For this animal, see Maekawa, ibid., 38–62, and J. Zarins, *JCS* 30 (1978) 4–11.

I 4: It is known that bear meat was eaten in Mesopotamia. For the most part, documentation dates back to the Third Dynasty of Ur; see A. Salonen, *Jagd und Jagdtiere im alten Mesopotamien* (Helsinki, 1976), p. 182; and for the wisen, ibid., pp. 164ff. However, in the Ebla texts, the bear is rarely mentioned; for example, in *ARET* I 11 obv. VII 12–13: šu-du_8 2 az.

III 1: This general total gives the sum of livestock registered in obv. I 1–III 1.

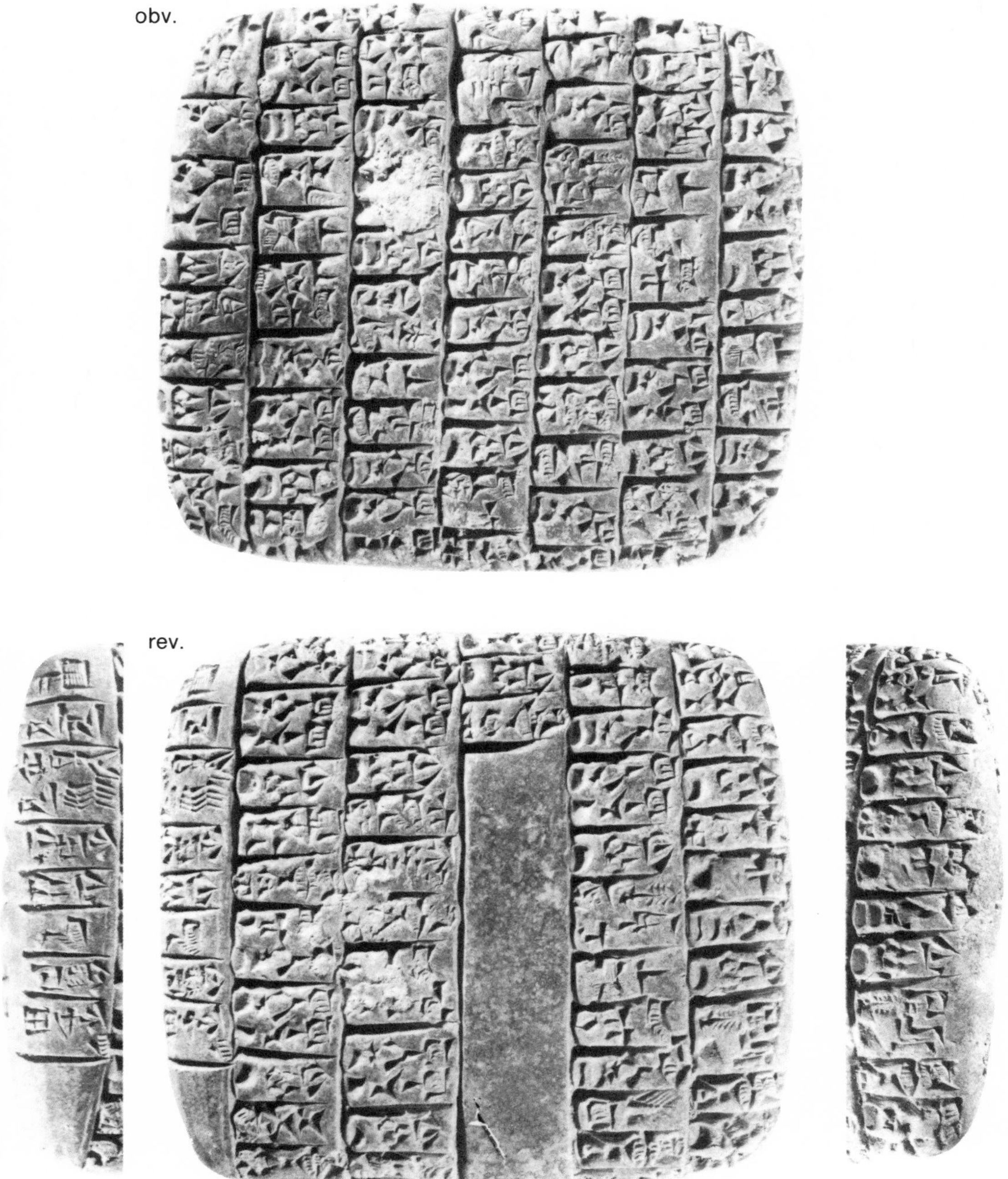

Figure 1. Text *A*. TM.75.G.2022.

obv.

rev.

Figure 2. TM.75.G.2283.

More on Ebla and Kish

ALFONSO ARCHI

Further study of the texts from Ebla has permitted the identification of 23 documents in which Kish is mentioned; these may be added to the other 45 which already have been treated elsewhere.[1] The publication of these new passages offers the occasion to reconsider some points regarding Kish.

Relations between Ebla and Kish

Fabrics are the goods most frequently consigned to people from Kish; see texts [1], [2], [4], [6], [7], [9], [10], [12], and [22]. But in [6], [7], [9], and [22] fabrics are also given to people from Ebla or from other cities who come to Kish. The texts always mention 3 (or 2) garments per person: a cloak, a tunic, and a gown: *ʾà-da-um*-TÚG aktum-TÚG *ib*+III-(sa$_6$-)GÙN-TÚG, or similar pieces. They are the standard consignment of the Eblaite administration, whether the recipient is a simple functionary or a sovereign. Sometimes the quality of the garment varies: a *ʾà-da-um*-TÚG may be of higher quality: -II, and a gown may be 'good' sa$_6$. For the king of Kish and his brothers, šeš en, see [9]. In [12] only Kish is mentioned as the recipient, but it is clear that the reference is to the sovereign of the city. In this case, an ingot of 40 shekels (313 g.) of gold is added to the clothing (and this is rather usual when it is a question of gifts to foreign kings). Therefore, Ebla did not export clothing to Mesopotamia; instead of documents recording exports, these texts must be concerned with gifts, which leads one to presume an exchange on a reciprocal basis.

To its messengers to Kish, the Eblaite administration gives silver, usually in modest quantities ([5]: 20 shekels = 156 g., as 'travel allowance', níg-kaskal). In these cases, the use of the silver is not specified. Instead, in another passage, [5], 11 shekels = 86 g. are destined to the purchase of 102 'turtles' (ba-ba) "in favor of Mari and Kish," and in [15] 70 shekels = 548 g. are delivered to a person in Kish for the purchase of fabrics.

In the passages in *SEb* 4, [19] concerns 8 minas = 3760 g. of silver for an expedition (kaskal) to Kish; [27] 5 shekels = 39 g. as 'travel allowance' (níg-

[1] A. Archi, "Kiš nei testi di Ebla," *SEb* 4 (1981) 77–87. Nos. [44] and [45], published there in the Addendum, are also included in the present article as nos. [6] and [20].

kaskal) of Ennai; [33] 30 shekels = 235 g. as "travel allowance" of Wana; [37] 2 shekels = 15 g. as 'gift' (níg-ba) to a personage of Kish. In [7], [13], and [20] the silver is destined as gifts to make votive offerings to the gods of Kish. In [13], 10 shekels = 78 g. of silver are for the purchase of a dagger for an Eblaite man who goes to Kish. In [5] 46 shekels = 360 g. is the price of two garments to be purchased in Kish. Elsewhere instead, as in [12], a merchant (dam-gàr) has the task of purchasing garments, but the quantity of silver at his disposal is not indicated.

Gold is sent as a gift to high personages of Kish in the form of ingots (DIB) and not as worked objects. In [12] there is 1 ingot of 40 shekels = 313 g. for (the king of) Kish; 6 ingots of 16 shekels = 725 g. for the elders; 6 ingots of 10 shekels = 470 g. for the singers;[2] in [16] 1 ingot of 40 g. = 313 g. for Ṭūbī-Suʾen (king?) of Kish; 1 ingot of 20 shekels and 6 of 16 shekels = 908 g. for the elders; 6 ingots of 10 shekels = 470 g. for the singers. In *SEb* 4 [16], an ingot of 30 shekels = 235 g. of gold is sent to a person from Abarsal residing in Kish.

Lapis lazuli and carnelian were purchased in Kish, according to [5], for 33 shekels = 258 g. of silver (calculating a ratio of 1:4 between silver and lapis lazuli, it amounts to approximately 1 kg. of stones).

There is frequent reference to the king of Kish in the documents, and he is referred to interchangeably with the titles of en ([9]; [10]) and lugal.[3] Gifts are also sent to the brothers of the sovereign (Irišum and Bušušum: [9]) and to his children (*SEb* 4 [20]). In [16], the ingot of gold of 40 shekels is the typical gift given by Ebla to foreign kings (see *ARET* I, "Glossary," *s.v.* DIB). This precedes (even if not directly) the gifts to the elders and to the singers of Kish. All this would suggest that Ṭūbī-Suʾen, even though the name is not followed by a title, was a king of Kish who is otherwise unknown to us. It was common practice at Ebla to omit qualifications and titles, even in the case of foreign kings.[4]

Therefore, in addition to Mari, Ebla maintained direct diplomatic and commercial relations with Kish. Of special importance in this regard is [10], a passage, however, whose syntax is not clear. According to this text, some garments and 2 bracelets decorated with lapis lazuli are "the gift of the king which (his son) Ibbi-Zikir gave on the occasion of the marriage . . . of Hirdut; (to the) king of Kish, PN, dependent of PN; delivered." Now, Hirdut was a daughter of Ibrium, and a very large dowry was given for her marriage (the marriage also was the basis of a year-name).[5] With due reservations, another interpretation of this passage is perhaps more likely: "on the occasion of the marriage . . . of Hirdut (and) the king of Kish"!

[2] In fact, the metal of this DIB is not specified, but it was this type of ingot which was used to store gold.

[3] See also *SEb* 4 (1981) 83. The same alternate is well attested also for the king of Mari (see A. Archi, in *MARI* 4, *Á propos d'un cinquantenaire: Mari, bilan et perspectives* [Strasbourg, 1985] 48–50).

[4] For the kings of Mari, see ibid.

[5] See in this volume A. Archi, "Gifts for a Princess."

The only other high functionaries of Kish mentioned in these texts are the elders in the passages cited above. In [16], it appears that 'singers' (nar) from Kish went to Ebla. On the other hand, Ebla (where metal-working was probably more developed than in Mesopotamia) sends 3 metal workers to Kish along with their children [20]. In general, the titles of the Eblaite envoys are not specified, except in [7], [17], and [22], where 'couriers' (kas_4) are mentioned.

The types of shipments and deliveries seem to be exchanges made on a reciprocal basis. There is also a certain amount of trade but, as has been seen, only in a few cases is it possible to know what goods were purchased.

Kish Civilization and Ebla

I. J. Gelb has pointed out the characteristics of the so-called Kish civilization—that is, of that Semitic culture which formed in the Pre-Akkadian Age in north Mesopotamia, in contact with the Sumerians—and has demonstrated that Ebla shared that culture.[6] But it is important to distinguish between elements which Ebla received from Kish and others which instead were a common patrimony of the Semites in the entire Syro-Mesopotamian area. Among the latter surely are the use of the decimal system and also the calendar, as is proved by some month names found at Abū Salābīkh as well as at Mari and Ebla. On the other hand, with regard to the weight system, the Semites of Mesopotamia adopted the Sumerian system, based on a mina of 504 g. divided into 60 shekels of 8.40 g. In contrast, from very ancient times Syria used a lighter mina of 470 g., which remained in use until the Hellenistic period. This mina was divided into 60 shekels of 7.83 g., and this unit of measure was used—at least from the third millennium—from the Mediterranean coasts up to northern Iran. Dividing that same mina (according to the decimal system) by 50 a shekel of 9.40 g. (1/100.2) is obtained, precisely the unit of which many examples were found at Ebla in Palace G (third millennium). During the second millennium this was the shekel in use at Ugarit, and it corresponded precisely to the Egyptian *qdt.*[7]

From the Semites of Mesopotamia Ebla received, above all, several features of the writing system,[8] and with it some literary and lexical texts. The fact that many of the texts of this sort found at Ebla are known to us also from the archives of Abū Salābīkh (a city approximately 12 km. northwest of

[6] I. J. Gelb, "Thoughts about Ibla," *Syro-Mesopotamian Studies* 1:1 (1977) 13–15; I. J. Gelb, "Ebla and the Kish Civilization," in L. Cagni, ed., *La Lingua di Ebla* (Naples, 1981) 9–73, but especially pp. 60–64 (henceforth *Lingua*).

[7] See A. Archi, "Considerations on the System of Weights at Ebla," in this volume. For Ugarit, see N. Parise, *Dialoghi di archeologia* 4 (1970–71) 3–36. For the shekel weighing 7.83 g. in first millennium B.C. Syria, see A. Archi and E. Klengel-Brandt, "I pesi provenienti da Zincirli," *SMEA* 24 (1984) 245–61.

[8] See n 6.

Nippur) and only in lesser number from other Mesopotamian cities[9] demonstrates with which region Ebla (directly or indirectly) was most in contact. Abū Salābīkh belonged to a Semitic milieu, as is shown by the fact that there the scribes had Semitic names.[10] But all these texts are of Sumerian origin, and therefore in this respect, the Semitized Mesopotamian centers were no more than channels of culture, even if some lists may have been rewritten by their schools of scribes. Perhaps the "Names and Professions List," in which some PNs are Semitic, was rewritten in these schools, as well as the "Geographical List," in which the GNs (often with Semitic endings) are in the majority to be placed in north-central Mesopotamia, while on the contrary the great Sumerian centers are not mentioned (with the exception of Nippur). But it is certain that the "Geographical List" also had a Sumerian forerunner. There is an archaic list from Uruk, preserved in two specimens, which begins with several important Sumerian cities but which also includes some GNs known only from the "Geographical List."[11] Similarly, with regard to the literary texts, *ARET* V 20 = 21 is a Sumerian epic which has only one known parallel: *IAS* 278, also from Abū Salābīkh; but since Aratta and the divinity from Uruk, Ama-ušumgal, are mentioned in it, it must certainly be a text originally composed in Uruk. Of the Sumerian incantations found at Ebla, the only duplicate known to us is from Fara, from south Mesopotamia.[12]

Some relation with Kish is attested by a mathematical document, that is, "a systematic list of composite signs for large sexagesimal number units," composed by a certain Išma-I(l), "scribe of Kish."[13] But one should note that this list, since it is based on the sexagesimal system, is part of the Sumerian tradition.

Instead, it is necessary to fix our attention on another document, *ARET* V 6, an epic dedicated to the Sun-god (^{d}Utu [zà]-me)—and in which Enlil, Enki, and Suʾen are mentioned—the subject of which seems to be trade. In fact, it speaks about 'sea-traders' ga-raš, 'deep-going boats' má-gur$_8$, gold, silver, copper, lapis lazuli, timber, and perfumes. There is a duplicate of this epic from Abū Salābīkh *IAS* 326,[14] about which R. Biggs (*IAS*, p. 91) writes: "The tablet

[9] For the "Names and Professions List," see A. Archi, *SEb* 4 (1981) 177–204. For the "Geographical List," see G. Pettinato, *Orientalia* 47 (1978) 50–73. For the texts from Abū Salābīkh in relation to those from Ebla, see R. D. Biggs in *Lingua*, 121–33.

[10] R. D. Biggs, *Inscriptions from Tell Abū Ṣalābīkh* (OIP 99; Chicago, 1974) 33–35 (henceforth *IAS*).

[11] M. W. Green, *JNES* 36 (1977) 293–94.

[12] Incantation *e* (= 1), according to the classification of M. Krebernik, *Die Beschwörungen aus Fara u. Ebla* (Hildesheim, 1984) 8–9.

[13] G. Pettinato, *Ebla: Un impero inciso nell'argilla* (Milan, 1979) 258–59 (henceforth *Ebla*) = G. Pettinato, *The Archives of Ebla* (Garden City, NY, 1981) 239–41 (henceforth *Archives*). See also A. Archi, *SEb* 3 (1980) 63–64. The interpretation of I. Vino and T. Viola *apud* G. Pettinato, *Testi lessicali monolingui della Biblioteca L. 2769* (Naples, 1981) 278–85, is not compatible with the mathematical knowledge of the scribes of the third millennium. See J. Friberg, "Three Remarkable Texts from Ancient Ebla," *Vicino Oriente* 6 (1986; in press).

[14] The identification is by M. G. Biga.

is not formed of a separate core and surface layer as are most Abū Salābīkh literary and lexical tablets." And so, perhaps "this tablet was not written at Abū Salābīkh but comes from elsewhere, possibly Kish or Ebla."[15] It is important to emphasize that it is a matter of whether or not this is a Semitic text; this would prove that documents of this kind were not written at Abū Salābīkh, but were imported, perhaps in fact from Kish, but certainly not from Ebla. This is proved precisely by the copy *ARET* V 6, which shows some peculiarities. (1) As in the tablet from Ebla of the "Names and Professions List," the cases are generally large: one normally corresponds to two cases of the Mesopotamian tablets. (2) In place of a logogram, frequently there is syllabic writing, as in the "Geographic List" from Ebla. Consider these examples: obv. I 6: ᵈEn-ki *ì-lú* (A.S.: . . . AN); 7: *nu-ru₁₂-um zu-bù-um* (A.S.: . . ud-ud dag-dag); V 5: ᵈEn-zu *kur-da-su* (A.S.: . . . ur-sag-*sù*); VII 1–3: *a-bar-rí-iš ti-ià-ma-dím ḫu-du-dè-iš in a-bar-rí-iš ti-ᵓà-ma-dím* (A.S.: ambar ab-zu *ḫu*[-]ambar [ab-zu].

For these reasons, even if the colophon of *ARET* V 6 is read only: [*En-na-I*]*l* dub-sar *Ìr-a-Il* dub-zu-zu, and *Ìr-a-Il* is not attested in other colophons,[16] it is clear that all these lexical and literary tablets found at Ebla were written in the same environment. This environment was certainly the school at Ebla, and it cannot be hypothesized that they were imported from Mari, the city which was the necessary point for every kind of contact with Mesopotamia. Proof is supplied by the colophon of the "Geographic List": *Ti-ra-Il* dub-mu-sar *A-zi* dub-zu-zu *En-na-Il* zi-lugal-da. Now, Tira-Il was also the scribe of a Word List, TM.75.G.2515: *Ti-ra-Il* dub-mu-sar [*Ib-dur-*]*I-sar* dub-zu-zu, and this text has a date formula which only makes sense if the text was written at Ebla: *in* u_4 dumu-nita-dumu-nita dub-sar e_{11} *áš-du Ma-rí*ᵏⁱ 'when the young scribes left Mari (= to return to Ebla).'[17] Tira-Il is also the scribe mentioned in the famous letter of Ḫamazi, TM.75.G.2342, which dates from Irkab-Damu, Arennum's predecessor. This is important for the relative dating of the tablets of Ebla. Whatever may have been the period of time elapsed between the texts found at Abū Salābīkh and their copies at Ebla, the latter date from three generations before the destruction of Palace G, that is, the time of the last administrative documents.

IAS 326 contains almost solely logograms. Now, in theory, it is true, a text in logograms can be read in various languages, but it is probable that the Eblaite scribe furnished the text with some syllabic writing, since it had been written originally in a language which he felt was rather close to his own.

This text constitutes a point of contact between two distant geographic areas, and therefore the Semitic of Mesopotamia, prior to the age of Akkad,

[15] R. D. Biggs in *Lingua*, 127.

[16] The identification with *Ìr-ar-Il*, scribe of the tablet of the "Names and Professions List," is doubtful.

[17] *A-zi*, along with *Ib-dur-I-sar* dub-zu-zu and *Dam-da-il* um-mi-a, was also the scribe of the Eblaite tablets regarding the "Birds List," the "Nagar List," "Ed Lu A," and a Word List (TM.75.G.1954+4592); see G. Pettinato, *Testi monolingui*, xxviii.

could not have differed substantially from the Eblaite. But despite this, the culture of Ebla was not that of the Semitic population of Kish and its surroundings; to be convinced of this it is sufficient to glance over the lists of the gods of Ebla, which are not those of Mesopotamia,[18] the personal names, which follow their own tradition, and in part the lexicon itself, which is attested by the bilingual lexical lists.[19]

Personal Names

The PNs of the persons coming from Kish, according to the Eblaite documentation, seem all to be Semitic (Table 1), and this clearly demonstrates the character of the population of that region for the Pre-Sargonic Age. This is a confirmation of the data furnished by the Sargonic texts of Kish and Mugdan.[20] In fact, according to an analysis conducted by B. R. Foster, the PNs of the tablets from Kish can be classified in this way: Akkadian 82%; Reduplicated 11%; Sumerian 6%; Unassigned 1% (total cases counted: 679).[21]

The theophoric names known from Ebla above all attest the Moon-god Suᵓen in this peculiar writing: *Zu-i-nu* (*Du-bí-Zu-i-nu* /ṭūb-ī-DN/ 'DN is my god'; *Ìr-an-Zu-i-nu*),[22] and then the Sun-god ^{d}Utu (*Iš-dub-*^{d}Utu). Eblaite names composed with Zuᵓen are not known, and those with Utu[23] are rare. By contrast, in the PNs of Sargonic Kish, Zuᵓen is certainly the god most mentioned (12 PNs), and Utu is less frequent only than Ea and Ishtar.[24] Further, according to the Eblaite writing system, -NI may be read *-ì* and express *-I*(*l*); and this ending is found in *I-da-ì* /yidaᶜ-DN/ 'DN knows', and in *Iš-má-ì* /yišmaᶜ-DN/ 'DN heard', the initial elements are rather frequent both at Kish (cf. above all *I-da*-DINGIR, *Iš-má*-DINGIR) and in general in Mesopotamia, and at Ebla.[25]

[18] See the offering lists published by G. Pettinato, *OA* 18 (1979) 87–215. For the gods which appear in the PNs, see the indexes in *ARET* I–IV.

The fact that the "god Zababa, king of Kish," is cited in the colophon of the Eblaite manuscript of the "Names and Professions List" means no more than that the Eblaite scribe faithfully also copied the final part of the Mesopotamian original. Zababa is cited only in this colophon: TM.75.G.2659+; see A. Archi, *SEb* 4 (1981) 189. G. Pettinato, *Catologo dei testi cuneiformi di Tell Mardikh—Ebla* (Napoli, 1979) pp. 198–99, no. 2095; p. 205, no. 2539; pp. 218–19, no. 4910, erroneously cites three tablets with that formula. In reality, all three fragments belong to a single text!

[19] An important study has been done on the Eblaite lexicon by P. Fronzaroli, "Materiali per il lessico eblaita," circulated in pre-print by the author in 1980 and unfortunately never printed for reasons beyond his control. And now see M. Krebernik, *ZA* 73 (1983) 1–47.

[20] I. J. Gelb, *MAD* 5, 93–123. A few texts are from the Pre-Sargonic Age, see p. xvi.

[21] B. R. Foster, *Orientalia* 51 (1982) 299.

[22] In the Old Akkadian period, this DN is written: ^{d}EN.ZU, with two exceptions in Pre-Sargonic texts, where it occurs as $^{(d)}$Zu-en; see J. J. M. Roberts, *The Earliest Semitic Pantheon* (Baltimore, 1972) 50.

[23] *En-na-*^{d}Utu; *Tíš-ma-*^{d}Utu; cf. *ARET* I.

[24] *MAD* 5, 123–24.

[25] Ibid.; I. J. Gelb, *MAD* 3, 17 and 274–75; for Ebla, see *ARET* III, 276ff. and 287.

TABLE 1. Kish Personal Names Attested in the Ebla Texts

A-ḫu-šu/d[*a*(-x)] [25]	*Iš-dub-bù* [11]
ᵓ*À-tum* [7]	*Iš-du-bù* [9]
Bù-šu-sum (šeš en) [9]	*Iš-du-bu*$_y$(NI) [2]
Da-da; *SEb* 4, 84	*Iš-du-bù-um* [9]
Da-li-lum [6]	*Iš-dub*-^{d}Utu [21]; *SEb* 4, 84
Dab$_6$*-si-ga* [21]; [26]; *SEb* 4, 84	*Iš-lum-a-ḫu* [9]
Du-bí-Zu-i-nu [16]	*Iš-má-ì*; *SEb* 4, 84
Gi-iš-ḪI [9]	*Lu-gu-si-lum* [9]
I-da-ì [7]; *SEb* 4, 84	*Sa-mu-nu* [4]; *SEb* 4, 84
I-du-NI-*i-du*; *SEb* 4, 84	*Su-i-du*; *SEb* 4, 84
Ìr-an-a-bù [8]	*Su-ma-núm* [9]
Ìr-an-mu [8]	*Su-mu-nu* [23]
Ìr-an-Zu-i-nu [8]	UR-*ni-zi* [8]
Ìr-kum-Nu-nu [31]	*Ur-ra-nu* [29]
I-rí-šu; *SEb* 4, 84	^{d}Utu-ERIN+X$_2$ [29]
I-rí-sum (šeš en) [9]	*Zi*-NE-*ḫur* [8]; [9]; [27]
Iš-dab$_6$*-bu*$_y$ [27]	

The verb *šaṭapum* 'to preserve (life)' appears in *Iš-dub*-^{d}Utu /išṭup-DN/ 'DN preserved', and in the hypocoristicon *Iš-du-bù/bu*$_y$(*-um*), *Iš-dub-bù*; it is rather frequent in Mesopotamian PNs (also from Kish), but is not used at all in those from Ebla.[26] Instead, Mari knows *Iš-dub-Il/ì*, *Iš-dub-*(*I-*)*sar*, *Iš-du-bù*(*-um*); and also in Tuttul (on the Balih River) is found *Iš-dub-Il/ì*.[27] This is one of the examples which demonstrates how Mari was more or less the point of contact between two different onomastic traditions, the Syrian (Ebla) and the Mesopotamian (Kish).

Further, *Da-li-lum* /dalīl-u-um/ 'praise', is attested in Mesopotamia (and also at Mari),[28] but not at Ebla; and this is also true for the hypocoristicon *I-rí-šu/sum* /yiᵓriš-u/ 'DN requested'.[29]

Also, *Sa/Su-mu-nu* /śa/um-u-nu/ 'Our progeny' (with the alternate *śam-/śum-* well known in Amorite),[30] and *Su-ma-núm* /śum-ān-um/ 'progeny' (with the hypocoristic ending *-ānu*(*m*), which is found particularly in Northwest Semitic names, but is a Proto-Semitic suffix),[31] present an element well attested

[26] *MAD* 3, 291; *MAD* 5, 108.

[27] See A. Archi, in P. Fronzaroli, ed., *Studies on the Language of Ebla* (Florence, 1984), 225–51; A. Archi, in *MARI* 4, *Á propos d'un cinquantenaire: Mari, bilan et perspectives* (Strasbourg, 1985), 53–58.

[28] *MAD* 3, 109ff.; *ARET* I.

[29] *MAD* 3, 67.

[30] See G. Buccellati, *The Amorites of the Ur III Period* (Naples, 1966) 180ff.; H. B. Huffmon, *Amorite Personal Names in the Mari Texts* (Baltimore, 1965) 247.

[31] See W. von Soden, *GAG* § 56r; H. B. Huffmon, *Amorite*, 135–38.

in Mesopotamia. But Ebla itself knows similar names, such as *Su-ma-Il/ì*, *Sa-mu-ù/um*, whereas *Su-ma-núm* is also the name of a man coming from Irrite.[32]

Su-i-du /śu-id-u/ 'He is the strength' contains the element *idu*(*m*), well known from names both Mesopotamian and Eblaite.[33] On the other hand, in *Iš-lum-a-ḫu* 'The brother is . . .' the element *išr/lu* is widespread in the Eblaite area and rare in Mesopotamia.[34]

For *Dab₆-si-ga* keep in mind *Si-ga*(*-ma-al*), *ARET* III, p. 297; the first element could therefore be /ṭāb/ 'is good'.[35]

Finally, *Da-da* is a "reduplicated name," in use both in the Sumerian as well as the Semitic area.[36]

These PNs, even if few, demonstrate how the language of Ebla was rather close to that of Kish, but also how the onomastic tradition of Ebla was different from that of Kish.

Dating

When the Ebla tablets were first discovered, it appeared that the dynasties of Ebla and Akkad were contemporaneous. In a tablet, TM.75.G.2428, rev. IV 9, the name of *Sa-rí-gi-nu* was read and it was thought that Sargon of Akkad[37] had been mentioned. Subsequently, however, the correct reading was recognized: *Ša*-NAM-*gi-nu*; furthermore, the name was not followed by a royal title nor by a place name which could be identified with Akkad.[38] Nevertheless, according to P. Matthiae, some stylistic elements in Eblaite works have a correspondence in Akkadian manufactures. He therefore posits a synchrony between the ceramic production of Mardikh IIB 1—which corresponds to ʾAmuq I and Hama J 8-5 (= EB IV A)—and a period which includes the last decades of ED IIIB and the first years of the reign of Naram-Sin.[39] In confirmation of this dating Matthiae was then able to offer the find, during the campaign of 1977, in a well-stratified level, of the lid of an unguent jar with a cartouche of Pepi I, whose period of rule traditionally has been thought to coincide with the second part of the reign

[32] *ARET* III, 297ff.

[33] *MAD* 3, 16ff.; *ARET* III, 277.

[34] Cf. *ARET* III, 398; I. J. Gelb in *Lingua*, 29ff.

[35] According to a suggestion of P. Fronzaroli.

[36] See T. J. Meek, *RA* 32 (1935) 51–55; I. J. Gelb, *OAIC*, 325; I. J. Gelb, *MAD* 3, 104; I. J. Gelb, *MAD* 5, 96; B. R. Foster, *Orientalia* 51 (1982) 302.

[37] G. Pettinato, *Ebla*, 124, n 24 = *Archives*, 109, n 24; P. Matthiae, *Ebla, un impero ritrovato* (Torino, 1977) 180–82 (henceforth *Ebla*) = P. Matthiae, *Ebla: An Empire Rediscovered* (Garden City, NY, 1981) 166–69 (henceforth *Empire*).

[38] G. Pettinato, *Ebla*, 124, n 24; G. Pettinato, *RBI* 25 (1977) 233; G. Pettinato, *Catalogo*, xxxvii.

[39] P. Matthiae, *Ebla*, 60, 76–106 = *Empire*, 66, 79–105. For the dating of the pottery, cf. H. de Contenson, *UF* 11 (1979) 860. Support was also provided by M. van Loon in a report delivered in Rome in 1980.

of Sargon and the beginning of the reign of Naram-Sin.[40] Matthiae does not rule out the possibility that the destruction of Palace G was the work of Sargon, but contends that it is more probable to attribute it to Naram-Sin, for two reasons: (1) Naram-Sin is the only one who explicitly says that he conquered Ebla; and (2) with the destruction of Mardikh IIB 1, Palace G was abandoned and the subsequent phase is constituted by Mardikh IIB 2, which more or less corresponds to Lagash II.[41]

Instead, G. Pettinato, once the groundlessness of the synchronism between Sargon and Ibrium was recognized, moved up the dating of the archives of Ebla considerably. In fact, he maintains that the dynasty of Ebla is "contemporary with the I Dynasty of Kish (2600–2500 B.C.) . . . and the IV Dynasty in Egypt," for these reasons: (1) Iblul-Il of Mari is contemporary with Arennum of Ebla; (2) Akkad is never mentioned in the texts from Ebla, but Kish is attested, "followed by Adab"; (3) there is a PN read Mesalim, and this must be the famous sovereign of the first Dynasty of Kish; (4) in two fragments of an oil lamp from Egypt found in the palace, the cartouche of Chefren is carved, and this constitutes a synchronism between the dynasty of Ebla and the fourth Egyptian dynasty; and (5) "the paleography and criteria of composition of the tablets are correspondent to those in force in Fara and Abū Salābīkh."[42] But in reality, of these points only (2) is valid[43] since: (1) a synchronism between Iblul-Il and a Mesopotamian dynasty does not exist; (2) the PN Mesalim in reality is to be read *Bar-za-ma-li*;[44] (3) the implication that the vase with the cartouche of Pepi I was not found in a stratigraphic level is gratuitous, and therefore "there can be no doubt that the cover of Pepi I, whatever be the absolute chronology that is attributed to this Pharaoh, constitutes a fundamental *terminus post quem* for the destruction of the Palace";[45] and (4) the typologies of the tablets are in fact similar to those of Fara and Abū Salābīkh,[46] but the order of the signs in the reading-sequence is respected (with rare exceptions) only in the tablets from Ebla; in addition, the lexical and literary

[40] P. Matthiae, *AJA* 82 (1978) 542ff.; P. Matthiae, *CRAI* (1978) 229–36; G. Scandone Matthiae, *SEb* 1 (1979) 37–40.

[41] P. Matthiae, *Ebla*, 53–54, 107, 208–10 = *Empire*, 59–60, 105–6, 191–93.

[42] G. Pettinato, *RBI* 25 (1977) 233ff.; G. Pettinato, *Ebla*, 80ff. = *Archives*, 72ff.; G. Pettinato, *Catalogo*, xxxviii.

[43] But for Adab I am able to supply only two passages from the administrative texts of Ebla, in which it is mentioned in connection with Mari and not with Kish: (1) TM.75.G.1918 rev. III 20–26: 1 ma-na bar_6:kù níg-ba *Šu-ga-du Ma-rí*^{ki} níg-AN.AN.AN.AN Adab (UD.NUN)^{ki} šu-ba_4-ti '1 mina of silver (as) gift: PN of Mari has received for votive offering (to the gods) of Adab'; (2) TM.75.G.2429 obv. xx 4–12: 15 gín DILMUN bar_6:kú níg du_8 1 dam Adab (UD.NUN)^{ki} ama-gal dumu-nita nar *áš-da Ma-rí*^{ki} '15 shekels D. of silver: payment for one woman from Adab, mother of the son of a singer from Mari.'

[44] See A. Archi, *SEb* 4 (1981) 227–30.

[45] A. Archi, *SEb* 2 (1980) 37 = *BA* 44 (1981) 153. For the lid with the incision of Pepi I, see G. Scandone Matthiae, *SEb* 1 (1979) 37–43, and especially n 12.

[46] According to R. D. Biggs, *IAS*, 24: "The Abū Salābīkh tablets were approximately contemporary with the so-called Schultexte from Fara."

texts from Abū Salābīkh (and Fara) are written "in a less explicit orthography, using a number of rare or even otherwise unique cuneiform signs of unknown reading, whereas the Ebla version uses ordinary syllabic signs."[47]

The explanation for this phenomenon may be found in the fact that the Eblaite scribes, being less familiar than their colleagues from Mesopotamia with the Sumerian language and the use of certain logograms, preferred syllabic writings.[48] But this may also be an indication that the tablets from Ebla belong to a phase slightly later than those of Abū Salābīkh. A precise comparison of the paleographic elements remains to be made, but with regard to at least some of the tablets from Abū Salābīkh published in photographs, the impression is that they are more archaic.[49]

It is true that the horizon of the lexical and literary texts at Ebla imported from Mesopotamia is the same as Abū Salābīkh, but nevertheless it is a question of a tradition which in some cases begins as early as Uruk III and continues to the Old Akkadian Age.[50] Therefore, placing the date of the texts from Fara "to the time of Ur-Nanshe or even a generation later,"[51] there are six generations to Urukagina and Lugalzagesi (but traditionally ca. 150 years)[52] in which to place Abū Salābīkh and Ebla.

On the other hand, as has been stated earlier, a part of the lexical tablets of Ebla which are copies of texts found also at Abū Salābīkh, on the basis of the names of the scribes, are to be dated to the reign of Irkab-Damu, and therefore three generations before the destruction of Palace G. This is a period estimated to be from 30 to 40 years long. That this period could not have been shorter is confirmed by the fact that Irkab-Damu must have been a contemporary of Iblul-Il of Mari, and that four generations of sovereigns of Mari—NI-zi, Enna-Dagan, Iku-(I)šar, Ḫidaʾar[53]—correspond to the successors of Irkab-Damu—Arennum, Ibrium, and Ibbi-Zikir.

From the paleographic point of view, the texts from Ebla can without difficulty be dated as late as Sargon; this is demonstrated by the Pre-Sargonic administrative texts from Kish, found "at Ingharra, in the south-eastern corner

[47] R. D. Biggs, *BA* 43 (1980) 78, 84.

[48] See the texts quoted above in "Kish Civilization and Ebla," and see J. Krecher, "Eine unorthographische sumerische Wortliste aus Ebla," *OA* 22 (1983) 178–89.

[49] Cf., e.g., the sign SUM in *IAS* 23. For a comparison between the paleography of Fara and that of Ebla, see for the moment S. Picchioni in *Lingua*, 119ff. According to E. Sollberger, in a report read in Rome in 1980, points of contact exist between the paleography of the Ebla texts and those from the time of Lugalzagesi.

[50] For example, of ED lu E there is an Old Akkadian tablet from Gasur, *MSL* XII, 16, and there is an early Ur III copy of the "Names and Professions List"; see F. M. Fales and T. J. Krispijn, *JEOL* 26 (1979–80) 39–46.

[51] W. W. Hallo, *Orientalia* 42 (1973) 235.

[52] W. W. Hallo in D. Schmandt-Bresserat, ed., *The Legacy of Sumer* (Bibliotheca Mesopotamica 4; Malibu, 1976) 37.

[53] The table in A. Archi, *SEb* 4 (1981) 161, is to be corrected; see A. Archi, *MARI* 4, *Á propos d'un cinquantenaire: Mari, bilan et perspectives* (Strasbourg, 1985) 48.

of the Kish complex of Mounds,"[54] which are very similar to the administrative texts of Ebla. Sargonic documents come from the same findspots, and it is therefore probable that these Pre-Sargonic texts date from a phase immediately preceding, and therefore from the reign of Sargon ("paleographically 'Pre-Sargonic' extends to include the reign of Sargon"!).[55] It is unthinkable that during the epoch of Naram-Sin tablets of a Pre-Sargonic shape and with a Pre-Sargonic writing were in use at Ebla. The contacts between Syria and Mesopotamia are too frequent to permit a "delay" of this nature. Rather minor phenomena, such as writings of the type šu-ba$_4$-ti and bar$_6$:kù with respect to šu-ba-ti and kù-bar$_6$ attested in the Pre-Sargonic texts from Mari[56] can be explained by a "delay."

The fact that in the documentation from Ebla the title "king of Kish" is often found, but not "king of Akkad," is not a determining element in favor of an earlier dating; instead, the fact that Kish is mentioned in approximately 70 tablets (sometimes in connection with other cities) and Akkad not even once is a fact which rules out the attribution of Ebla's destruction to a successor of Sargon. On the other hand, if the Dynasty of Ebla had been more or less contemporary with that of Akkad, it would be strange indeed that in the documents from Ebla (even if they are only administrative) there is no mention of the political activities of the king of Akkad. Certainly, Naram-Sin is the only king to call himself "*conqueror* of Armanum and Ebla,"[57] and he explicitly states that "never, since mankind was established, had any king among kings subdued Armanum and Ebla."[58] This inscription gives a rather detailed summary of the Syrian expedition, and it is expressly stated that Naram-Sin's adversary was the king of Armanum, whereas Ebla is mentioned only indirectly. Very different instead were the power relationships in Syria around the age of Ibrium and Ibbi-Zikir; Armi (corresponding to Armanum) was an important city, but there is no doubt that it was Ebla which held supremacy throughout the territory to the west of the Euphrates.[59] We know from Gudea statue B that Ebla was traditionally considered the route to reach the mountains from which valuable timber was imported.[60] It is therefore probable that the mention of

[54] I. J. Gelb, *MAD* 5, ix; the texts are listed on p. xvi, and the photographs are published in pl. XI (no. 25), pl. XII (nos. 26, 27); pl. XV (no. 38); pl. XVIII (no. 47); pl. XXXVI (no. 90). Nos. 25, 26, and 27 were found in Locus: Red Stratum; no. 38 in Locus: C 6; no. 47 in Locus: YWN. Later tablets come from all these Loci.

[55] I. J. Gelb in *Lingua*, 57.

[56] These data were given by D. Charpin in a report read in Rome in May, 1984.

[57] *RGTC* 1, 38.

[58] *IRSA*, 107ff.

[59] Beside *Ar-Mi*^{ki} note also the writing *Ar-mi-um*^{ki}; cf. *ARET* III, 318. GNs with the suffix *-ānum* are not frequent at Ebla. For an etymology of the name, see P. Fronzaroli, *JSS* 22 (1977) 148f. The identification of Armanum with Aleppo (cf. C. J. Gadd, *CAH* 1/2, 426), is based solely on the fact that some scholars want to attribute to Aleppo (not mentioned in the texts of the third millennium) the same importance which it enjoyed in subsequent epochs.

[60] Cf. A. Falkenstein, *AnOr* 30, 52.

Ebla after Armanum[61] was influenced by a literary *topos*. In the epic texts dedicated to Naram-Sin, but from a later epoch, only Armanum and not Ebla appears among the king's rival states.

Sargon, *IRSA* IIA1b, also mentions Ebla, but in generic terms: "(Dagan) gave him the upper land, Mari, Yarmuti, Ebla, up to the cedar forest and the silver mountains." It is precisely the nature of this inscription, a summary of all the king's exploits, that does not however allow the underestimation of the mention of Ebla.[62] If, instead, in accord with what Naram-Sin stated, one wants to maintain that the memory of the destruction of Ebla was not a part of the historical tradition of the Dynasty of Akkad, then it would be necessary to date the destruction of Palace G to a phase immediately prior to Sargon.

Archaeological documentation shows that Palace G was destroyed, sacked, and burned. The architectural structures of the later phase are of rather minor importance and are characterized by the painted caliciform pottery which is usually attributed to the end of the third millennium.[63]

APPENDIX

BAN-*ga*^{ki} = *Ti-rí-ga*^{ki}: Terqa

It is difficult not to notice that the only places where men from Kish receive fabrics from Ebla, namely, BAN-*ga*^{ki} and *Ti-rí-ga*^{ki} in [7] and [9] (in addition to Tuttul), have the same ending. The suspicion that these two names are merely variant spellings for just *one* city and that BAN therefore has the phonetic value of *tir*$_x$ is confirmed if the following facts are considered.

The PN BAN-*kab-Du-lum* is not rare. Since the beginning of this name recalls the element *Ìr-kab-*, rather frequent at Ebla,[64] the reading *ir*$_x$[65] has been proposed for BAN. But a reading *Tar*$_x$*-kab-Du-lum* is just as plausible, and in some cases necessary, since a feminine name is expected here, as in *MEE* II 41 obv. XI 5–7: *Tar*$_x$*-kab-Du-lum* šà-zu dumu-mí 'T., midwife of the daughter.'[66]

The GN BAN-*ḫa-tum*^{ki} now must no longer be identified with *Ar-ḫa-du*^{ki}, as was proposed in *ARET* III, p. 400, but with *Dar-ḫa-du/tum*^{ki}, *Da-ra-ḫa-du*^{ki} (see *loc. cit.*).

[61] See A. K. Grayson and E. Sollberger, *RA* 70 (1976) 127.

[62] A later literary text which describes the empire of Sargon also mentions "From Ebla to *Bit-nanib*: the land of the Armanaeans"; see E. Weidner, *AfO* 16 (1952–53) 12ff.; A. K. Grayson, *AfO* 25 (1974–77) 59. But perhaps this expression was suggested by the inscription of Naram-Sin cited above.

[63] J. Boese, *WZKM* 74 (1982) 33–55, lowers the chronology of the Akkadian Dynasty. Accepting the lower chronology would make possible a correlation between the last years of Pepi I and the reign of Sargon.

[64] *Ìr-kab-ar*; *Ìr-kab-Da-mu*.

[65] G. Pettinato, *Testi amministrative della Biblioteca L. 2769* (*MEE* 2) (Naples, 1980) 262.

[66] For the formation of the feminine PNs, see P. Fronzaroli, *UF* 11 (1979) 278. For the vowel alternation *tar*$_x$/*tir*$_x$, compare *àr*/*ḫur*: ḪUR.

The GN BAN-*ḫa-tum*^{ki} also occurs in the "Geographical List" *IAS*, p. 72, line 46. But in the duplicate from Ebla, in the place of BAN, there is a sign which is not clear.[67]

There is no doubt that the Tir(i)ga of the Ebla administrative texts is the *Ter-qa*^{ki} of the Mari texts of the second millennium, and is to be identified with the modern Tall al-^{c}Ašara on the Euphrates. However, it is possible that the *Tir*$_x$-*ga*^{ki} of the "Geographical List" is to be identified with the other Terqa, located in the Diyala region.[68] This second Terqa is surely mentioned in an Old Akkadian document, Gelb, *OAIC* 33, 46 (writing: BAN-*ga*^{ki}). In fact, immediately following, in line 50, *Ki-te*^{ki}, a city not far from Ešnunna, is mentioned.[69]

D. O. Edzard has pointed out that the Pre-Sargonic god ^{d}Lugal-BAN-*ga* (T. 66) is typologically analogous to the god ^{d}Lugal *ter-qa* (T. 142).[70] We now know that there are variant spellings for the same god.

The sign BAN

(1) Normal form in the administrative texts, see *ARET* I 6 rev. VIII 4: GIŠ-BAN. (2) *ARET* I 12 obv. X 11: GIŠ-BAN. (3) Bilingual lexical texts *A*, *C*, *D* and Sumerian forerunner TM.75.G.2422 obv. IX 25: GIŠ-BAN. (4) "Names and Professions List": Ban-maš-kalam. (5) *ARET* II 6 rev. III 3: GIŠ-BAN.

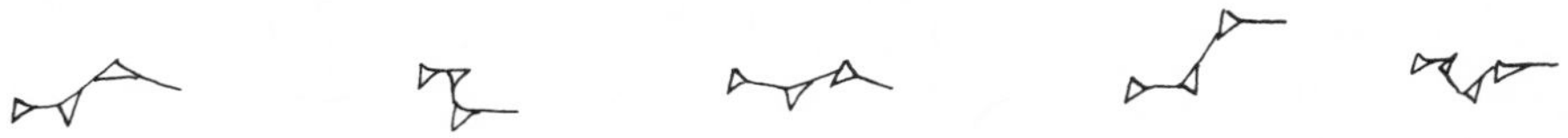

1 2 3 4 5

[67] See the photograph published by G. Pettinato, *Orientalia* 47 (1978), Tab. XI.
[68] See the bibliography in *RGTC* 3, 236.
[69] See *RGTC* 1, 94ff.
[70] D. O. Edzard, *CRRA* XV, 54. T. 142 is published by G. Dossin, *RA* 61 (1967) 97–104.

TABLE 2. Ebla Texts Mentioning Kish

[1] TM.75.G.1249 obv. V 10–13: (fabrics) Kiš^{ki} *in Ì-ab*^{ki} šu-ba$_4$-ti.

[2] TM.75.G.1254 obv. X 8–9: (fabrics) *Iš-du-bu*$_y$(NI) Kiš^{ki}.

[3] TM.75.G.1783 obv. VI 3–8: *En-na-ni-Il* maškim *Ḫa-ra-Il* ì-ti *mi-nu* Kiš^{ki}.

[4] TM.75.G.1792 obv. IV 3′–4′: (fabrics) *Sa-mu-nu* Kiš^{ki}.

[5] TM.75.G.1918 rev. IX 10–16: 20 gín DILMUN bar$_6$:kù níg-kaskal *Wa-na wa A-da-ar* du-du Kiš^{ki};

rev. XVII 3–9: 11 gín DILMUN bar$_6$:kù níg-sa$_{10}$ 102 ba-ba iš$_{11}$-*ki* Kiš^{ki} *wa iš*$_{11}$*-ki Ma-rí*^{ki}.

[6] TM.75.G.2241 obv. IV 13–14: (fabrics) *Da-li-lum* Kiš^{ki};

rev. I 8–II 2: (fabrics) *Za-mu Ma-rí*^{ki} maškim-e-gi$_4$ *Ḫi-da-ar Ma-rí*^{ki} *áš-da* GIGIR-*ra-ar Gi-te si-in* Kiš^{ki};

rev. III 11–15: 1 *LAK* 670-TÚG mu-DU Kiš^{ki} *wa* šu-ba$_4$-ti-*sù Du-bu-ḫu-*$^{d\supset}$*A-da* (cf. *SEb* 4, p. 87 [44]).

[7] TM.75.G.2250 obv. X 10–14: (fabrics) *ᵓÀ-tum* Kiš^{ki} *in Tir*$_x$(BAN)-*ga*^{ki} šu-ba$_4$-ti;

obv. XI 2–8: (fabrics) *I-da-ì* Kiš^{ki} šu-du$_8$ *in Tir*$_x$(BAN)-*ga*^{ki} al-tuš *Ìr-ku*^{ki};

rev. II 13–23: (fabrics) *Na-gàr*^{ki} du-du *si-in* Kiš^{ki} (fabrics) *Ìr-ì-ba Ìr-da-lum* lú kas$_4$-kas$_4$ du-du *si-in* Kiš^{ki};

rev. V 13′–VI 7: *Ar-si-a-ḫu*$^!$ *Áš-da*-NI EZEN-NI *A-ḫu-ma-da Ma-rí*^{ki} du-du *in* Kiš^{ki};

obv. VIII 14–IX 2: (fabrics) Ma-rí^{ki} è *in* Bàd^{ki} *wa* maškim-e-gi$_4$ *si-in* Kiš^{ki}.

[8] TM.75.G.2270 obv. X 7–12: (fabrics) *Ìr-an-Zu-i-nu Zi*-NE-*ḫur* UR-NI-*zi Ìr-an-a-bù Ìr-an-mu* Kiš^{ki}.

[9] TM.75.G.2277 obv. I 8–13: (fabrics) *Ši-ḫi-lu Da-la*-NI 2 maškim *I-bí-Zi-kir* du-du Kiš^{ki};

obv. VIII 17–18: (fabrics) *Iš-du-bù-um* Kiš^{ki};

obv. IX 7–10: (fabrics) *Zi*-NE-*ḫur Lu-gu-si-lum Su-ma-núm* Kiš^{ki};

obv. XI 19–24: (fabrics) *En-na-ni-Il* lú *Ša-ù-um Gi-ra-Ma-lik si-in* Kiš^{ki} šu mu-DÚB;

rev. V 9–12: (fabrics) *I-rí-sum* šeš en Kiš^{ki};

rev. V 23–VI 10: (fabrics) *Iš-du-bù Gi-iš*-ḪI Kiš^{ki} (fabrics) *Gi-iš*-ḪI Kiš^{ki} šu mu-DÚB udua$_x$ 2 šu-ba$_4$-ti (fabrics) *Iš-du-bù* Kiš^{ki} *in Du-du-lu*^{ki} šu-ba$_4$-ti;

rev. VI 21–22: (fabrics) Kiš^{ki} lú *Ib-la*^{ki};

rev. VII 26–28: (fabrics) *Wa-ru*$_{12}$-*tum* Kiš^{ki} šu-mu-DÚB;

rev. VIII 14–20: (fabrics) *Iš-lum-a-ḫu* Kiš^{ki} šu mu-DÚB udua$_x$ *in Ti-rí-ga*^{ki} šu-ba$_4$-ti;

rev. IX 4–6: 1 túg-GÙN 1 *ᵓà-da-um*-TÚG-II 2 aktum-TÚG 1 íb+IV-TÚG-sag 1 íb+IV-TÚG ú-ḫáb en Kiš^{ki};

rev. X 22–24: (fabrics) *Bù-šu-sum* šeš en Kiš^{ki}.

[10] TM.75.G.2327 obv. IX 6–21: 1 dùl-TÚG *Ib-la*^{ki} 1 aktum-TÚG 1 íb+III-sa$_6$-GÙN-TÚG *wa* 2 *gú-li-lum* GIŠ-PA gìn:za kù-gi lú níg-ba en lú *I-bí-Zi-kir* ì-na-sum *in* u$_4$ níg-mu-sá bur-KAK *Ḫir-du-ud* en Kiš^{ki} *En-na-ni-Il* lú *Ša-ù-um* šu mu-DÚB.

[11] TM.75.G.2330 obv. IV 13–14: (fabrics) *Iš-dub-bù* Kiš^{ki}.

[12] TM.75.G.2335 obv. VI 19–VII 10: 3 *ᵓà-[da-]u[m*-TÚG-II] 3 aktum-TÚG 3 íb+III-TÚG-sa$_6$-GÙN 3 DIB 40 (gín) *Na-gàr*^{ki} *ᵓÀ-du*^{ki} Kiš^{ki} 7 *ᵓà-da-um*-TÚG-II 7 aktum-TÚG 7 íb+III-TÚG-ša$_6$-GÙN 1 DIB 20 (gín) 6 DIB 16 (gín) AB×ÁŠ-AB×ÁŠ Kiš^{ki} 6 gu-dùl-TÚG 6 aktum-TÚG 6 íb+III-TÚG-ša$_6$ 6 DIB 10 (gín) nar Kiš^{ki};

obv. VIII 3–7: (fabrics) *A-zi Kab-lu*$_5$-*ul*^{ki} du-du *si-in* Kiš^{ki}.

[13] TM.75.G.2336 rev. IV 18–V 3: (fabrics) ì-giš-sag *Si-ti-Ma-lik* du-du *si-in* Kiš^{ki}.

[14] TM.75.G.2353 obv. V–VI 3: *Si-t[i-]M[a-lik] Ša*[- . . .] du-du *si-in* Kiš^{ki}.

[15] TM.75.G.2359 v. VI 15–VII 9: 30 (gín) bar$_6$:kù níg-sa$_{10}$ 2 zara$_6$-TÚG 40 gín DILMUN bar$_6$:kù níg-sa$_{10}$ 1 níg-lá-gaba 3 níg-lá-sag *I-in-zé*

in Kiš^{ki} 20 gín DILMUN bar$_6$:kù níg-du$_8$ *Dam-da-Il Ib-su*^{ki} in Kiš^{ki} lú *Na-zu-mu* níg-du$_8$.

[16] TM.75.G.2426 obv. VI 16–24: 4 DIB 40 (gín) *Du-bí-zu-i-nu* Kiš^{ki} *En-na-ni-Il* *ᵓÀ-du*^{ki} *Sá-ù-mu Na-gàr*^{ki} *Íl-ba-Zi-kir Kak-mi-um*^{ki};

obv. VII 23–VIII 17: 4 ma-na 50 (gín) bar$_6$:kù šu-bal-ak 1 ma-na 56 (gín) kù-gi 2½ 1 DIB 20 (gín) 6 DIB 16 (gín) SAL AB×ÁŠ-AB×ÁŠ Kiš^{ki} 2 ma-na 30 (gín) bar$_6$:kù šu bal-ak 1 ma-na kù-gi 2½ 6 DIB 10 (gín) SAL nar Kiš^{ki} lú ì-ti *in* níg-kas$_4$ *Ma-rí*^{ki} *in* SA.ZA$_x$^{ki} šu-ba$_4$-ti.

[17] TM.75.G.2441 obv. V 8–10: 12 udu kas$_4$ Kiš^{ki};

obv. VII 17–21: 4 udu kas$_4$ Kiš^{ki} en ì-na-sum.

[18] TM.75.G.2455 obv. IV′ 1′–15′: *Na-zu-mu* ḫi-mu-DU níg-kaskal *si-in* Kiš^{ki} 3 mí-TÚG 3 ib+III-GÙN-TÚG maškim-*sù* 1 mí-TÚG TAR.TAR maškim-*sù* 1 gír mar-tu *ba-du-ud* bar$_6$:kù *En-na-Il* lú GIBIL-*za-Il* du-du [*si-*]*in* Kiš^{ki}.

[19] TM.75.G.2556 rev. III 6–13: (fabrics) *Bar-zi Ar-si-a-ḫu Da-*NE-*lum* simug *wa* 3 dumu-nita-*sù* du-du Kiš^{ki}.

[20] TM.75.G.2643 obv. I 1–7 (= *SEb* 4, p. 87 [45]); 1 *ᵓà-da-um*-TÚG-II 1 aktum-TÚG 1 íb+III-TÚG-SAL 1 *gú-li-lum* ŠÚ+ŠA(= 20)+7-II kù-gi NA$_4$ a-mu-*sù* en Kiš^{ki} GIBIL-*Ma-lik T*[*i-t*]*i-nu* šu-mu-DÚB.

[21] TM.75.G.2649 rev. I 8–17: (fabrics) *A-ku-gú-nu Íl-e-I-sar I-in-zé* du-du *si-in* Kiš^{ki} (fabrics) *Iš-dub-*^{d}Utu *Dab*$_6$*-si-ga* Kiš^{ki} (cf. *SEb* 4, p. 82: [42]).

[22] TM.75.G.10156 rev. VII′ 12′–14′: 2 *ᵓà-da-um*-TÚG 2 aktum-TÚG 2 íb+III-TÚG-sa$_6$-GÙN 2 kas$_4$ Kiš^{ki}.

[23] TM.75.G.10251 rev. IV 2–3: (fabrics) *Su-mu-nu* Kiš^{ki}.

[24] TM.76.G.199 obv. 7–11: *wa a-la-ga* Kiš^{ki} *šu-ul-ma Kam*$_4$*-mu*

obv. VI 6–9: bar?-x̣ Kiš^{ki} *wa* kalam^{tim}.

[25] TM.76.G.541 obv. V 4–5: (fabrics) *A-ḫu-šu*/*d*[*a*(x)] Kiš^{ki}.

ADDENDUM

[26] TM.75.G.2277 obv. III 11–IV 1: (1+1+1 fabrics) *Dab*$_6$*-si-ga* Kiš^{ki}.

[27] TM.75.G.2401 obv. VI 19–VII 1: (2+2+2 f.) 1 *gú-li-lum* bar$_6$:kù-gi 30 (shekels)-II 1 *gú-li-lum* bar$_6$:kù-gi 20 (shekels)-II *Zi-*NE*-ḫur Iš-dab*$_6$*-bu*$_y$ (NI) Kiš^{ki}; obv. X 13–19: (5+5+5 f.) 1 mí-TÚG níg-bar-du-*sù En-na-ni-il* lú *Ša-ù-um* du-du Kiš^{ki}.

[28] TM.75.G.10109 obv. III 1–6: AN.ŠÈ.GÚ 70 lá-2 ma-na bar$_6$:kù *wa* 1 *li* 1 *mi-at* 53 še *gú-bar* al-"taka$_4$" *in* Kiš^{ki} [x-*a*]*r*? [x] x̣; rev. IV x+1–10:] kù-gi 1 níg-tur *wa* 30 (shekels) kù-gi še[-] [(x)] ⌜a⌝-mu lugal *In-Ma-lik* lú *Ib-rí-um* [šu-]mu-"taka$_4$" (lugal = the king of Kish?).

[29] TM.76.G.542 obv. VI 1–3: *Ur-ra-nu* ^{d}Utu-ERIN+X$_2$ (see *ARET* III, 407) Kiš^{ki} (cf. the literary text *ARET* V 6 VII 1: am-am x ^{d}Utu u$_5$ (MÁ.ḪU) = *OIP* 99 326 IV 3′–4′: . . . am ERIN+X$_2$ ^{d}Utu u$_5$, and again *ARET* V 6 XII 3; for MÁ.ḪU = u$_5$, see P. Steinkeller, *OA* 23 [1984] 34, n 8).

[30] TM.76.G.704 obv. I′ 1–3: lu⌈gal⌉ Kis^{ki} *ḫu*$^{?}$*-lu*.

[31] TM.76.G.540 obv. VII 16–VIII 5: (3+3+3 f.) 1 ma-na 2 (gín) kù-gi 1 DIB na$_4$ 50 kù-gi 1 DIB na$_4$ ša-pi 5 (gín) kù-gi 1 DIB na$_4$ níg-ba en Kiš^{ki} *wa* dumu-nita-*sù* *Ìr-kum-Nu-nu* Kiš^{ki} *In-Ma-lik* lú *Ib-rí-um* šu-mu-"taka$_4$".

[32] TM.75.G.1945 obv. XI 14–17: 6 udu kú maškim-maškim Kiš^{ki}.

It is worth noting the large amount of barley, 9,153 kubār, delivered to Kish, according to [28].

TABLE 3. People from Ebla Traveling to Kish

A-ba-da-an (dam-gàr): *SEb* 4 [12]. *A-da-ar*: [5]; *SEb* 4 [33]. *A-ku-gú-nu*: [21]; *SEb* 4 [42]. *A-mur-Li-im*: *SEb* 4 [17]. *Ar-si-a-ḫu*: [19] (simug). *A-zi Kab-lu*$_5$*-ul*^{ki}: [12]. *Bar-zi*: [19] (simug). *Da-la*-NI: [9] (maškim *I-bí-Zi-kir*). *Dam-da-Il Ib-su*^{ki}: [15]. *Da*-NE-*lum*: [19] (simug). *En-ba*$_4$*-zé*: *SEb* 4 [14]. *En-na-ì/Il*: *SEb* 4 [7]; [24]. *En-na-ì/Il* lú GIBIL-*za-Il*: [18]; *SEb* 4 [12]; [13]; *En-na-ni-Il* maškim *Ḫa-ra-Il*: [3]. *En-na-ni-Il* lú *Ša-ù-um*: [9]; [27]. GIBIL-*Ma-lik*: [20]. GIGIR-*ra-ar*: [6]; *SEb* 4 [34]; [40]. *Gi-ra-Ma-lik*: [9]. *Gi-te*: [6]. *I-bí-Zi-kir*: *SEb* 4 [1]. *I-bí-Zi-kir* lú *Zi-da*: *SEb* 4 [12]; [18]. *I-in-zé*: [15]; [21]. *Íl-e-I-sar*: [21]; *SEb* 4 [42]. *Ír-an-Ma-lik* lú *Ib-ga-iš-lu*: *SEb* 4 [16]. *Ìr-da-lum*: [7]; *SEb* 4 [9]. *Ìr-ì-ba*: [7]; *SEb* 4 [9]. *Ì-rí-ik-ì*: *SEb* 4 [38]. *Na-zu-mu*: [15]; [18]; *SEb* 4 [7]; [39]. *Si-ti-Ma-lik*: [13]; [14]. *Ši-ḫi-lu*: [9] (maskim *I-bí-Zi-kir*) [9]. *Ti-ti-nu*: [20]. *Wa-na*: [5]; *SEb* 4 [17]; [33].

TABLE 4. Cities Mentioned in Connection with Goods Exchanged Between Ebla and Kish

A-bar-sal$_4$: *SEb* 4 [16] (PN from A. residing in Kish).

ᵓÀ-du: [12] (1 man from Nagar, 1 man from A., 1 man from Kish); [16] (PN from Kish, PN from A., PN from Nagar, PN from Kakmium).

Du-du-lu: [9] (PN from Kish has received in D.).

Ì-ab: [1] (a man from Kish has received in I.).

Ib-al: *SEb* 4 [2] (Kish, I.).

Ma-rí: [5] (tortoises for M. and Kish); [7] (3 men from M. went to Kish); [16] (a singer from Kish traveling to M.); *SEb* 4 [19] (caravans to M. and Kish); [21] (Ebla merchants, dam-gàr, to M. and Kish); [31] (Kish and M.); [32].

Na-gàr: [7] (a man from N. went to Kish; further, see *ᵓÀ-du*); *SEb* 4 [1] (PN, who went to Kish and N.); [6] (king of Kish and king of N.); [22] (2 men from N. went to Kish).

Tir$_x$*-ga*: [7] (PN from Kish has received in T.).

Ti-rí-ga: [9] (PN from Kish has received in T.).

The Lugal of Mari at Ebla and the Sumerian King List

M. J. GELLER

The political implications of the terms lugal and en were treated in Thorkild Jacobsen's seminal article on early political development in Mesopotamia,[1] although many difficulties remain in distinguishing between the meanings of lugal, en, and ensi.[2] The potential for confusion is now increased by the Ebla documents, which refer to their own ruler as "en"[3] while

* I would like to thank Professor Thorkild Jacobsen, who collated the Weld-Blundell Prism with me during his stay at St. John's College, Oxford, and to Dr. M. W. Green and Professor Erle Leichty for collations, and Dr. I. L. Finkel for suggestions and comments. A version of this paper was read at the Leningrad Rencontre, July, 1984.

[1] *TIT*, 132–56, according to which the kernel of the Mesopotamian polity was the assembly, which chose one type of leader, the "en," to handle banditry and internal problems, while a second elected official, the "lugal," was war leader. As warfare became more common, the authority of the lugal increased until he became the householder presiding over the é-gal or palace. Whether one accepts Jacobsen's theoretical model or not, it is clear that the title en never seems to have lost its priestly associations, while the term lugal gradually acquired regal status, especially in the grandiose titles of lugal-kalam-ma and lugal-kiši implying larger political units.

[2] Cf. D. O. Edzard, "La Royauté dans la Periode Présargonique," in *Le Palais et la Royauté*, ed. P. Garelli (Paris, 1974) 141–49, and I. M. Diakonoff, "Structure and Society in Early Dynastic Sumer," *MANE* 1/3 (1974) 9–11; and I. M. Diakonoff, *Oekumene* 3 (1982) 27, treating this en as 'priest-ruler'.

[3] G. Pettinato, *The Archives of Ebla* (Garden City, N.Y., 1981) 74, states that the "king of Ebla bears the Sumerian title en 'lord'," sharing this unusual feature with Uruk. (He is followed by A. Archi in *ARET* 3, 347, although Edzard, *ARET* 2, 123, translates en as "Herrscher"). In Uruk, however, both titles lugal and en remained as political nomenclature (cf. e.g., H. Steible, *FAOS* 5/II, 293). Nevertheless, there has been some philological justification for rendering en as 'king', based upon references in Ebla documents to the en *wa/ù ma-lik-tum*, and the bilingual equation of nam-en with *ma-li-gú-um* (*MEE* 4, 318), but such an assumption leads to impossible complications. One text, TM.75.G.411, for instance, refers to food allotments for the en, as well as the en-en, which G. Pettinato, *The Archives of Ebla* (Garden City, N.Y., 1981), 78–79, is compelled to translate as 'former kings', then allotments for the dumu-nita-en-en 'sons of the former kings', followed by allotments for the elders and *maliktum*. Moreover, the presence of "kings" and "former kings" is explained by reference to a colophon in another text which totals votive gifts for years 7-6-5-4-3-2, which was Pettinato's basis for assuming an elected kingship in Ebla serving in a seven-year cycle (cf. *The Archives of Ebla*, 72; and *MEE* 2, No. 48), so that Ebla

often using "lugal" in a relatively mundane meaning to indicate an official or overseer.[4]

One significant exception to the general usage of lugal at Ebla is the specific designation of the lugal of Mari,[5] either by title or by name, in addition to the many references to Mari officials or the Mari elders,[6] all of which suggests that the presence of the lugal of Mari was felt at Ebla. This fact is particularly noticeable in the date formulae of the Ebla documents, which offer decisive evidence for the relationship between the two cities, in the following samples of colophons:

MEE 2 No. 6 rev. vii–viii: (total of gold and silver) *áš-du En-na-*^{d}*da-gan* lugal 1 mu 'from Ennadagan lugal, year one'.

MEE 2 No. 16 rev. iv: *in* ud NI-*zi* til-til 1 mu iti *ga-sum* 'in the reign of Nizi, completion of records of one year, month of Gasum'.

MEE 2 No. 35 rev. x: (total of gold and silver) dub-gar níg-ba *En-na-*^{d}*da-gan* [til] 1 mu 'record of a *gift* of Ennadagan, [completion] of one year'.

Both Ennadagan and Nizi are known as rulers of Mari (see below). Another similar colophon is dated by reference to the Mari elders:

SEb 4, p. 161: (total of silver) AB×ÁŠ.AB×ÁŠ *ma-rí*^{ki} *áš-du* 4 mu 'the elders of Mari, from year four'.

Similar date formulae are occasionally incorporated into the texts themselves, rather than as colophons:

SEb 4, p. 132: (amounts of silver and gold) níg-ba e-gi$_4$-maškim e-gi$_4$-maškim *in* ud-ud *Ip-lul-Il* lugal *ma-rí*^{ki} '*gift* of the e-gi$_4$-officials in the reign of Iplulil, lugal of Mari'.

---

is seen as developing from monarchy into a family oligarchy. At the same time, the en of Ebla is considered to be an international figure at the center of an empire, despite the lack of distinction between the title "en of Ebla" and the "en" of numerous other localities mentioned in Ebla documents (for references, cf. *ARET* 2, 123; *ARET* 3, 348; and *MEE* 2, 354); the "king" of Ebla bears no august title such as "en of en's" or "en of the land," or anything comparable. It is therefore difficult to support the argument on purely philological grounds that the en of Ebla was 'king'.

[4] Cf., for example, the term lugal-BAR.AN-BAR.AN (*MEE* 2, No. 27 × 7–8, No. 26 vi 5–6, and Edzard's discussion in *ARET* 2, 120) and lugal-ir$_{11}$-ir$_{11}$ (*MEE* 2, No. 27 rev. iv 4–5), together with parallel terms ugula-BAR.AN-BAR.AN (*ARET* 2, No. 23 iv 4) and ugula-ir$_{11}$ in *ARET* 3, No. 941 iv. 5. Cf. also *MEE* 2, No. 42 lugal-sa-za$_x$-ki.

[5] The term lugal was also used to refer to the lugal of Kish, but these references are much less prominent in the published corpus than those to the lugal of Mari; cf. A. Archi *SEb* 4 (1981) 77–87.

[6] Many references to Mari have been usefully collected by A. Archi, "I Rapporti tra Ebla e Mari," *SEb* 4 (1981) 129–66. Cf. also *MEE* 2, No. 1 rev. ii 3–4, and No. 6 rev. v 1–2, as well as *ARET* 3, No. 278 ii 3–4 (lugal *Mari*^{ki}); Mari officials are mentioned in *ARET* 2, No. 940 iii 7–8, and No. 15 v 3, *MEE* 2, No. 1 rev. ii 17–18, No. 12 rev. i 10–11.

ARET 2 No. 4 xv 7–10: šu mu-DÚB *Ip-lul-il* lugal 1 mu til 'the *deposition*? of Iplulil, lugal, completion of one year'. This text contains a colophon which reads: (total of silver and gold) lú GAL.LÚ *áš-du* 4 mu 'betrifft den König, (den Zeitraum) seit vier Jahren (umfassend)' [Edzard, *ARET*, 2, p. 18]

Not only is the Mari king Iplulil known from votive inscriptions from Mari itself, but the type of year annotation used, 1 mu (til), is not too dissimilar to that used in Old Akkadian date formulae.[7] One other interesting example occurs in the following colophon:

MEE 2 No. 43 rev. x: (total of silver and gold) dub-gar lú šu ba_4-ti *in* ud NI-*zi* lugal 3 mu 'the record which one received in the reign of Nizi, lugal, year three'.

In all of the cases cited above, the notation "x mu" may either refer to "year x" (as in mu-iti dates), or to the span of reckoning of the document itself (i.e., "over four years").

Note that every lugal mentioned by name in a colophon is a lugal of Mari. It is inconceivable that any king of Ebla as ruler of an independent state would date his documents by the reign of a foreign power.[8] An exception to the examples cited above is the colophon in which Ebrium's name appears: (total of garments) 1 mu til *eb-rí-um* (*MEE* 2 No. 1 rev. x), perhaps indicating a greater measure of independence while Ebrium was en of Ebla, but Ebrium is never referred to as lugal.[9]

[7] Cf. *MAD* 3 277, and *RLA* II 132–33 ("Datenlisten"). For Iplulil and possible synchronisms with Ebla, cf. C. Kühne *ZDPV* 93 (1977) 307–8.

[8] Similar misconceptions occurred in the identifications of Lagash and Girsu. If Mari had never been found or excavated, it would be logical and natural to assume that archaeologists had discovered at Tell Mardikh the early dynastic city of Mari.

[9] The fact that lugal does not refer to the ruler of Ebla, but refers either to the lugal of Mari (or Kish) or to minor officials may reflect differing normalizations of the term lugal in Eblaite. The problem, however, is how to normalize lugal into Eblaite, since the main evidence comes from a lexical text described by Pettinato as a "Liste di Nomi di Persona Sumerico-Eblaiti e Parole Sumeriche" (*MEE* 3, No. 59, photo *MEE* 3/A, pl. 33), in which columns ii and iii appear to list seven Sumerian personal names all beginning with lugal-, followed by a list of Eblaite personal names all beginning with *sar*-. Since the tablet is broken at the bottom, it may be possible that the Sumerian list of col. ii also contains eight names, with the final name completely broken, but it is difficult to judge from the photograph. Although the lists seem to be parallel, the names do not appear to correspond in meaning: lugal-*LAK* 586, lugal-nir-gál, lugal-gaba-gál, lugal-AN.GI.DUB, lugal-UD, lugal-ḪUR-sa, lugal-[. . .], [lugal?-. . .?], with the Eblaite names *sar*-X-*tu*, *sar*-KU-*da*, *sar-ma-ì-lum*, *sar*-NI-*sa*, *sar*-BÀD, *sar-ma*, *sar-ma-ni*, *sar-a-*ba_4. Several of the Eblaite names have parallels in OAkk. names, such as *sar-ma-ì-lum* (*MAD* 3, 287), *sar-ru*-BAD (ibid. 107), *sar-me-ni* (ibid. 179), and X-*ni-sa* (ibid. 208), and the name *sar-a-*ba_4 appears elsewhere in Ebla as LUGAL-*a-*ba_4 (*ARET* 2, 109). Since the meanings of these names are generally uncertain, only tentative inferences can be drawn: (1) The Eblaite names corresponding to Sumerian names lugal-X all show *sar*-X forms, in contrast to OAkk. names which show both *sar*-X and *s/šar-ru-X*, with the latter form being more common (*MAD* 3, 286–89). (2) Although

The three lugal Mari named in Ebla colophons and date formulae are Iplulil, Nizi, and Ennadagan,[10] the latter of whom is known from his letter to the en of Ebla. According to this important document, three rulers of Mari, namely Saʾumu, Ištupšar, and Iblulil, conquered numerous cities in the region, including Emar and Ebla, implying that Ebla's fortunes were inextricably tied to Mari, the ruling power in the region.[11] Ennadagan's assertion of Mari's hegemony in Syria finds support in the Sumerian King List, which omits any reference to Ebla and cites Mari as the only western city of sufficient prominence to be included within a survey of history. Unfortunately, the Mari section of the King List is damaged in all exemplars, but the appearance of Mari kings in Ebla documents provided good reason to collate the Weld-Blundell prism and the University Museum duplicate, with interesting results.

The collations of *SKL* v 23–30 read as follows:

PBS 13/1 v 11–14: *ma-rí*^{ki}*-a* AN.BU lugal-àm 30 mu *ì*-AK
⌜*ná*⌝*-zi* dumu ⌜x⌝ [x]
(break)

W-B prism: [*ma-rí*^{ki}]-šè AN.BU
[lugal-àm] mu 30 ì-AK
[x x] dumu AN.BU-ke$_4$
[. . . mu x] ì-AK
[x (x) l]ugal mu 30 ì-AK
[x (x) lu]gal-gal$^?$ mu 20 ì-AK
[x (x) *s*]*a-ʾu-me* mu 30 ì-AK
[x (x) lu]gal mu 9 ì-AK

---

the distinction between the Eblaite name *sar*-BÀD and OAkk. *sar-ru*-BÀD may be interesting if a definite pattern can be established, the formal difference between *sar* and *šarru* is insignificant since the two words are etymologically and morphologically related. The *semantic* difference, however, between West Semitic *sar* 'official' and East Semitic *šarru* 'king' is relevant, since Ebla texts employ both meanings. In *ARET* 2, 25, for instance, a large quantity of oxen and sheep are enumerated in groups assigned to an ugula. The colophon (viii–ix) reads (total of oxen and sheep) in-na-sum lugal-lugal 'given by the lugal's', using lugal as the generic term for ugula. On the other hand, references to the lugal *Mari*^{ki} (cf. *ARET* 3, 367), may suggest that the meaning of lugal as *šarru* was reserved primarily for the king of Mari, i.e., using the logogram lugal as it would have been understood in Mari itself.

[10] Cf. A. Archi *SEb* 4 (1981) 161.

[11] D. O. Edzard, *SEb* 4 (1981) 89–97; G. Pettinato, *OA* 19 (1980) 231–45, and B. Kienast, *OA* 19 (1980) 247–61. Pettinato's reading of *qá-nu-um eb-la*^{ki} as 'il 'canneto' di Ebla' (*OA* 19 [1980] 239, v 1–2) and Kienast's translation 'Kolonie' (*OA* 19 [1980] 256) can both be rejected in favor of Akkadian *qannu*(*m*) 'border, environs' (*CAD* Q 81f.), although the word is previously attested only as early as the Amarna period. The expression *qannum Ebla*^{ki} may imply the city proper plus surrounding villages and towns, and this idea is supported by an Ebla colophon which reads, "total of 17 'countries' (kalam^{ki} kalam^{ki}) in the possession of the en of Ebla" (TM 75.G.2136; cf. Pettinato, *The Archives of Ebla*, 106–7), and by the preamble to the treaty between Ebla and A-bar-sal$_4^{ki}$ (E. Sollberger, *SEb* 3 [1980] 135).

SKL v 29: 

For the sign me (not maš), cf. *SKL* ii 24, in which the me sign of en-me-nun-na-ke$_4$ appears as .

SKL v 30: The first visible sign is .

PBS 13 1 v 14 (*SKL* v 25): M. W. Green's collations read:

 -zi dumu 

The first Mari king mentioned in the King List is AN.BU, whose name has also been found on a macehead from Ur. The second name, completely missing on the Weld-Blundell prism, may be read on the Philadelphia duplicate as ⸢*ná*⸣-*zi*, as confirmed by two independent collations from M. W. Green and E. Leichty.[12] This name ⸢*ná*⸣-*zi* can plausibly be identified with NI-*zi* lugal Mari, who appears with his title in several Ebla administrative documents.[13]

Although the names of the next two Mari kings in the King List are irretrievably broken, the name of the fifth king can now be read on the Weld-Blundell prism. Although Jacobsen in 1939 could offer no satisfactory reading for the name, read as ⸢bi⸣-MUŠ$_4$-MAŠ (*SKL* v 29), collation suggests reading the line as *s*]*a*-ʾ*u*-*me* mu 30 ì-ak, 'Saʾume reigned for 30 years'; it is tempting to identify this Saʾume with *sá*-*ù*-*mu*, the first ruler of Mari cited in Ennadagan's letter to the en of Ebla. The following name is also broken on the Weld-Blundell prism, but collation indicates that it is the end of [-lu]gal or [-*š*]*àr* (*SKL* v 30), which at least allows for the possibility that this sign could be the ending of the name Ištupšar, the successor to Saʾumu in the Ennadagan letter. Consequently, if these collations are correct, the names of at least two Mari rulers, Nizi and Saʾumu, are to be found both in Ebla documents and in the Sumerian King List.

All of this data can be seen to reflect a pattern, as follows: The idea of the en at Ebla representing kingship, with the sovereignty and independence which that term implies, must be subject to serious doubt.[14] Although the en was holder of the highest political office in Ebla, evidence for Mari's hegemony is everywhere attested in the Ebla documents, whether in the form of payments to Mari or in votive gifts from the lugal and elders of Mari to Ebla. The Ebla documents which are dated to Mari kings support the evidence of Ennadagan's letter that Ebla, like Emar and other states, was a satellite of Mari, whose own kings may have had international reputations extending to Mesopotamia itself.

[12] The independent collations of both Green and Leichty agree with the possibility of reading ⸢*ná*⸣-*zi* dumu⸢x⸣-[x] in *PBS* 13 1 v 14, which should correspond to *SKL* v 25 (cf. S. H. Langdon, *OECT* II pl. 3 v 25), which reads [x x] dumu AN.BU.ke$_4$, but unfortunately both Green and Leichty affirm that the sign after dumu in *PBS* 13 1 is not A[N.

[13] Cf. A. Archi, *SEb* 4 (1981) 133, 137–39.

[14] Even at Ebla the title en may have retained its meaning of 'priest', in such expressions as en dam-dingir (*ARET* 3, No. 723 iii 2), nídba en ^{d}*à*-*da* (*ARET* 3, No. 417 iii 8–10), or en é ^{d}*à*-*da* (*MEE* 2, No. 49 ii 3–5).